EDUCATION
Means of Instruction Delivery

EDUCATION

Means of Instruction Delivery

Editors

Monica Tomar
D.S. Srivastava

ISHA BOOKS
DELHI-110 033

Education: Means of Instruction Delivery

Rs. 790

ISBN: 81-8205-167-3

Published in 2005 in India by
Isha Books, D-43, Prithviraj Road,
Adarsh Nagar, Delhi-110 033

Laser Typesetting at: Shree Vaishnavi Creations, Delhi
Printed at: Mehra Offset Press, Delhi

PREFACE

Teaching is an art as well as a science. Knowledge of what constitutes effective teaching has increased significantly in recent years. Today teachers recognize that education is an interactive process, and that students need to be actively involved in tasks that are achievable, useful, relevant, and challenging if they are to respond successfully to the curriculum challenges posed for them. To make the process of instruction effective, teachers use a number of teaching aids.

With the help of teaching aids teachers can enable the learners to improve reading and other skills; illustrate or reinforce a skill, fact, or idea, and relieve anxiety, fears, or boredom, since many teaching aids are like games. Some of the major teaching aids used by teachers include books, calendars, charts, graphs, easy readers, flash cards, field strips, OHP, slides, etc. Today, teachers are also using computers, video, audio and multimedia technologies as means of instructional delivery.

The present book aims to provide a comprehensive information of various teaching aids commonly used by teachers of various levels. The functions and using methods of teaching aids and skills needed by teachers to use them effectively are also elaborately analyzed. The content of the book will be of immense help to practising teachers, teacher-educators and student-teachers.

Editor

CONTENTS

1

Teaching Aids

A teaching aid is a tool used by teachers, facilitators, or tutors to

— help learners improve reading and other skills

— illustrate or reinforce a skill, fact, or idea, and

— relieve anxiety, fears, or boredom, since many teaching aids are like games.

Here are some kinds of teaching aids:

— alphabet book

— alphabet chart

— calendar

— chart

— easy reader

— flash card

— flip chart

— poster

— sentence building cards

— sentence building grid

— syllable whee

— word building card

— word slide

Today teachers are also using computers, video, audio and multimedia technologies for the purpose of instruction

ALPHABET BOOK

Alphabet books are sometimes used

— as motivational tools to attract people's attention to books

— as supplements to primers

— to help transfer reading skills from one language to another, or

— to introduce the sounds and letters of an alphabet.

Definition

An alphabet book is a collection of pages that lists and illustrates the entire alphabet.

Features

Here are some features of an alphabet book. An alphabet book usually contains the following for each letter:

— one or more keywords

— an illustration of each keyword, and

— the letter(s) in small and capital letters.

Variations

An alphabet book might include

— all the letters in a language

— only the vowels

— selected vowels and consonants

— sentences using the keywords and letters

— paragraphs or stories featuring the key words or letters

— an entire page of examples of the use of one letter, or

— several letters on each page.

ALPHABET CHART

An alphabet chart is useful for displaying the alphabet letters, either

— on a wall

— as part of a book, or

— by itself.

It can be a tool from which letters are introduced and taught.

Definition

An alphabet chart is a single page that lists the entire alphabet, or selected parts of the alphabet.

Features

The size of an alphabet chart can range from a wall chart large enough to be seen by a group to a small leaflet. An alphabet chart usually contains the following for each letter:

— a keyword using the letter

— an illustration of the keyword, and

— the letter in small and capital letters.

CALENDAR

Calendars are a popular item in most parts of the world. Here are some ways to use calendars in a literacy program:

— As a teaching aid
— For fund raising
— As gifts, incentives, or awards
— As motivation to read
— For reading practice

Definition

A calendar is a page or a series of pages that shows the dates, days, and months of one year.

Features

A calendar usually contains numbers, text, and illustrations.

Text

Here are some kinds of text to use on calendars:

— Months and days of the month in the local language and possibly in other appropriate languages
— Proverbs and folktales
— Quotes from famous people or literature
— Scripture portions
— Self-help information
— Stories

Illustrations

Here are some kinds of illustrations to use on calendars:

— Charts
— Diagrams
— Line drawings

— Locally drawn pictures

— Photographs

Here are some kinds of calendars:

— Calendars with
  - — every month printed on one large sheet of paper, and
  - — enough room for some pictures and text.

— Calendars with
  - — one picture and some text on a large coloured piece of paper, and
  - — pages for each month written on smaller pieces of white paper and stapled on to the large coloured paper.

— Calendars with
  - — a separate page for each month, with
  - — an illustration, and
  - — some text on each page.

— Commercially produced calendars with handwritten local language text added

— Pocket or desk agendas

CHART

A chart is a useful way to present and display information or instructions, especially in a classroom or other educational situation. It can range in size from a large wall chart to a single piece of paper.

Definition

A chart is a group of related facts presented in the form of a diagram, table, graph, or other visually organized model.

Kinds

Here are some kinds of charts used in literacy:

— Alphabet chart

— Consonant chart

— Enlarged primer page

— Number chart

— Punctuation chart

— Song chart

— Vowel chart

EASY READER

Easy readers are good for beginning readers. They can help motivate beginning readers by giving them a whole book that they can read by themselves.

Definition

An easy reader is a short book with a small amount of text and large illustrations. The illustrations are designed to give clues to what the text says.

FLASH CARD

Flash cards are useful for drilling new letters, syllables, words, and other information. They are normally used in a classroom, but can also be used more informally.

Definition

A flash card is part of a set of cards on which are written items to be studied. They are "flashed" (shown quickly) one by one to a learner to elicit a quick response.

Uses

Here are some other uses for flash cards:

— Use two matching sets of them with games such as How to play the Memory game .

— Have learners practice tracing the characters on the cards with their fingers.

— Make up your own games using the cards.

Features

Here are some features of flash cards:

— Flash cards are sets of cards printed with information to be studied, such as

— definitions

— formulas

— letters

— multiplication tables

— prefixes

— syllables, or

— words.

— If there is an answer or solution to what appears on the front of the card, it is printed on the back so that the person showing the cards can see if the learner's answer is correct.

FLIP CHART

Flip charts are a useful teaching aid. You can purchase prepared or blank flip charts, or you can make them. Flip charts are useful in teaching situations where you need to teach a number of people at a time. They are used

— when books are unavailable, scarce, or too expensive for individuals to have their own copy

— when other media such as overheads and slides are not available, and

— where group learning is most culturally appropriate.

Definition

A flip chart is a collection of large pages which are bound together at the top. The pages are "flipped" or brought up and to the back as they are used.

Features

A flip chart is bound together at the top in such a way that the pages can be easily turned and lie flat.

Variations

Some flip charts have a reduced version of the page that faces the group printed on the back of the preceding page. This makes it possible for the leader to see the same thing the group is seeing.

Others have teaching notes printed on the back.

Use

— Flip charts can be placed on an easel or held. The leader stands beside or holds the flip chart, referring to the text printed on the back if necessary. As each page is finished, the leader flips it over to the back.

— Flip charts are easiest to use when the pages facing the group have large print and illustrations.

— The back of the pages can have

— the same text and illustrations in a smaller size

Kinds

- Here are some kinds of flip charts:
- Here are some kinds of flip charts used in a literacy program:
  - Community development information
  - Discussion outlines
  - Parts of a lesson
  - Primers
  - Songs
  - Stages of a process
  - Steps of a procedure
  - Stories
  - Textbooks

How to make a flip chart

Flip charts are often used instead of individual books in group situations. If you decide to produce multiple copies of a flip chart to use instead of individual books, you may need more sophisticated printing methods than hand printing. Although having charts printed is more expensive than producing them by hand, it is still more economical to produce, for example, 100 charts than 5,000 books.

Materials

Here are the materials needed to make a flip chart:

- Premade blank flip charts (may be purchased in most countries) *or* large sheets of paper
- Heavy cardboard

— Marking pens
— Materials to bind the pages
  — rings
  — string
  — glue
  — tacks
  — pole or stick, or
  — wooden slats.

Steps

Follow these steps to make a flip chart:

— Print the front of each page with a large version of the text and illustrations.

— Collate the pages, including as a last "page" a piece of heavy cardboard if you want the flip chart to stand up.

— Bind the pages together at the top.

Alternatives

Here are some alternate ways to make a flip chart:

— Print a reduced version of the text and illustrations on the back.

— Print the front of each page as above.

— Print a small version of the first page on the back of the cover page.

— Print a small version of the second page on the back of the first page.

— Continue in this manner with all the pages.

— Collate and bind as shown above.

- Print notes on the back.
- Print the front of each page as above.
- Print appropriate notes for the first page on the back of the cover page.
- Print appropriate notes for the second page on the back of the first page.
- Continue in this manner with all the pages.
- Collate and bind as shown above.

POSTER

A poster is an informative, often decorative way to attract attention to the information it contains. Here are some ways to use posters in a literacy program:

- To advertise events or products
- To display information or instructions
- To teach some kinds of information

Definition

A poster is a bill or placard usually displayed in a public place. It is often decorated with designs or illustrations.

Kinds

Here are some kinds of posters:

- Posters you make yourself.
- Ready-made posters from
  - business organizations
  - community development organizations
  - government offices

— medical companies, or

— tourist agencies.

How to print a poster with a silk-screen printer

Using a silk-screen printer to print posters is similar to printing on regular size paper. Most of the steps in this module will refer you to instructions for printing on paper. Posters usually have larger text and designs than regular printed pages. Preparing the designs and stencils for posters, therefore, requires some different techniques. Some of the steps will refer you to instructions for printing on fabric because they are more appropriate for posters. If you want to print large posters, you will need to use a printer large enough for the size of poster you want, or adapt the printing procedure.

— To adapt the instructions for making a silk-screen printer to make any size you need,

— Instructions for printing the poster one section at a time will be provided in the future.

Materials

Here is a list of the materials needed to print a poster with a silk-screen printer:

— Ink

— Stencil

— Paper or poster board

— Masking tape

— Cleaning materials:

Steps

Follow these steps to print a poster with a silk-screen printer:

— Design and draw a graphic.
— Prepare the stencil.
— Select the proper ink for the job.
— Prepare to print.
— Print trial copies.
— Print multiple copies.
— Dry the copies.
— Clean the printer.

Designing and drawing a graphic for printing on fabric

Appropriate designs for printing on fabric require some extra thought and care to make them easily printable.

Materials

Here are the materials needed for drawing a graphic for printing on fabric:

— Paper
— Stencil
— Stylus

Guidelines

Here are some guidelines to follow to help you design a graphic that is attractive and easy to print:

— Keep the design as simple as possible.
— Use large letters and design parts because they are easier to cut out than small ones.
— Remember, though, that the design must be small enough to fit on the stencil and the printer.

— As much as possible, avoid creating loose pieces, especially with small designs and letters like *a* and *o*.

  — One way to avoid loose pieces is to leave thin connectors to the circle centers. This will, however, cause "broken circles" because circle centers will be attached to the background rather than loose.

Illustration

— If you do not want to have "broken circles" in your design, do the following:

  — Cut out centers of letters.

  — Moisten centers slightly and place them in the correct positions on the screen. The moisture will hold the loose pieces in place until the first printing. After the first printing, the ink itself will make the loose pieces adhere to the screen.

Steps

Follow these steps to design and draw a graphic for printing on fabric:

— Draw the design on paper.

— Place the paper design on the stencil, centering it carefully.

— Trace the design on the stencil.

Caution

— Press hard, using a stylus that will leave an impression on the stencil but will not cut through it.

— Make sure the impression is clear enough to follow when you are ready to cut the stencil.

PREPARING A LARGE HAND-CUT STENCIL

Designs for printing on fabric or postersare larger and usually more complicated than regular stenciled text and illustrations. You probably need to hand-cut a stencil from cardboard or sturdy plastic.

Guidelines

Here are some guidelines to follow when you prepare a large hand-cut stencil:

— Use a very sharp blade.

— Cut all the way through the stencil as cleanly as possible.

— Be extra careful to cut corners very neatly.

— Cut the inside parts of the design first and work outward.

— Cut *toward* angles in the design. Starting from the angle might tear the stencil.

Illustration

— To cut smaller designs on mimeograph stencils

Deciding what ink or paint to use with a silk-screen printer

You can use various kinds of ink or paint to print with a silk-screen printer. The kind you choose depends on

— the material to be printed on, and

— the kind of stencil you use

Guidelines

Here are some guidelines to follow when you decide what ink or paint to use with a silk-screen printer:

If you want to print...	Then use...
Typed-size letters on paper	Mimeograph ink.
Larger letters or a design on paper	Mimeograph ink, or Poster paint.
Larger letters or a design on a poster	Poster paint.
A design or large letters on fabric	Textile ink or paint.

Preparing a silk-screen printer for printing on fabric

Before printing anything, you must prepare the silk-screen printer and properly attach the stencil. The procedure may vary somewhat, depending on the kind of printer you use.

Steps

Follow these steps to prepare a silk-screen printer for printing on fabric:

— If there are hinges on the printer, remove them.

Tip: The screen is easier to manipulate without them.

— Place the screen frame face down.

— Lay the stencil face down on the side of the screen facing up.

— Tape the stencil onto the frame. Tape all around the edges to prevent the ink from leaking.

How to print trial copies with a silk-screen printer

The first copies you print with a silk-screen printer are usually uneven and unusable. Before you print on good paper, make some trial copies that you can throw away.

Guidelines

Here are some guidelines to follow when you print trial copies with a silk-screen printer:

— If the applicator is not wide enough to cover the print area in a single pass,

  — pull it along one edge of the frame, then

  — start again at the top and pull it down along the other edge.

— Notice that when enough ink has gotten through the stencil, the stencil will stick to the fabric screen.

— Remember that the idea is to press the ink evenly through the fabric screen and the openings on the stencil onto the paper.

— Try not to use more than one stroke over a section.

Caution

If you use more than one stroke, you may cause the stencil to shift position and the printing to be unclear.

— Use ink sparingly or it will be wasted and the working area will be messy. Excess ink can ruin equipment and clothes.

— Use old, used paper for making trial copies.

Steps

Follow these steps to print trial copies with a silk-screen printer:

— Put a line of ink about as thick as your little finger along the top edge of the fabric screen .

Illustration

— Pull the applicator down firmly and evenly across the screen, holding it at a 60-degree angle to the fabric surface.

How to print multiple copies with a silk-screen printer

Printing with a silk-screen printer is a good option if you need a fairly small number of copies. A stencil is usually good for 20 to possibly 50 copies. After that, it is likely to tear or wrinkle from repeated use.

Prerequisite

Here is a prerequisite for printing multiple copies on the silk-screen printer:

— Prepare the printer and print a good quality trial copy.

Guidelines

Follow these guidelines for printing multiple copies:

— Add more ink as needed.

— Lift the stencil and straighten it if it gets wrinkled or it may tear.

— Print pages one immediately after another without cleaning the ink from the screen.

Steps

Follow these steps to print multiple copies with a silk-screen printer:

— Put a clean sheet of paper in place and lower the screen frame

Illustration

— Pull the applicator firmly down across the fabric screen.

— Remove the paper.

— Put each sheet aside to dry for at least 5-10 minutes before stacking or printing the other side.

Drying silk-screened copies

Once you have printed copies with a silk-screen printer, you must be careful to dry them well. If you touch or stack them while the ink is still wet, you will ruin them.

Alternatives

Here are alternative ways to dry the silk-screened copies:

— Lay each of the first 10 printed sheets in a different place. Place the next 10 on top of these, and so on, until the printing is finished.

— This allows the ink to dry partially on one sheet before another is put on top of it. Putting the sheets in stacks of 10 makes them easy to count.

— Put "blotters" (old paper or newspaper) between the sheets.

Tip

In the case of two-sided printing:

— Print all odd numbered pages first so they can dry.

— Then print the even pages on the other sides.

Cleaning a silk-screen printer

It is important to thoroughly clean a silk-screen printer after using it. Leaving ink to dry on the screen will ruin it. Use plenty of rags or soft absorbent paper and the appropriate cleaning solvent to remove all the ink as soon as possible after using the printer.

Warning

— Keep flammable cleaning solvents away from flames.

SENTENCE BUILDING CARDS

Sentence building cards are a teaching aid that is inexpensive and easy to make and use. They are useful to give learners practice in

— word recognition, and

— sentence recognition and building.

Definition

Sentence building cards are a teaching aid. They allow learners to build sentences by matching individual words to words in a sentence that has already been written.

Features

Each set of sentence building cards consists of

— a large sentence card with pictures and sentences, and

— several small word cards.

The large sentence card has several illustrations drawn in boxes down the left side of the card. Each illustration has a sentence written in a box beside it. The illustrations serve as clues to the sentences. The small word cards have words that match the words in the sentences on the sentence card.

The learner

— looks at the pictures

— reads the sentences, and

— builds the same sentences by placing the matching word cards in the space below the sentences.

SENTENCE BUILDING GRID

A sentence building grid is a simple way to help learners put parts of sentences together to form whole sentences. It is useful to give learners practice in sentence recognition and building.

Definition

A sentence building grid is a teaching aid that allows learners to construct sentences by choosing parts of sentences and putting them together to form whole logical sentences.

Description

A sentence grid is a chart arranged in columns. Each column contains words that are a specific part of a sentence, such as

— articles

— subjects

— objects, or

— verbs

How to use

Follow these steps to use a sentence building grid:

— Have the learner choose any *one* word from each column so that, when the words are put together in order, they form a sentence that makes sense.

— Have the learner write the sentence or just read it.

— Have the learner make as many logical sentences as possible.

Example

Here is an example of a sentence building grid.

A	horse	has	grass.
An	house	protects	legs
The	table	eats	people.

apple	is	sweet.
man	was	Henry.
		empty.
		set.
		rough.
		hungry.
		new..
		windows.

Here are some logical sentences made from the grid:

— The table was set.

— A horse eats grass.

SYLLABLE WHEEL

A syllable wheel is a teaching aid that is inexpensive and easy to make and use.

It helps learners develop the following word attack skills:

— Blending consonants and vowels into syllables

— Breaking syllables into component parts

— Recognizing syllable patterns

— Recognizing symbols for consonant sounds

— Recognizing symbols for vowel sounds.

Definition

A syllable wheel is a teaching aid that allows a learner to substitute letters in a designated position in a syllable. The learner rotates an inner wheel to line up letters printed on it with letters printed on an outer wheel.

Features

Here are the features of a syllable wheel:

— Two circles of heavy paper: a large circle with a smaller one on top of it.

— The two circles are fastened together in the centre so that they can be rotated independently.

— The large circle has the first letter or letters of syllables printed all around the edge.

— The small circle has letters for the end of syllables printed around the edge.

— The circles or "wheels" are rotated to line up the letters to make various syllables.

— The syllable wheel may have a long "window" attached to frame a syllable as it is lined up. This focuses attention on a specific syllable and eliminates the distraction of the other letters.

WORD BUILDING CARDS

Word building cards are a teaching aid useful

— to give practice in syllable recognition

— to give practice in word building

Definition

Word building cards are a teaching aid. They allow learners to build words by matching individual syllables to syllables in a word that has already been written.

Contents

Each set of word building cards consists of

— a large word card, and

— several small syllable cards.

The large word card has three built words written across the top with blank space under each word.

The small syllable cards have syllables that match the syllables in the words on the word card.

HOW TO MAKE WORD BUILDING CARDS

Materials

Here are the materials needed to make word building cards:

— Large (8" x 8") pieces of paper or other material to make word cards

— A long strip of paper or other material for each word to make syllable cards

Steps

Follow these steps to make word building cards:

— Rule lines on the large card.

— Print three built words that the students are learning in the top half of each box.

— Print the same words on the strips, one on each strip.

— Cut the word strips into individual syllables.

How to use

Follow these steps to use word building cards:

— Give the learner a large word card.

Have the learner do the following:

— Read the words on the card.

— Build the same words from the syllable cards by placing the matching syllable cards in the space below the words.

— Read the words they build.

WORD SLIDE

A word slide is a teaching aid that is inexpensive and easy to make and use. It can be used to help learners practice specific sounds in the context of a word. It helps learners develop the following word attack skills:

— Blending consonants and vowels into syllables

— Breaking syllables into component parts

— Recognizing syllable patterns

— Recognizing symbols for consonant sounds, and

— Recognizing symbols for vowel sounds.

Definition

A word slide is a teaching aid that allows a learner to substitute letters in a designated position in a syllable or word.

Features

A word slide consists of two pieces of paper.

— One has part of a word printed on it lengthwise.

— The other has letters or syllables that could complete the word printed on it from top to bottom.

— The second piece of paper slides through slits cut in the first piece. The letters or syllables printed on it complete words which change as you slide the paper from one position to another.

TEACHING AIDS FOR THE NEW MILLENNIUM

Teaching and training users how to operate laboratory equipment is a time-intensive practice. Many new users are students, who have generally high turnover rates; after they complete a class project or degree program, they leave the facility. In addition, users often divide their time among a variety of techniques and equipment. With episodic usage, researchers tend to forget details of instrument operation and need to be retrained. Academic core facilities must balance their productivity against the time it takes to train and retrain an ever-changing parade of users. Site-specific multimedia teaching and training resources, such as films, CDs, videos, or DVDs, if easily available in the laboratory, would enable users to refresh and retrain themselves on equipment operation.

Videos, CDs, and websites that highlight the use and theory of operation of equipment, already exist [e.g., 1-4]. However, these resources provide only general information; they are not applicable to training users in the operational procedures and maintenance guidelines for particular instruments in *your* laboratory. Popular software such as PowerPoint can incorporate instructional video clips into slide shows, but PowerPoint[1]s inability to edit video clips and modify soundtracks limits its overall utility in this regard. In the past, producing training videos or equivalent teaching aides about equipment operation required expensive resources: camera, crew, editing equipment, and the like.

However, recent advances in consumer digital image electronics have powered the development of inexpensive cameras and software for dealing with video images. There are now several low-cost, easy-to-use programs for digitizing and editing video images, inserting them into a sequence along with title boards and still images, then exporting this edited session to a CD, DVD, or video tape. The Electron Microscope Facility at San Diego State University is already using video editing software to create training CDs for in-house equipment. These CDs introduce new users to microscopy equipment in a format that enables users to see and hear a demonstration of the step-by-step operation protocol.

After studying the CDs, new users are tested for their understanding of the instrument and its operation. They must demonstrate the operation of the instrument to a satisfactory level to receive Facility clearance to operate the equipment independently. Using these CDs has reduced the required training time by half. More importantly, the training CDs ensure a standardized presentation so that each user receives uniform instruction. The CDs are inexpensive to duplicate, and, given the ubiquity of CD drives in computers (DVDs in the future), are readily viewable on or off site at the researcher's convenience. Users who desire a refresher session need only review the CD.

The production methodology for creating equipment training CDs in the SDSU EM Facility is highlighted below. The approach is similar to that of presenting a laboratory demonstration. Note that the following example describes the production equipment and programs we use but that other software and hardware options exist.

Develop a storyline and production scenario.

As with so many other aspects of life, planning reduces the need for subsequent manipulation. You must consider the instructions you wish to impart, the scientist who will present the tutorial, and the roles of any other participants in the demonstration. From these ingredients, you create a detailed script. If you have been training users for any length of time, you have already created your script[1]: it is your well-honed presentation of the standardized protocol for a given piece of equipment. Keep in mind that the ŒScript serves as a resource not only for the people who will perform on camera but also for the camera operator. For the camera operator, your 'Script[1] must indicate the sequence of activity, the approximate timing of each shot, whether the camera is zoomed in or out and at what rate. Before recording the tutorial, be sure the camera operator understands how to record the parts of the demonstration.

Also, have the camera operator practice zooming‹too fast a zoom, or changing shots too rapidly can be disorienting to the viewer. Make sure that there is sufficient lighting and that you will not be blocking the lighting, the camera, or the equipment during the recording. Be sure to have all accessory equipment or supplies in place. Lastly, remember that these recordings will take on a life of their own‹whatever you wear, and whatever your hairstyle, will be seen for years to come; so dress appropriately and comb your hair! Try a short practice tutorial and critically review it before embarking on the final shoot. You may notice mannerisms you would prefer not to record on the final tutorial, and you may find better ways to describe your protocol after watching and hearing yourself. Although this may sound daunting, in practice, after producing your first tutorial, the rest come easily.

Record the tutorial.

We use a tripod mounted digital video camera, available on loan from SDSU Instructional Technology Services, to record our sessions. This makes our subsequent editing much easier. Any video camera is appropriate, however, even one of the laboratory cameras that has no sound input. You can always add a soundtrack later, during editing. Before starting to record, post signs at all entrances to your laboratory that recording is in progress. Turn off pagers and telephones to avoid the recording of rogue sounds during the recording session. If something goes wrong or if the presenter misspeaks during the shoot, redo that part of the scene immediately. It is easier to redo a part of a scene while equipment and supplies are in place than it is to edit a mistake later, or to plan to reshoot on a different day. Set up the camera and record all sequences for a given camera orientation before moving to a different location, even if it means that your protocol is filmed out of sequence. You will rearrange the sequences in correct order during the editing. Include short pauses in the narration‹these pauses make it easier to insert, remove, or replace video clips or text during the editing.

Digitize the recording.

The tutorial, once recorded, needs to be transferred to the computer. For this step, you need a *video out* connection from the camera, and a *video in* connection to the computer. Digital video (DV) cameras and newer Macintosh computers running OS 9.1 and higher are configured to exchange video data via Firewire and the software program iMovie. Plug the DV camera into the Mac using Firewire, open iMovie, and the video clip playing on the camera is automatically transferred to the computer. A Wintel machine running Windows XP requires an optional Firewire card to exchange digital video clips. To exchange video from an analog video camera or VCR, you need a video capture board and driver, such as the ATI All-In-Wonder card. You can transfer between analog and digital sources with a card like this.

Edit the recording.

The latest computer operating systems contain simple video editing software: iMovie for the Mac running OS9.1 or higher and Windows Movie Maker for Wintel machines running Windows XP. These bundled programs, and other commercially available programs, generally open a video viewing window with side and bottom editing control areas. You can then edit each clip for content in the viewing window and drag it to its proper position in the video timeline below [Figure 1C]. You can modify soundtracks, if necessary, as part of the video clip editing. You can create or select new text slides and various effects and insert them for effective transitions between segments, much as one would do in PowerPoint. The final tutorial is thereby assembled step by step in the bottom video timeline. You can save the tutorial as you create it, but note that it will occupy a significant chunk of storage space. One hour of uncompressed video fills about 13 GBs of memory. To free this space, save the final product in compressed format as a movie.

Store the tutorial.

To save the recording as a movie at a particular resolution, select Export in the File window. Depending on your hardware, you may choose DVD, videotape, CD, or Web-compatible format. DVD or videotape provides the best image quality; the others suffer various degrees of degradation of resolution. DVD movies display at 720x480 pixels and run at 30 frames per second. Web movies display at 240x180 pixels and run at 12 frames per second. The CD-ROM format, which can store about 75 minutes of video, gives an acceptable intermediate resolution and has the advantage of being a standard accessory on most computers. In addition, tutorials on CD are easy to copy and distribute. As DVD players become standard accessories, this high quality format will be the best choice for recording and distributing tutorials. If you choose to record your tutorial to videotape, you will have a high quality image but will need a VCR and monitor to view the tape.

2

Effective Teaching Practices

Teaching is "helping people to learn". Everything else is a gloss. But since that needs a little unpacking, it is about

— setting up a purposeful exchange with a learner about a pre-determined topic, including

— telling them something new, and

— carrying through that exchange while monitoring its success and modifying it as necessary, so that

— the learner ends up knowing and being able to do more as a result.

The significance of the terms used should become apparent as you go through the site, as well as the ideas and techniques they embrace.

HANDOUTS

The Internet and Virtual Learning Environment may or may not radically change teaching, but the technology which has probably made most differ

ence in the past fifty years has been cheap, on-site, duplicating copying and printing. Among other things, it has radically changed student expectations — and the more conversant teachers become with computers and printing, the higher the expectations get.

Handouts are an integral part of the teaching and learning system.

That is to say, they make a difference to other elements in the system: they are not neutral add-ons.

— Give out a comprehensive handout at the start of the class: why should anyone stay to hear you say it when they can read it? They may be reading it rather than listening anyway.

— Give out a skeletal handout at the beginning: it acts not only as a form of "scaffolding", but also as a form of contract or promise — "This is what I am going to cover". It exposes your digressions.

— Give out an orientation handout for next week's session at the end of this week's class: it is a statement of expectations of what students will do.

— Give out a handout at the end of the class without announcing that you were intending to do so: this is a vote of no confidence in student's note-taking, and some of them may feel cheated because they took notes unnecessarily.

— Do you want students to take notes? Would it help them to understand the material for themselves? Then don't use handouts.

— Do you want them to concentrate on the session itself? Do you want them to look at OHTs or a video, or proceed via question-and-answer (in either direction). Then use handouts.

— Handouts shift some of the burden of conveying information from the taught session to themselves. They free you to be non-linear in your presentation and to pursue interesting angles raised by students. (Except when literal-minded students complain that you are not sticking to order of topics on the handout.)

— Distributing handouts to a large class is not a trivial enterprise, and can cause considerable disruption. In such cases you can either have piles for people to collect on their way in or out, or perhaps distribute smaller sets to students throughout the lecture theatre to pass around on cue.

So using handouts or not, and their form, is an act of class management, not simply of information-giving.

Design considerations

The design of handouts also sends a message to learners about your approach to teaching: out-dated or scruffy handouts and third generation barely-legible photocopies are an insult to learners when the technology is available to up-date them and produce pristine copies. At the other end of the scale, glossy and slick productions by some commercial training providers acquire a spurious authority, and often suggest that the trainer is a mere functionary rather than a professional who generates her own material.

— All handouts should have plenty of white space for students' own notes: use wide margins, and leave substantial gaps between topics.

— They should clearly flag the structure of the topic, using headings and sub-headings to show the relative importance of points — the structure is easily lost in a lecture.

— Relevant graphics are useful, particularly if they are used in the actual presentation and students may have difficulty in copying them down: but be careful about clip-art merely to "brighten up" the presentation.

— Students can be intimidated by vast wodges of paper: try not to make them too big.

Some kinds of handout and their peculiarities:

— *Reading lists*: Consider annotating them, and particularly indicate functional alternatives where possible.

— *Gapped Handouts*: these pre-structure the session. They list the headings, and at their simplest then leave enough space for the kinds of notes the students are expected to make.

  — They may also include any complex graphics or charts or tables of statistics used, perhaps without legends or labels so students have to listen to you to make sense of them, and then write them in.

  — The gaps may include the appropriate number of bullets or numbers for the points to be made

  — For less able students, they may outline the main points but leave gaps for key words to be inserted.

  — They ***can*** be patronising, and perhaps mechanistic, but they do balance guaranteeing accurate information with student activity.

— *Primary sources*: Brief excerpts or quotations from authors to be discussed, pictures or sets of figures. There is no real substitute for each student having their own copy of such material, but beware copyright regulations!

— *Worksheets*: handouts are not necessarily substitutes for, or complements to, your own presentation. They can include examples to be completed by the students and then discussed in class. If you are going to use them in this way, think through the whole process before you do so:

  — How are you going to distribute them at the right time?

  — How are they going to be marked?

  — Will you identify and correct common mistakes?

  — If there are no single correct answers, how are you going to deal with alternatives?

Effectively, this is using handouts as the equivalent of "activities" or "self-assessment questions" in resource-based learning. Experiment, and ask for reactions from students. Be specific in your questions, and they will not only realise that you want genuine answers, but also that you take seriously the development of your teaching.

WRITING ON THE BOARD

Whiteboards and chalkboards are no longer the staple technology of the classroom, but they are still important. Assuming that you are also using other equipment such as an overhead projector or data projector, the board (or flip-chart) has a complementary role to play, but it needs to be used well.

— It communicates spontaneity: you may be able to refer to a slide in response to a question or an issue which comes up out of the planned sequence, but often you can't. Either you have not got it with you, or it would take too long to find. Using the board is about being reactive to the class.

— Use it for key-words, which stay on the board for the duration of the session. Usually, if you use the OHP or data projector, there is only one of them, and each image is transient. Material on the board can stay there.

— This involves a little thought about how to organise the board. This may be sophisticated, as in the example below, or it may just be a matter of putting your first key word at the top-left corner, and using the rest of the space systematically rather than jotting words at random.

— Flip-chart sheets can be even more permanent: clumsy though they are, they can provide a reminder of discussions from session to session.

— Use it to map the course of a lecture or argument by adding to a developing picture. One of my former students who teaches drug-dealers (sorry — pharmaceutical company representatives) has this to a fine art. Alongside her sophisticated OHTs and models, she builds up a

— mind-map of the topic as the session develops. It acts as a sort of concurrent

— organiser, clarifying where each point fits with the others.

Pens

Everyone has their little obsessions (don't they?), like not throwing away pieces of string. One of mine is using the correct pen. It is not that silly: permanent markers on white-boards take a long time to remove, even with the special solvent. Whiteboard markers and OHP pens used on paper dry up at a phenomenal rate, leaving you struggling to get a decent line, not to mention the cost. For most purposes, a chisel tip (as opposed to a bullet-tip) pen is more flexible. It permits thicker and thinner lines, which not only makes drawing easier, but also can make writing more legible.

Writing for legibility

Writing on a vertical surface so that the result can be read at a distance of up to ten metres is a craft skill which needs practice. Find an empty classroom and practise. Best of all, find a colleague to practise with. One of you can sit at the back while the other writes, and you can provide each other with feedback.

— The single best piece of advice is: write from the shoulder. Let your shoulder do the moving, with the elbow and wrist, and certainly the fingers, hardly moving at all. Don't hold them rigid — it is too much of a strain — but there should be no need to move them. This single change will precipitate others which will improve legibility.

— If your handwriting is really awful, you may have to PRINT, but it is slow (and speed does matter to some extent), and only easier to read than script if your handwriting is worse than the average doctor.

— Even on a flip-chart, aim to have the body of lower-case letters, (the "x" height) of about 5 cm/2". The risers and descenders help to give shape to a word, so make them clear.

— What does this say? If you tend to this kind of angular script, writing from the shoulder will make it more pronounced, so try not to let letters run into each other: lift the pen occasionally. This is my most common failing in this area.

— If you have occasion to write coherently on a board for whatever reason — as opposed to odd words — keep the line length short. A line which goes all the way across a landscape format board is hard to follow, particularly given the wobbliness of much handwriting. And move yourself as you write: staying in the same place will almost invariably result in the line drooping at the end.

— Finally—don't stretch. If you are short, this will be a problem, particularly since the demise of roller-boards in most classrooms: but if you are stretching you can't form your letters properly.

Writing and the Class

— When you are writing, you should not be talking. You will be facing the board, and you will not be heard as well as if you were facing the class. Moreover, people with a hearing difficulty, who need to see you speak, will certainly not be able to follow.

— Left-handers rule! At least we do with western left-to-right scripts. A left-hander's writing hand is progressively moving away from the script, revealing it: a right-hander will be progressively covering it. You can't change your handedness for the sake of board-writing, but it's nice to know there are circumstances when left-handedness is a positive advantage! In any event, try to stand to one side of your writing, rather than directly in front of it. Somehow, that just seems rude.

— You do have an obligation to spell correctly if possible, but it is difficult to see just what you have just written from up close. Stand back and view it briefly to pick up errors. If you do spell badly, and the class is mature enough, ask them to proof-read for you.

HUMOUR

Humour is an important spice to use in teaching—but like any spice, you don't want too much of it. Many teachers, like myself, will have found their jokes being solemnly repeated back to them in assignments and particularly in exams. There is something about the culture of dependence characteristic of the classroom group which diminishes the ability to discriminate between the serious and the humorous. Nevertheless, gentle humour—never at the expense of anybody, except perhaps yourself (and then only occasionally and in an atmosphere of trust)—leavens the session wonderfully, and can rouse students from mid-lecture torpor. If it fails to do so, they are too far gone to be learning anything, either, so you might as well give up on that session.

Rules of Thumb

— The best kind of humour is not the discrete joke, but humour integrated into the main substance of the material, so that it is not merely a contribution to the maintenance needs of the group, but aids memory and understanding.

— Even when it is integrated, humour is an optional extra, and so there is no excuse for any kind of humour which is potentially offensive to anyone, whether represented within the group or not.

— If your jokes always fall flat in ordinary social conversation, they probably will in class. You may for some bizarre reason wish to acquire a reputation as a groan-monger rather than laughter-monger, but otherwise leave it to others.

- If you can't remember whether you have told this joke to this class before—don't tell it. If you have told it before, it also sends the message to the class that they are not that memorable to you, and therefore diminishes their importance, which is likely to inhibit that fragile frame of mind in which they can really learn.
- Keep humorous interludes short, but identifiable. Classes are not places for one-liners: comedy requires a particular frame of mind, which is different from that for learning. Students need to be able to frame an utterance as a joke—or else they'll take it down in their notes (and possibly resent the wasted effort when the punch-line arrives).
    - The exception is the humorous anecdote which nevertheless makes a teaching point.
- Natural banter between the students and yourself is the best kind of humour in the classroom:
    - It signals an appropriate, comfortable relationship—as long as you are comfortable with it, and you don't feel that they are "taking the mickey".
    - Take your cue from the students: banter which you initiate can be experienced as a put-down and an abuse of your power.
- Beware of inter-student joking behaviour which is at the expense of a member of the group. It may be wise to be careful about sanctioning against it too heavily (unless it is clearly abusive), because there may also be an agenda about "winding you up", but make your disapproval clear, and do not collude with it, however seductive it may be. Ask yourself why they need to do this in this class—it could tell you something about the group.

A word of apology: there are few things more depressing/pompous/boring/pretentious than being serious about humour!

ASSUMPTIONS

All this bumf is based on certain assumptions about teaching and learning. In the terms of Learning theory they are broadly constructivist, but in practice they have been adopted by successful (and some unsuccessful) teachers since the year dot, of whom 99% at least have never heard of that label. They are more or less congenial to any practitioner (as opposed to theorist) who believes that teaching is more than "take it or leave it" presentation of material.

1 The object of teaching is that learners should change — the extent of this change however is a matter of considerable debate. Behaviourists talk about changing behaviour, cognitivists about changing minds, humanists about changing lives, critical reflectors about changing society.

2 It is generally assumed that learners change more than teachers. But if teachers can/do not change at all, it is unlikely that they are teaching effectively (particularly when teaching adults). Mowing machines cut grass, but eventually the grass blunts the blade.

3 This is because, in order to get people to change, you have to know "where they are coming from". That means entering into a dialogue with them. Crudely, if you don't know how someone misunderstands something, you have got little chance of correcting him effectively.

4 So teaching is all about creating a task-centred dialogue, in which you — the teacher — understand the learner's experience of the subject, so that you can modify it.

5 Sometimes, if you have a class of 300, or if you are preparing resource-based learning materials, you can't have this live dialogue, so you have to speculate about potential

misunderstandings by putting yourself as best you can in the shoes of the learners: and try to offer something for everyone. But wherever possible, evidence is better than speculation.

6 The learning frame of mind is fragile: people find it difficult to sustain. Drama depends on the willing "suspension of disbelief" on the part of the audience. If I go to the cinema, and the film is out of focus, I can't suspend disbelief — I am too conscious that I am watching a film. In the same way, if teaching is not performed competently, it is difficult to maintain the learning frame of mind. Note that there are all kinds of other factors which may disturb this frame of mind, which are beyond your control, but that does not absolve you from getting right those which are within your control.

The other side of the coin is that if everything is perfect in the cinema, I forget the film is being projected. Teaching (like film editing) is the "art which conceals art". Few people come out of a sesssion saying how good the teaching was—if they "never forget a good teacher", as the TTA would have it, it is only with the benefit of hindsight.

7 However, the learning frame of mind is not conscious. If you — as a learner — are conscious that "I am learning this", you are less likely to really learn it than if you are framing the experience as "I am interested in this" or "I am practising this" or even better "I am doing this".

8 So the best guarantee of effective teaching is to keep your eye on the ball: concentrate on the learning and the teaching will follow. Think about the teaching and you might produce a great performance, but the main thing your students will learn is merely that you have a high opinion of yourself as a teacher.

THE TEACHER

Your principal working medium is yourself. That includes your voice, your presentation, your positioning, your mannerisms, and your personal qualities and values... Like many features of teaching, excellence in any of these areas is unlikely to enhance the process, but problems can severely inhibit it. There is no substitute for seeing and hearing yourself in action. With readily available video equipment, there is also no excuse. Video a few sessions, and then put the tape away and look at it a few weeks later (when you have forgotten all the considerations which influenced your self-presentation on the day).

— Watch it on your own, and make a note of what strikes you about your performance.

— If you can bear it, watch it with someone else who has never seen you teach, but who will be prepared to give you realistic feedback.

— Watch it with the aid of a classroom observation schedule, such as those used on teacher education courses, and rate yourself on the factors which the form draws attention to.

— Watch it on fast-forward, and see how your movements and mannerisms come to the fore.

— If you identify things which need to be changed, do not try to change everything at once: select one or two specific items and work on them. If you try to do too much you will become distracted by the "performance" aspects of teaching and forget about helping students to learn.

Non-verbal Communication

Positioning

Where do you put yourself? There are obvious points such as not obscuring students' views of screens or boards, but there are others which are often forgotten. In my view, for what it is worth, you should only sit down if you want to communicate that you are refusing to take the conventional teaching role (which may be quite often, depending on your classes).

Otherwise, students need to be able to see you. Seeing you speak is important additional information, which may help them to make sense of the occasional mis-heard word. If anyone in the class has a hearing impairment, whether aware of it or not, they need to see you.

So do not silhouette yourself against a window. Do not move so far away from the OHP or the board that students cannot see both you and it in the same glance. If you must move about, make a point with your movements: if you are presenting a debatable point, make the "pro" points from one side of the room and the "con" points from the other. Do not pace like a neurotic caged animal in a zoo!

Gestures

The British are not known for their demonstrativeness, but relevant gestures are an additional channel of communication which you can utilise. Some, such as making quotation signs in the air, are cliches, but that does not matter: if they make the presentation more comprehensible, so much the better.

Voice

Physical issues

— Your voice is an important tool of your trade, and it is worth looking after it. Do not strain it: no-one can sustain shouting for an hour (or listening to a shout, either).

— Breathe from the diaphragm: if you don't or you don't know what I mean, find an acting or singing coach to help you.

— Keep your throat open and relaxed.

— Lubricate your voice with frequent drinks. Centrally heated institutions are not a good environment for the voice, anyway.

— If you do end up straining your voice, it could be because you are talking too much!

Presentation

Listen to your own voice on audio-tape, recorded from the back of the class.

— Is there sufficient and appropriate variation in pitch? Monotonous voices are the stock in trade of hypnotists, remember. A predictable sing-song can be almost as bad. Does the variation of pitch support the sense of what you are saying? In the UK (before the advent of "Neighbours") it was standard "received pronunciation" practice to drop the voice at the end of a sentence. A rising inflexion conveyed a question. That is no longer the case, but at least a change of inflexion may indicate punctuation.

— Can you catch every word? It seems to be natural to change the register of the voice according to the speaker's distance from the hearer, so this is often a self-adjusting process. As we get further away, we articulate more clearly—but it is worth checking.

— How about pace? Do you gabble or drawl? Pacing is intimately linked to the extent to which you want students to dwell on every word, and your practice of saying things once or more frequently. Assuming you can be understood (remember that not everyone in your class may be listening in their first language), the important thing is the pacing of the ideas, rather than the words.

— How formal is your expression? This is a question of appropriateness, but be ware of using expressions which any of your listeners may not understand, such as idiomatic constructions or slang.

— Do you have irritating mannerisms? "Um...er...well" I am continually impressed by the ability of radio and TV presenters to speak without such mannerisms. Unfortunately, the evidence of my tapes of myself is that if I try not to use them, my delivery becomes even more stilted and self-conscious than usual: but when I am "in full flood", they disappear anyway. You can practise some of them away, but not all of them.

— Be more careful of habitual "padding" phrases, such as "OK?", "You know...", "Kind of..." They can be intensely irritating.

VALUES

"Values" may be a loaded word, but there are two personal qualities which will more than make up for deficiencies in practically everything on this site—although they are consistent with everything.

Enthusiasm

Genuine, not fake. Not chat-show-host enthusiasm (which works with no-one), or geeky self-absorbed obsessional enthusiasm (which works only very occasionally but is incompatible with the second quality), but genuine interest in and even love for your subject. It's infectious, and motivation is one of the principal determinants of effective learning.

It's difficult to be enthusiastic about some things: company law isn't riveting, and COSHH lights up few people's lives but there are stories to be told in either area which can show how much they matter. At the very least, never show that the subject is boring. Your students may think you a little strange, at worst, but if you are bored, what are they going to be?

Not everyone can be a charismatic teacher—I know, I've tried, but it doesn't come from trying—but excite yourself about the ideas, and you may not only excite the students, but you will also want to find exciting and effective ways to help them to learn, and what good practice there is on this site will follow almost automatically.

Respect

Sorry it sounds so pompous, but you do have to respect your students (however unworthy they may at first appear). If you don't have respect for the difficulties they have in learning—if you see them as merely "stupid" or "lazy", or other dead-end labels—there is no chance of finding a way to relate to them which will help them to learn.

Moreover, it is when you respect your students that you appreciate how much they are capable of, and so how much you can push (or even pull) them. Making demands of someone you don't think capable of meeting them is a futile and inevitably frustrating exercise. But to do so in a way which shows that you do think they are capable of rising to the challenge is quite different.

Advance Organisers

Isn't it nice to find out that something you have been doing all along has a jargon name? It's like M. Jourdain in Molière's *Le Bourgeois Gentilhomme* who was gratified to discover that he had been speaking prose all his life. Advance Organisers are like that: they are simply devices used in the introduction of a topic which enable learners to orient themselves to the topic, so that they can locate where any particular bit of input fits in and how it links with what they already know. Ausubel's major principle — that the most important determinant of learning is what the learner already knows — calls for an image or example which directs the learner to relevant prior experience or learning and also points forward to new material.

Common examples are:

— A simple statement of,

"We have been handling joints of meat in the kitchen a lot, so in this class we are going to look at cuts of beef.

We'll find out which part of the cow each one comes from, what its characteristics are, and how you might prepare it."

Because this is just verbal, it is transitory. In the example it did not matter because the session had a sort of rhythm to it, repeating the same headings in relation to a succession of different cuts; but in a more complex area, it would be wise to have something more permanent to re-visit.

— An OHT with a list of the topics and sub-topics on it, which you can return to at intervals during the session in order to mark how far you have got, and show how the new material fits in with established knowledge.

  — A useful variation on this is to use a concept- or

  — mind-map: you can put it on a whiteboard, and start with the major branches identified and add sub-branches as you get further into each topic. This also permits linkages between topics.

  — Even better, of course, is for students to build their own mind-maps, because those will almost necessarily establish linkages in terms of their prior learning.

  — Or an poster on the wall which is permanently there to refer to.

— A handout with the same kind of information on it, perhaps laid out with lots of white space so that students can fill in their own notes under each heading—again, linking back to what they already know. It could contain more information, of course, as a gapped handout.

— On a larger scale, a study guide to the course, or a handbook, can locate all the different bits: encourage students to keep it with them and to use it by making frequent reference to it.

— And don't forget the humble story or anecdote which may be memorable in its own right, but also serves to relate the abstract material to a more-or-less familiar situation in the students' own world.

Scaffolding and the ZPD

Bruner has another model of similar status, that of "scaffolding". Although applied principally to a description of the way in which we naturally teach young children, it also comes readily to mind in taking anyone through new material or skills. The teacher provides the external structure (the scaffold) within which the learner can build their building. This includes engaging the learner's interest, demonstrating, progressing from the simple to the complex, encouraging practice, providing feedback, and so on.

— Scaffolding, of course, is something which is taken down when no longer needed. So aids such as vocabulary lists in language learning, crib-sheets with formulae in engineering, mnemonics for memorising procedures (like the old "ABC" for first-aiders), can all be useful but are left behind as competence develops.

Vygotsky's wonderfully named "Zone of Proximal Development" has elements of the same process. This points out that learners can achieve more with help and guidance than they can left to themselves. Such an observation is commonplace in assessing the capabilities of people with learning disabilities, where achievement is categorised as "can do alone", "can do with guidance", "can do with physical assistance", and so on. However, there is more to it than that: judging how it is reasonable to "stretch" learners requires complex assessment. Too little and they don't get anywhere and get bored: too much and the task is overwhelming and they are almost sure to fail.

Models and Metaphors

Similarly fairly intuitive, as a way of structuring new ideas is the use of simplified models, metaphors and analogies:

— A simplified model: this is routinely used in science teaching. You start with the simplest possible case of something, and then you elaborate and move on to those which are closer to the real world. In discussing forces acting on an object, for example, you may start with an object falling vertically in a vacuum, and go on adding variables and forces until you are discussing a car going round an uphill corner in a cross-wind.

— In vaguer subjects, an artificially pure and perhaps mythical example or anecdote can serve the purpose. Indeed, that is in part what myths are all about.

— Analogy and metaphor: "The structure of the atom is like a solar system...", "Think of the hard disc as a filing cabinet", "White blood cells are like guards", "Teaching is like gardening..." This needs care, precisely because it can be so vivid, that learners get hooked on it and may not see where the analogy begins to break down. Metaphor is even more problematic: you are asserting that one thing is something else. However, it has its place. While potentially confusing, you can use more than one analogy to emphasise that each one points to just one aspect of a phenomenon. The classic example is that light behaves both like a wave and like a particle.

— A variant is the physical or visual arrangement of ideas or topics to depict their relationship. See the pyramidal arrangement of the levels of Bloom's taxonomy as an example. Or the diagrammatic representation of legitimate peripheral participation — which is interesting because the authors specifically reject any such representation of their model.

— ...or, more interesting, get the learners to tell you their metaphors, or to draw them. This may give you more insight into the way in which they are construing the material than anything else. I remember the lecturer, who, when asked for a drawing of his metaphor of teaching, drew an aircraft dropping bombs. He explained that his first job was to destroy his students' preconceptions, before he (or they?) could rebuild.

EXERCISES

What is the difference between an exercise and an assessment? Even a formative assessment is basically backward-looking, to what has already been learnt or achieved. In my book, exercises are ways of setting an agenda, of raising issues which can then be explored in more detail, of looking forwards. Of course, this is not incompatible with assessment, and the terms don't matter much anyway.

The page links below will take you to descriptions of a few exercises which meet my definition, with a few remarks about how to make them work most effectively, born of bitter experience! The list is not of course exhaustive, but each one represents a "family" of exercises which can be elaborated for your own purposes:

The Basic Rules

— Make sure that the instructions are clear. If students can possibly misunderstand, they will. Time spent trying to explain the procedure, again and yet again, is time wasted. Written instructions on a handout or OHT indicate that the exercise has been planned in advance and engender confidence. (Of course, there is also scope for spontaneous ones, too.)

— Make sure that the outcomes of the exercise will be relevant to the learning even if it does not "go well". Exercises are usually open-ended, so you have to work with whatever they produce.

— Always give value to students' efforts. This may take the form of comments and using the ideas in a plenary session, or marking any work produced, but it is a strange feature of the culture of courses that even sophisticated students are likely to feel that their effort has not been worthwhile unless it has received the legitimation of the teacher's recognition.

Musical Mnemonics

Objective

To help students to learn all those boring things which still have to be learned, such as names and dates. This may be the freaky fringe of rote learning, but the point of including it is to encourage a degree of creativity about this chore. This may not be the kind of thing you would want to do in class—it might well be experienced as patronising and reminiscent of primary school—but put it on the VLE or make it available on CD, and it becomes something different, and even "fun". I'm suspicious of efforts to make learning fun, as such, but there is no harm in complements and adjuncts to mainstream teaching.

Considerations

Ever since Ebbinghaus' experiments with learning nonsense syllables, it has been clear that people learn things better when they have a meaning. In the ideal world of adult learning, people would just memorise all this stuff from sheer familiarity, just as gardeners remember the names of plants, or we learn the names of people at work. Unfortunately, the taught curriculum often demands that we have to learn stuff without much of a context or a pre-existing structure. So the best thing is to find a structure which will serve, even if it bears little resemblance to the real-world context.

Many memory aids or mnemonic systems rely on visualisation: "Imagine the rooms in your house, and place the objects you need to remember in them..." or sometimes on word association; "Richard Of York Gained Battles In Vain". This exercise goes a little further, particularly for those people who have a principally auditory perceptual learning style.

Method

Music is one of the most structured phenomena in our world, and because of this, song lyrics are highly memorable. In them:

— sense

— rhyme

— rhythm

— tune

all come together, reinforcing each other so that if you forget a few words, you are prompted to remember the few possibilities which meet all the requirements. Poetry is almost as good, but without the "tune" channel, of course.

So: set the students the task of setting the material to music. They can use it as the basis for a new lyric to a song of their choice, or they can make up a new tune for it. The cleverest example I know of is Tom Lehrer's "The Elements", in which he sets the names of the chemical elements to the tune of "I am the very model of a modern Major-General" by Sullivan (replacing Gilbert's lyrics). The interesting feature of this exercise is that even if the students don't succeed in setting the stuff to music, by the time they have wrestled with it for a while, they'll know it anyway!

Posters

Poster sessions are established features of academic conferences. They are periods in which people with contributions which do not add up to full papers, or those wanting to up-date on work in progress, are each allocated a table or space in a hall, where they put up a stand or simply stick a poster on the wall. They stand by it, and other delegates wander around reading the posters and talking to their "owners".

— There are several ways in which this idea can be adapted for teaching purposes.

— It can be used instead of a series of presentations, especially when the group is large, and a succession of presentations would take too much time.

— Designing the poster in small groups is a useful way of breaking up a long and perhaps rather arid teaching sequence. Encourage members to express theoretical ideas in some graphic and metaphorical way, using flip-chart paper and felt-tip pens, then display them during a coffee- or meal-break.

— Teacher-designed posters can be used to inform students about by-ways of the subject which do not justify taking up time in main classes, but which are nevertheless valid aspects of it.

— Mini-posters: anything from the size of a Post-it note upwards can be stuck on a wall to note student reactions to a teaching sequence: people can anonymously ask the teacher to vary the pace, use simpler language, or spend more time on particular topics and less on others. Again useful for large groups.

— Reporting-back from large numbers of small groups can be done in this way, too. Instruct the group reporters to write just one point on each piece of paper or card. Wandering around the groups, pick up a general idea of the main themes which are likely to emerge. Use this to start a mind-map on the whiteboard, or divide it into columns or areas. Reporters then post their individual findings onto this in the appropriate place, and everyone gets a chance to have a good look at the result before the next session.

— Use a similar system to match up students with information to provide, with those who want to know it. We used to do this as part of an induction programme when students came with very different experiences of working in disparate areas of social work. Each would be asked to list their experience ("working with young offenders", "day care for dementia sufferers" etc.) on cards, and also their areas of ignorance, on different coloured cards. Matching these up provided the basis for informal student-led seminars for the best part of a week, and ensured that when we started "teaching proper", there was a much more consistent base of shared experience to work with.

— Posters give something to do as well as something to look at, and enable students to get out of their seats.

As ever, always make sure that you give value to what is offered by commenting on it both formally and informally, and refer back to it in formal teaching.

Role-Play

Many students hate role-play. That is a problem, because it is undoubtedly one of the best methods of developing interpersonal skills in a safe situation, and of bringing alive material which would otherwise simply be "academic" in the pejorative sense of the term. For anyone who has not encountered it, role-play is a way of improvising a mini-drama to practise skills in interpersonal practice, whether it be sales technique, job interviewing, technical advising, counselling, or whatever. Role-plays can last for a matter of fifteen seconds or fifteen minutes or even longer when they are part of more complex simulations. Useful though they are, learners often feel very exposed by participating in them, particularly if they take place under the scrutiny of the rest of the class, or if they are videotaped.

The commonest complaint is that they are "unrealistic": in practice this usually means that they are too realistic for comfort! However, they stand in the same relationship to real life as cartoons do to photographs. They point up certain features and ignore others. In this respect, they present fairly well-defined problems (much more clearly defined than in real life, and usually not mixed up with other issues as real life invariably is).

There are however some points which can minimise the negative aspects:

— Be up-front in course information about whether role-play will be involved, and what the expectations are about participation. It is better if people do not come at all, than if they turn up and then interrupt the proceedings by complaining that they don't like role-play.

— If you have got a group in which some people are likely to be reluctant to participate, check it out explicitly, in a way which means that they can opt out without confrontation. Use methods such as small syndicate groups working to brief one member to participate in the role-play on their behalf: it promotes involvement without everyone being "exposed".

— Be matter-of-fact about it. For example, many manuals emphasise the importance of "de-roling" (communicating to other members of the group, and to yourself, that you are no longer in role after a session), and certainly there are occasions when that requires considerable work—but those are largely situations bordering on psychodrama, rather than practice of professional skills (with the possible exception of counselling, if you have taken the role of client). De-roling can be done in a simple and ritualised way, very effectively. If you are anxious about the process, the anxiety will communicate itself to the course members, and undermine the effectiveness of the method.

— If role-play is likely to be central to the learning process, use it frequently throughout the course, rather than building up to THE ROLE-PLAY as a climax.

— Participate yourself. If you are demonstrating points, invite a member of the group to act as your "foil", feed or straight man (excuse the dated/sexist language, but "straight-person" sounded so odd, as if opposed to "gay-person"). Use such opportunities to routinise aspects of role-play: get your partner to move out of her or his seat and to take up an appropriate position in relation to you, for example. Thank her and let her sit down again as soon as you have finished.

— Make the instructions and procedures very clear, perhaps with a handout. In particular, be clear about time-limits if anyone is nervous: a time-limited commitment is easier to handle than an open-ended one.

— Try getting participants to role-play doing something as badly as possible, for the first try. Not only is it an effective ice-breaker, but it is easy to draw out the teaching points in discussion afterwards.

— Be focused. Be clear about why you want to/need to use role-play (as opposed to simple discussion, or the use of video demonstration, etc.). If it is to practise a particular technique or method, bring it in step by step, rather than plunging people in with "now you try it".

— Give plenty of thought to the role-play scenario. It needs to be focused so that it brings out the relevant skills above all. All participants also need to have a common understanding of the situation and the background. This can be tricky: you don't want to go into tremendous detail because it is a distraction, but on the other hand it is not uncommon for a participant to "hi-jack" a role-play by trotting out a piece of information which in real life would be known to both participants, thereby forcing their partner to adjust to it—"As you know, the student welfare service has been abolished in the last round of cuts...!"

— Remember that it is often the person taking the "client", "consumer", etc., non-professional role who learns most from the experience: do not neglect this in the interests of the "professional" role.

— If there are technical points at issue, feel free to adopt a convention of "time-out", when you can stop the process in mid-flow and have a few moments to think (or even consult with others). Agree a clear signal for time-out in advance (a sweeping "cut" gesture works quite well, for example, and is not likely to be part of the role-play action). The other participant, of course, has to remain "frozen" during the time-out.

— Never let a role-play pass without comment. Have a clear procedure for review, included in the briefing and strictly followed, such as:

  — Participants give their reactions first, usually starting with the person who took the more/most difficult/vulnerable role, or that furthest from her or his "normal" self. This is usually sufficient de-roling, and permits cathartic laughter, swearing etc.,

  — If the participants have been working on behalf of a group which briefed them, the other members of that group get the next opportunity to comment.

  — The rest of the course group get their say

  — Finally, the tutor comments. You should by now have heard everything from everyone else: you may simply need to confirm or build on points which have already been made. Just occasionally, the participants will have totally missed the point. Even so, start with the positives, and if you can, draw out the critical comments *via* questioning. This has the effect of dividing the responsibility for being critical—it's partly yours because you asked the question, and partly that of the person who answers—and this makes it easier both to make and receive critical comments.

Sculpting

"Sculpting" here refers to any technique which uses physical objects to represent elements within a system. It offers the opportunity for activity, and for the discovery of relationships which might not otherwise be apparent. It also provides an additional visual, and sometimes tactile, channel of communication with fellow-students or the teacher when talking about complex relationships, which is why it is included in this selective list of exercise types. The use of objects (which can be neutral or symbolic — what is represented by using a key, for example?) gives an extra dimension which cannot be gained from mere diagrams.

Unlike a drawn diagram, too, the sculpt is ephemeral: you can move it about and change it without hassle, which encourages experimentation. If you arrive at a perfect arrangement, you can always draw it, after all. The "Learner, Subject and Teacher" model is a sculpt: when used in a class, the students have pieces of card which they are asked to arrange to depict the respective positions of the elements of the system. They can move them around to represent alternative aspirations, or "what if?" questions. When talking about patterns of relationships in class groups or work groups, students can readily use the contents of their pockets or bags to represent the members and arrange them physically to add an extra dimension. Coins, keys, scraps of paper, polo mints — anything small with a distinctive shape can be used.

The arrangement can be done on the stage of an overhead projector if the whole class needs to see it. An advantage of using physical objects is that there are three dimensions in which they can be manipulated. The attribution of the dimensions is often intuitive, but it can be formalised. In the Learner, Subject, Teacher example, the "vertical" dimension is formally designated as that of authority. Proximity and distance, clustering, size of objects, even colour can all be used to represent different features of the system. A further development—only applicable on "touchy/feely" courses—is to use other students to produce a living tableau of a system, perhaps making use of socio- and psychodrama techniques such as "doubling", to help with the exploration of its dynamics, but that is best left to people who know what they are doing and who can contain the sometimes unpredictable outcomes!

Skeletal Cases

Want to develop students' investigatory skills? Then instead of presenting complete case-studies, provide only the initial "presenting information", and only add to it in response to their questions. There are a number of variations on the theme:

— *Background*: Provide just the superficial information with which a student might be confronted on first acquaintance with the situation. Feed in additional background only if asked about it: this is useful for fairly basic professional skills of gathering data on cases. After a set period of time or number of questions, see how efficiently the students have got at the important material.

— *Investigation*: A more sophisticated variation, perhaps starting from a higher information base, is to offer to answer questions, but only when the student explains why she is asking. This identifies the issue of testing hypotheses, and the question of what evidence might be gathered in order to test an hypothesis. It applies clearly to medical diagnosis, but it could also apply to fault-finding in a computer network, or a car engine.

— *Potential accounts*: Almost the reverse strategy, particularly useful on in-service courses with practitioners who are locked into recipes of the order of "When such-and-such happens, I always...": outline the presenting situation and asked them to multiply as many potential explanations as possible, before eliminating any of them. This is a good exercise for the divergent thinkers in the group, and for any occasion when you wish to encourage what John Keats called "negative capability"—the art of not jumping to conclusions, but tolerating uncertainty and confusion where necessary.

— *Raw data*: a variant on the above is to start with raw statistical or documentary data.

ROOM LAYOUT

The physical surroundings of a class can encourage or inhibit the kind of interaction, and hence learning, which you want. Making distinct efforts to arrange the furniture of a classroom to promote a particular kind of interaction also sends strong messages to participants who are used to conventional layouts that this class is something different. It may be a hassle (particularly when there are instructions to "leave the room as you found it") but it is worth it. The ability to "make eye-contact" (look someone in the eye, however fleetingly) is—at least in Western culture—the key to establishing communication in a group, and it is particularly important for the teacher.

— The traditional classroom layout, in rows, allows the teacher to make eye-contact with all the students (although it is important to keep looking around to move beyond a narrow arc of vision, if you want everyone to feel included). It facilitates traditional teacher-student delivery and questioning, or "teacher-centred" teaching.

— The students can also readily see a screen or board at the front.

— But in order to talk to each other, they need to turn in their seats or address the back of a fellow-student's neck.

— For whole-group discussion, the U-shape layout is more effective. The students can make eye-contact with each other (although they still have to twist to talk to a person along the same side of the table). However, apart from those along the back, they also have to turn to see whatever the teacher is presenting.

— If the group is too large to get around a U-shaped layout or a board-room table, the "fishbowl", with concentric circles of students, maximises the possibilities of discussion. Clearly this works better without tables, and it is useful to make efforts to ensure that over several sessions, everyone has their turn in the "inner circle".

— For sessions involving small group working, it is useful to arrange tables at which four or five students can sit, to promote the easy formation of the small groups from the start of the session. It avoids the disruption caused by people moving about half-way through (although that is sometimes a useful "punctuation mark" in the session).

The moral of the story is, as ever, that there is no single solution: it all depends on what it is you want to do.

LEARNING CONTRACTS

Learning contracts are agreements between a teacher (or teaching team) and a learner (or occasionally a group of learners). They normally concern issues of assessment, and provide a useful mechanism for reassuring both parties about whether a planned piece of work will meet the requirements of a course or module: this is particularly valuable when the assessment is not in the form of a set essay title, or an examination. However, there is more to the principle of the learning contract than a convenient administrative device. It is based on the principle of the learners being active partners in the teaching-learning system, rather than passive recipients of whatever it is that the teacher thinks is good for them. It is about their ownership of the process.

Merely using the technique, however, does not automatically bring about this ownership and involvement. As Collins has pointed out, the contractual bargain is often one-sided, with all the obligations being on the side of the student, and none on the part of the teacher. The teacher does not even undertake unequivocally to award a pass mark to the resultant work: she will do so only if in her judgement it meets the required criteria. After all, all assessments are based on a contract, which usually remains implicit. It is of the order of:

"The teacher undertakes that:

— if the student produces such work as the teacher specifies,

— to a standard which the teacher will determine (whether or not that standard is based on fixed criteria or personal whim, and regardless of whether the standard is known to the student),

— the teacher will award a mark to that work.

— The student indicates acceptance of this 'agreement' by producing the work"

That is a slightly unfair version, but only slightly. Matters can be improved by being explicit and transparent about the marking scheme. Learning contracts seek to make explicit this implicit deal, which should at least expose any one-sidedness, and ideally provide a basis for addressing it.

Initially, there may be considerable student resistance to learning contracts: they are not part of the rules of the educational game they are familiar with. The common cry is, "Just tell me what to do!" Nevertheless, if their negotiation is taken seriously (by the teacher as well as the student, and recognising the time which has to be put into tutorial consultations about them), they are very valuable ways of focusing attention on things which matter.

Form of the Contract

There are many forms which the contract can take, but the following represents a general example:

— *Student name and details:* This is pretty obvious

— *Course name and level:* So is this, but the course level is important, because that sets the expectations of the piece of work: the level criteria should be set out clearly somewhere—perhaps in the handbook.

— *Outcomes to be addressed:* They may not be expressed as outcomes, but this is where the student puts the course requirements about the piece of work.

— *Form of submission:* It could be a project, a portfolio, a videotape of practice, an object the student has made, a computer program ... If the tutor signs the form, she is agreeing that a submission of this type will be acceptable.

— *Outline of submission:* This is the crunchy bit: this is where the student sets out her intentions for the submission. Much of the rest of the form may be governed by course regulations, but this has to be original. It is a statement of the student's solution to the problem, "How am I going to produce evidence that I can meet these outcomes?"

— *Resources and assistance:* So far, the contract has been one-sided, as Collins comments. This is where the student can request input from the tutor, such as looking over a draft, or providing copies of some material not in the library, or an introduction to an interviewee.

— *Signatures:* These are what make the magic work: the contract is not worth anything until it has been agreed and signed by both student and tutor. Usually the student keeps the main copy to submit with the completed work, but the tutor can keep one on file for security purposes if necessary.

The tutor's signature makes explicit the implicit bargain above. She is agreeing that if the student delivers what is promised, credit will be awarded. Practically, then, the contract allows for considerable variation in the form of submission, and clarifies in advance such thorny problems as collaborative working and how much help the student can expect from the tutor. At the level of principle, however, it changes the student from being merely reactive, in the sense of responding to set demands to produce a 4,000-word assignment on this or that, to being proactive in taking the initiative in proposing work to meet the requirements.

QUESTIONING

Questioning class members is one of the defining features of teaching. It is the single most common variation from the direct presentation of material, and the basic mechanism for creating a dialogue with students.

Questioning in school classes in particular has spawned quite a lot of research. So let's start with some questions!

— Why do you use questions? This is not a rhetorical question. (Rhetorical questions are not a good idea in teaching—they accustom students to the idea that if they wait long enough you will answer any question yourself.) Please think of some answers before proceeding.

If you have some answers ...

Call me a cynic, but I wonder whether you have arrived here the second time around? Either way, let's have a look at some of the potential answers:

To check on understanding

This is probably the most common usage: but it is important to emphasise the "understanding" element, because if you are not careful, your questions can end up testing something quite different. The most familiar questions are "closed" ones, much used in school.

— "What is the formula for calculating speed from time and distance?"

— "What is the first person plural subjunctive of 'docere'?"

They are closed, because they are searching for a single correct answer (or possibly one of a range of correct answers) based on what has already been taught. The other kind of question is "open": it calls for an answer in which the student draws on her experience, knowledge or judgement beyond the confines of the class. Open questions may well have incorrect answers, but potentially many correct—or more accurately, useful—answers.

One well-known problem with questioning is that students frequently assume that all questions are closed, sometimes despite the teacher's protestations. This is the heritage of schooling, and leads to the "Guess what I'm thinking" game, which stems from ill-thought-out questions, and to my mind has no place in post-school education.

> *What's the major difference between Trollope and Conrad?*
> Conrad's more exciting
>
> *I suppose you could argue that... Can you think of another?*
>
> Conrad writes about the rest of the world. Trollope's all about England.
>
> Well, that's right, but...
>
> Conrad is a twentieth-century writer, but Trollope is firmly in the nineteenth.
>
> True—can you think of anything in the structure of the novels?
>
> Trollope digresses, with all those long boring passages about...
>
> *Well, you could argue that Conrad digresses, too. Still, you are onto something... The major difference is in their approach to plotting the story*

The teacher had that answer in mind when he asked the question, and the principal task of the students was to find out what it was. In the end, the teacher had to supply it, by a rather convoluted route. The effect of the interchange was to devalue the suggestions made by all the students: the lead-in to the teaching point (about plot) in fact came from the least accurate of all the answers. Closed questions test knowledge, but not understanding. As familiarity with Bloom's taxonomy will remind you, knowledge is a necessary but not sufficient condition for comprehension.

Closed questions have their place, but usually it is as a follow-up to a broader question which sets the scene, as it were, and which can get at the context. They then serve as a focusing device:

"In the next few sessions we are going to look at language. What do you think are the issues psychologists are most likely to be interested in, about language?

Why people in different countries speak different languages?

That's a fascinating question, but it's more to do with the languages themselves, which is a linguistics issue, and perhaps history and social factors. Psychologists are more concerned with individual competence in using language.

So would they be interested in why some people talk a lot and others don't say much? Can they explain why O'Connor over there never shuts up?

(Laughter: someone chips in, "Can they explain the effect of kissing the Blarney Stone?")

He's not the only one! Well, social psychologists are indeed interested in that kind of thing, and how conversations are structured—we'll be getting onto that, later.[...]

How about how we learn a language?

Yes indeed. In fact, that's where we're going to start. [...] From what we've done so far, have you any ideas about different approaches to language acquisition? Nature and nurture?

Yes! What would that mean in practice?

Nature theories would [...] say language was sort of built in to us.

And...? Someone else?

Nurture would say we learned it all from scratch.

Good: that's it, more or less exactly. Who would you expect to emphasise

learning?

Behaviourists?

Exactly...

In the above example—which is not meant to be perfect—the initial question is open, and although the first answers are not exactly on target for the rest of the lesson, they are taken seriously and linked in to the main theme.

The later questions are more closed, but make sense in the context of earlier ones, so that what is really quite a sloppy question, "have you any ideas about different approaches...?" nevertheless "hits its target". For better or for worse, closed questions are a means of control. They emphasise the teacher's authority. Nominated questions: *"O'Connor, tell me the name of a prominent behaviourist."* (OK, it's an order, not a question) are an even stronger form of control. At least one textbook in the field recommends the following procedure for questioning:

— Pose: Ask the question

— Pause

— Pounce: Nominate someone to answer

This implies a very tight structure: it is the "teacher as Predator" approach. As with all these things, it has its place, but it is not always appropriate.

To get students thinking

Here, we are moving up Bloom's taxonomy in the cognitive domain, beyond knowledge to understanding or application and beyond. Nevertheless, because each level presupposes those below, a question of this nature gets at the lower levels, too.

> "Why do you think the trusses are constructed with cross-bracings?
>
> Because it makes them stronger?
>
> But it also adds to the weight
>
> So it must make them stronger than the additional weight matters [...]
>
> OK, but why does it make them stronger? Gerry? Because it stops the top and bottom moving relative to each other.

Good point. Why does that matter? Sam?
Well, it's like you had a thicker beam, but not as heavy.

You've answered the weight question! But we can still be more explicit [...] Think about why the bracings are criss-crossed. Why don't they go straight across? Ali?

Is it something to do with compression?
Could be—go on..."

This is the kind of questioning which is often neglected, because really, it would be a lot easier to tell them the answer. The students are building on their pre-existing knowledge (strength vs. weight, compression and tension) and groping towards the answer. The fact that the answer is already known is not relevant—they don't know it, yet, and they are constructing it for themselves. There may be more vivid ways of getting them to understand the point (building something for themselves, for example, or just a demonstration with a model), but routinely, this kind of questioning is an effective stock-in-trade for the teacher.

As ever, it is respect for the answers which is central to success. Some students might have been discouraged by the initial objection to the first answer, and it is debatable whether the teacher should have moved on so fast to the next student, but there is nevertheless a sense of building something between teacher and student. This is the so-called Socratic method (only Socrates wasn't very good at it—he asked too many leading questions). See the discussion of the Conversational Model.

To get examples, to check out principles

"Does this ring any bells with anyone? Is Gestalt actually relevant to your teaching?

Yes, I think it is, only I'm not sure it's Gestalt—it's more of a way of thinking...

Can you say a bit more about what you're getting at, Judy?

> Well, with my marketing students [...] sometimes they'll learn all the stuff, and you can test them on it, and they know it, but they still haven't got a clue what it's all about. [...] but some of them, who may not be as good, technically, they just think in a marketing kind of way, if you know what I mean...
> [Another member] Doesn't that say something about the assessment?
>
> Perhaps it does, but can we stay with this point for a while? Judy?
>
> Marketing is more of a perspective—in business—than a subject. Some students just get it, and some don't—and I'm not sure how to ensure that they all get it..."

The question is open-ended: it calls for students to search their experience for anything which might possibly be related, and then to check out whether they are on the right lines by linking experience and theory. In this instance, the material the student brought up could have been considered under a number of theoretical perspectives, but she was testing ("I'm not sure it's Gestalt") her understanding. A pre-requisite of such a discussion is that students have to know that their ideas will not be dismissed. This example might well not have been the kind of thing the teacher was thinking of when he asked the question, and the answer posed some problems in terms of discussion management (it might easily have gone off the point, into a discussion of assessment methods, and it was important not to be dismissive of the other student's contribution). However, the point was firmly task-related, even if not a central example of Gestalt.

There are many other potential headings under which we could discuss questions, but these three subsume most of the variants, and there is no virtue in multiplying categories for the sake of it.

SCHEDULING

There is very little in the literature about the scheduling and pacing of teaching, which is not surprising, because:

— It is something over which we often have little control: we are likely to be stuck with a timetable governed by all kinds of factors, such as staff and room availability, which are much more clear-cut, and

— time is something teachers fight over: there rarely seems to be enough time to "cover the syllabus" and

— judging how long something is going to take (with this group of students *etc.*) is a high-level and rather inexact skill. You may know how long it will take to *teach,* but how long will it take for an acceptable proportion of these students to *learn?*

So scheduling and pacing (the speed at which topics are tackled and the relative amounts of time devoted to them) receive much less attention than they deserve. The following notes represent what appears to me to be a broad consensus of experienced teachers:

Scheduling of sessions

— Put lectures (if you have them) and intellectual activities in the morning: put practicals after lunch. There tends to be a dip in people's ability to concentrate between 2 and 4pm: they need the extra stimulation of activity.

— If you have the choice, teach intellectually demanding and academic topics on a "drip-drip" basis: relatively short sessions with time between for reading and perhaps exercises.

— Practicals clearly demand more time, if only because of the need to complete experiments, and the investment of time needed for setting up equipment. Apart from this, however, practical inter-personal activities, such as interviewing or counselling training, benefit from an "immersion" approach. A great deal can be lost between sessions, so better one whole day than an hour a week for six weeks. The group needs time to work through its developmental cycle.

— Consider planning your schedule on a "working backwards from the end" basis. The big learning pay-offs often come in the last 15% of the session or the sequence (assuming you have not lost your learners — physically or mentally — by then), but they may well be diminished if you are having to rush to catch up with yourself.

— If necessary, include "slippage" time in your sequence. An almost guaranteed way to lose your students is not to be prepared to answer their questions or follow their arguments because you are pressured to keep to an inviolable schedule. Prioritise your taught material so that you know what you may be prepared to drop in the interests of capitalising on an opportunistic moment.

— Plan the whole sequence in advance: but re-visit each session before you actually teach it, and modify in the light of the experience of the previous sessions.

Scheduling within sessions

— "Advance organisers": these may be outlining handouts, statements of objectives, introductory orienting remarks or a variety of other techniques. They give the students confidence that you know where you are going, as well as helping them to get a handle on the session — and to register that something new is coming when they have switched off. Everyone, no matter how motivated, switches off some of the time.

— Change the pace at least every 15-20 minutes. Exercises which really engage the learner can go on longer than this, but under no circumstances that I can think of should you rabbit on for more than 10 minutes at a time.

— Even so, remember the ending. The shape of a teaching session is similar to that of most other task-related conversations, from selling to counselling: note that this operates at a number of scales, from the minute-to-minute presentation/incorporation of each new idea, to the month-to month, even year-to-year, scale of a whole programme

— The Opening is about setting the scene, establishing the rules, and introducing the topic

— The Middle expands on the topic, in this case referring both back to previous material, and probably forward to later material, in order to place it in context

— Then it is important to get Closure, so that students have something relatively clear and manageable to take away — even if that is a question, rather than the teacher's answer

WORK PRACTICE

Many professional and vocational programmes use work practice (under various different names, including "placement", "practicum" and "internship") as a means of enabling students to test their learning in the "real world". The establishment of the pattern of these placements is generally undertaken at the level of large-scale curriculum planning, and hence largely beyond the scope of this site, and the topic is far too large to say much of value at that level, but these notes are intended to guide thinking about how the individual teacher relates to her or his students' work practice. Don't forget that in many cases part-time students already have a substantial amount of work experience: that is what makes them so much more challenging and rewarding to teach.

In very broad terms, work practice has two broad functions:

— Application of college learning to the real-world workplace, or taking learning out, and

— Facilitating testing of learning against the experience of the work-place, or bringing experience in.

The image of the bridge is a useful one, which can inform the role of the tutor in assisting with learning through and from work practice. If the student is concerned with the practicalities of what "they" do in the work-place—look at what principles underlie it. If the student is concerned with theoretical issues, emphasise questions about how practitioners use them in practice, or how they account for practice.

The Partners

It goes without saying that work practice involves engagement with outside employers, and the relationship with them can vary enormously.

— For some employers and some disciplines, taking students is an obligation: some regard students as an asset, some as a liability.

— Some get recompensed for their investment in training, some provide workplace supervisors or mentors out of goodwill, and yet others duck the task.

— Some will actively select their students, others have to take whatever the college or university decides to send.

— In some cases it is up to students to find their own placements, in others the college is more active.

— Some employers pay their students, others do not.

— Some will have long-standing relationships with courses, others may be one-offs

All of these factors will affect what you can legitimately expect: but in every case there needs to be a contract. It may be negotiated with a light touch, and simply take the form of a confirmatory letter about the placement arrangements, or it may be the product of high-level negotiations, sometimes even at a national level, but whatever the form, it sets out clearly the expectations and responsibilities of each partner. If the contract is not spelt out, it will still exist implicitly, but there may be different understandings of crucial provisions, and there may be unacceptable variations in the opportunities offered to different students.

The Student

This part is similar to (although naturally less detailed than) a contract of employment/job specification. It needs to set out what will be expected of the student, including hours of work, role and responsibilities, accountability, etc. It may specify the facilities available to the student, and the circumstances under which expenses may be claimed from the employer. A significant issue for students undertaking professional training is the extent to which the placement agency or company is able or willing to allow them to take responsibility in their work: this can be defined in this section. Some thought may need to be given to whether students are covered by the company's insurance, and legal liabilities.

There may also be a section setting out the student's individual learning needs, and the opportunities sought from this particular placement. This is particularly important if the student is to undertake a specific project, either in the form of an assessment task for the course (where information control and confidentiality may also be issues) or for the employer.

The Employer

This part similarly defines the level and limits of commitment of an employer, including the arrangements for mentoring and supporting the student, and their role in reporting on progress and summative assessment.

The Course

The programme's part of the contract will define the purposes and objectives of the placement, and the arrangements for monitoring and visiting by programme staff. It may also cover the financial arrangements if any.

Objectives

Much of the potential of work practice can be lost if there is a lack of clarity about objectives. There may well be a general set of objectives, included in the "Course" part of the contract, and a specific set negotiated at the outset of the placement for this particular student. In some circumstances, students may be assessed on a specific set of competences. This, of course, assumes that every placement can offer appropriate opportunities, and that the mentor or supervisor is able to devote the time to such assessment.

In other cases, the emphasis may be much more on the value of the experience of a real-life working placement, and it will be up to the student to make of it what she or he can, with a reflective journal or similar task to be assessed back on the course. This is more flexible, and may make fewer demands on the employer, but assessment is much more difficult — particularly in terms of what the student does not mention.

Support

Most students will survive without any particular support. Some will even learn something from the experience. But really to learn does require support.

- Support in the work-place is most likely to come from colleagues with whom the student strikes up an informal relationship. This is good at the level of survival, but limited at the level of learning. Career workers have to arrive at an accommodation with their practice in which they take a lot for granted and are not given over much to penetrating beneath the surface. They may not even know why things are done as they are. They may be locked into a grumbling culture, which locates all problems outside themselves and their responsibility—there are innumerable possibilities. However, really to learn, students need more than this.
- Work-based support from a trained mentor or practice teacher is probably the ideal. It is found in professional settings with a high commitment to training, but rarely

elsewhere. The mentor has regular meetings with the student, helping him to address a defined practice curriculum. The downside of this is that the student role may be very restricted by the setup, giving little idea of what working life is like for the "real" staff.

— Tutor support from college is an effective complement to mentor support, but realistically it is rarely frequent or intensive enough to do much more than to remind the student she is still a student. Even so, the tutor has an important role in ensuring that the contract is respected and implemented.

Follow-up

Follow up is essential, and in practice it is often driven by the students, who want to share their work experiences and to test their ideas with tutors. Tutors may find students re-vitalised and re-motivated, able to make connections with practice on issues which before were merely theoretical. This needs to be respected:

— Seminars in which students can report on their experience and share it in a more disciplined way, are valuable.

— Course credit can attach to the placement in many ways, and the reflective journal is one useful one. It does not directly assess the practice on the placement, but the extent to which the student gives evidence of thinking through its rationale, and relating it to college input.

— Tutors can make a conscious effort to recognise the students' recent experience, and draw on it in routine classes.

LECTURES

Lecture: "The process by which the notes of the lecturer become the notes of the student without passing through the mind of either". The lecture is still the standard teaching event in higher education—although nowhere else—and thus an illustration of Atherton's law, "The amount of attention paid to teaching and learning is in inverse proportion to the perceived ability of the students."

For once, there is a standard text in the field. Bligh (5th edition 1998, with a 6th edition imminent) may tell you more than you ever wanted to know, but it is very clear and well laid out for skimming by busy academics. It includes 23 pages of references, in double columns and 8-point text: admittedly, some of them relate to dubious research on the memorisation of nonsense syllables, but he has covered all the angles.

Use

Lectures are relatively effective for conveying information, but—unsurprisingly—not for developing skills or changing attitudes. Used in conjunction with other methods, such as set reading, seminars and student presentations, they can provide a useful overview of a field and help students to make sense of their other work. Attending a lecture is a passive experience for the student. Of all teaching events, the lecture is most likely to promote basic assumption dependence. Note-taking is up to the students, their level of motivation and their skill, so—

Signposting

It is useful—nay, vital—to enable the students to appreciate the shape of the argument. The biggest single problem with note-taking is not appreciating the level of the point which is being made. Lectures unfold over time, and students do not always know whether what they are listening to is a major substantive point, its elaboration, or a gloss or even digression. You can signpost aurally—"The next major issue to consider is ..." —but an outline presented visually and returned to at appropriate points is much more effective. A gapped handout serves much the same purpose.

Attention

Bligh's evidence suggests a fairly steady decline in student attention (and lecturer performance) from the start to the end of a traditional one-hour (50 minute) lecture. Students blip upwards about 10-15 minutes before the end, but this has little effect if the lecturer continues to go downhill. He suggests that the limit to students' effective attention is 25-30 minutes. The good news is that even half a minute's respite has beneficial effects, and that a change is almost as good as a rest. So

— inviting questions

— posing a simple multiple-choice question, answered by a show of hands

— setting a simple exercise for buzz groups

or anything else which varies the pace may produce the desired result.

Rehearsal

A relatively rapid rehearsal of the content can make a considerable difference to retention. A seminar or lab session immediately following the lecture is perhaps the best way to achieve this —and "Any questions?" with two minutes to go, probably the worst (apart from not inviting any questions at all).

3

MODELS

USING ANALOGY

Although some research studies prior to the 1980s have been conducted on the use of analogies, a new interest in this area has produced several in-depth studies that indicate that using analogies assists in concept development. This is particularly true when students have alternative conceptions about a particular concept. Research in this area tends to be qualitative in nature, and the conceptual change that occurs may not result in higher scores on multiple choice science tests of facts and concepts.

In the Classroom

Textbooks and teachers sometimes use analogies to help familiarize students with concepts that are abstract and outside their previous experience. To be effective, analogies must be familiar to students, and their features/functions must be congruent with those of the target. Since adult perspectives are not identical with those of adolescents, it is not surprising that, even though students are familiar with the physical phenomena or event that might be used as the analogy, they are not always familiar with those features that provide the similarity to the target. Once a suitable analogy is found, considerable time must be spent by students in discussion of similarities between the analogy and the target.

It is also important for students to understand how the analogy and target differ. Sometimes this can be done by using multiple analogies to teach the same concept. Studies of chemistry and biology instruction show that some students, who are exposed to and who become skilled in the use of multiple analogies, develop a more scientific understanding of particular science concepts than do students who concentrate on one acceptable analogy. Use of multiple analogies in a bridging sequence has been successful in helping students make sense of initially counter-intuitive ideas.

Analogies occurring in texts may be simple-based on surface similarities—or more complex (particularly in chemistry and physics)-based on similarities of function. The use of functional analogies appears to be more appropriate at the secondary level, where students have developed appropriate reasoning strategies. The discussion that occurs when using analogies not only helps students construct their own knowledge but also assists teachers in basing instruction on students' prior knowledge and existing alternative conceptions. Analogies may also motivate students to learn by provoking their interest. Finally, having students create their own analogies also appears to be an effective instructional strategy.

Role of Analogies in Teaching Science

In the elementary and middle school years, a conceptual foundation for learning science is established. The children progress from concrete to abstract thinking and begin to develop mental models of science concepts. Teachers often use models and analogies to facilitate this process, introducing concepts in ways that are concrete, meaningful, and relevant to the children. The teachers use physical models to show the children simplified representations of concepts. The teachers use analogies to help the children form initial mental models of concepts (e.g., the human eye is like a camera, the heart is like a pump, and an electric circuit is like a water circuit).

Scientific Discovery

Analogies often play an important role in scientific discovery--not as proof, but as a source of inspiration. For example, Joseph Priestley was thinking analogically when he proposed a law of electrical force. Priestley was familiar with Newton's Law of Universal Gravitation, which holds that the gravitational force between any two bodies varies inversely as the square of the distance between them. Priestley speculated, correctly as it turned out, that the electrical force between two charges also varies inversely as the square of their distance. This law of electrical force was experimentally confirmed by Charles Coulomb, and today bears his name. The analogy between Newton's Law of Universal Gravitation and Coulomb's Law of Electrical Force is a good one. Like any analogy, it breaks down in places. Gravitational force only attracts, whereas electrical force attracts or repels. And G is a small constant, whereas k is a large one.

Teachers' Analogies

Recently, in an in-service workshop conducted by Shawn Glynn, science teachers discussed their use of analogies during lessons. Many teachers reported drawing an analogy between a water circuit and an electric circuit. Other popular analogies were:

— A DNA molecule is like a ladder,

— A cell is like a factory,

— A heart is like a force pump,

— A kidney is like a waste filter,

— An eye is like a camera,

— A pulsar is like a lighthouse, and

— Photosynthesis is like baking bread (both are food-making processes in which the ingredients are combined and converted by energy).

Double-edged Swords

Analogies can hinder as well as help learning. When stretched too far, analogies lead to misconceptions. For example, the analogy between the camera and the human eye breaks down with respect to focusing. A camera is focused by changing the distance between the lens and the film, whereas a human eye is focused by the cornea, and the ciliary muscle around the lens.

Teaching-With-Analogies (TWA) Model

The TWA model provides guidelines for using analogies. The TWA model was developed by examining the analogies of exemplary teachers and textbook authors. In this model, the goal is to transfer ideas from a familiar concept (the analog) to an unfamiliar one (the target). If the analog and the target share some similar features, an analogy can be drawn between them. The process of comparing the features is called mapping. The basis of the TWA model consists of six operations that the teacher carries out when drawing an analogy:

— Introduce target concept (e.g., the human eye)

— Review analog concept (e.g., a simple camera)

— Identify relevant features of target and analog (e.g., retina and film)

— Map similarities (e.g., lens)

— Indicate where analogy breaks down (e.g., focusing)

— Draw conclusions (e.g., about lens aberrations)

For children, an analogy functions as an initial model of the target concept--a model that draws on the children's existing knowledge. Later, when the children learn more about the target concept, they will "outgrow" the analogy and adopt more sophisticated models of the concept.

Analogies in Teach General Biology to Non-Biology Majors

Biology can sometimes be difficult, particularly when describing things that we cannot see or abstract concepts that we cannot fully comprehend the first time round. Some students have the notion that Biology is boring, and that the subject requires only memory work to get one through. Others find the subject irrelevant. Yet others find it extremely technical with bombastic terms littering every other sentence in a typical Biology text. Many students base such perceptions on how they were taught Biology in school.

Teachers in primary school and even kindergarten often use actual models or play things to facilitate the learning process and introduce new concepts in ways that are understood by the children. Such supposedly simplified presentations of concepts help students to make connections with the new knowledge. Similarly, an analogy allows students to form an initial mental model of concepts to be learnt based firstly on what they are already familiar with and then transposing it to the new knowledge. Analogies work because human reasoning is said to be primarily based on sparse data and the identification and comparison of patterns instead of logical inference: we look at a new experience and try to match it with similar experiences in the past. Analogies are thus something one can use to establish and organise links among experiences and make them available for retrieval in the creative problem-solving process.

Glynn, Russel and Noah describe a Teaching-With-Analogies (TWA) model (first proposed by Glynn, Duit and Thiele) that shows how analogies can be used in the teaching process. In this model, the goal is to transfer ideas from a familiar concept (the analog) to an unfamiliar one (the target). If both the analog and target share some similar features, an analogy can be drawn between them. The process of comparing the features is called mapping. When using analogies, one has to go through the following steps:

— Introduce the target concept (e.g. the DNA molecule).

— Review the analog concept (e.g. a long, twisted 'ladder').

— Identify relevant features of target and analog (e.g. the two side handles of the ladder contain sugar and phosphate units; the 'rungs' are made of pairs of chemicals called bases).

— Map similarities (e.g. 'side handles of the ladder' and DNA backbone; 'rungs' and bases).

— Indicate where analogy breaks down (e.g. a ladder is rigid; a DNA molecule can open up and be replicated).

— Draw conclusions (e.g. about the structure and function of DNA or about mutations occurring at the bases).

Ruhl describes how analogies can be used to communicate complex medical concepts to patients. Ruhl also suggests that in order to construct and use analogies effectively, one must understand what works and what does not. Five rules are suggested (adapted below) for teaching students (instead of patients):

— *An analogy works best when the concept being taught is new*. If the student already has some understanding of the topic, it may be better to build on the already available framework.

— *Use analogies only if the concept is hard to grasp*. Analogies take time to set up and explain. If the concept is simple, a straightforward explanation may be quicker and will not open the student to possible misconceptions from misapplication of the analogy.

— *Make sure the student understands the analog*. If the students do not even understand the analog, it would not help in the understanding of the target concept.

— *Explain the specific similarities*. Simply stating the analogy does not focus the learners' attention on how it is similar.

— *Be aware of misconceptions the analogy may leave.* Ruhl warns that one of the greatest hazards of teaching by analogy is that the student may transfer inappropriate knowledge from the analog to the target and leave with misconceptions. Analogies can hinder as well as help learning. When stretched too far, analogies lead to misconceptions: "An analogy is like a car. If you take it too far, it breaks down."

After the target concept is learnt, the student should be able to learn new things without always going back to the analogy. Once the analogy has helped the student to understand the skeleton of the concept, the learner can now add further insights directly to this outline and build his own knowledge base. Thus the learner is 'weaned' from use of the analogy.

SPATIAL DYNAMICS TEACHING TOOL IN THE SOCIAL STUDIES.

In elementary school classrooms students are typically engaged in active learning; however, as students progress into middle school, high school, and college, their teachers use less activities-based instruction and more "intellectual" classroom methodologies. Yet active learning has proven to increase motivation, develop valuable skills, and enhance learning in students of all ability levels and grade levels. Teachers at the middle school and high school levels, therefore, need to incorporate more active learning into their classes.

A Key to Active Learning

Spatial dynamics is an instructional strategy wherein students create large-scale models that capture their interest by allowing them to participate in learning. That participation is maximized because students help design and construct the models. Spatial dynamics activities motivate and enhance the learning of students of all ability levels and grade levels. Learning styles not accommodated by more traditional teaching methods are addressed by spatial dynamics. For example, concrete sequential learners prefer direct, hands-on activities; a spatial dynamics classroom activity provides abundant opportunities for such learners.

Spatial dynamics activities also demonstrate a teacher's enthusiasm and commitment to the subject, which further motivates students and yields high-level cognition and learning. Teachers who use only one teaching style day after day are denying opportunities for achievement to their students who may learn more effectively through a variety of teaching approaches. Furthermore, those teachers quickly become stale and boring to students. The students then perceive the subject matter as uninteresting when it is not the subject matter that is boring, but the teacher's instructional style.

Teacher creativity is essential to enhance the educational experience in the classroom, but it is also needed to keep teachers and their students active as learners. Spatial dynamics activities enhance student learning in ways that traditional classroom instruction does not. In 1994, the National Council for the Social Studies published EXPECTATIONS OF EXCELLENCE: CURRICULUM STANDARDS FOR SOCIAL STUDIES as a statement of purpose and standards for the social studies. In a section of this document on teaching and learning, a "powerful" social studies curriculum was advocated—one that would maximally enhance student achievement.

A "powerful" social studies curriculum was identified as one with solid content, containing various instructional approaches and active learning experiences. Spatial dynamics is part of this "powerful" social studies curriculum because it is based on sound social studies content, involves a unique instructional approach, and allows for active learning. "Powerful" social studies teaching, then, requires teachers who can create and implement various creative curriculum plans that actively involve students in the learning process. Finally, exemplary teachers use a variety of instructional techniques, including physical examples. Using spatial dynamics, classroom teachers can easily develop activities which provide physical examples. Spatial dynamics, therefore, is one aspect of a "powerful" social studies curriculum.

CLASSROOM FLOOR MODELS

There are two types of spatial dynamics activities. One type involves large-scale classroom floor maps or floor models. In such an activity, the concrete details of an historical event are replicated and laid out on the classroom floor. The chairs are moved next to the walls or into the hall for these activities. One such activity on the John F. Kennedy (JFK) assassination uses a large-scale map of Dealey Plaza.

The students, using poster paper, draw the Texas Textbook Depository building with the famous sixth-floor window. They then build a small car out of balsa wood for Kennedy and Connally, lay out the street plan, create the grassy knoll, and make a small replica of Mr. Zapruder, who shot the famous 8 millimeter film of the assassination. Using this large-scale model on the floor, the teacher walks the students through the JFK assassination. A creative teacher can also use primary sources on the assassination such as newspaper articles, CD-ROMs, videotapes, and oral history information to enhance the lesson. Whatever ancillary materials the teacher uses, the floor map remains the focal point of the JFK classroom activity.

Another activity using a large floor model is based on the attack on Pearl Harbor. In this activity, the classroom floor becomes Pearl Harbor, Ford Island, and the surrounding Hawaiian waters. Students draw the outlines of the harbor and Ford Island on the floor and make the various ships in the harbor that day using flat poster board. After the "ships" are placed in the correct locations, the teacher walks the students through the attack. The size and visual appeal of the model stimulates student interest. Again, additional sources such as videotapes, oral histories, and Franklin D. Roosevelt's "Day of Infamy" speech can be used to enhance this activity.

This type of teaching activity can be used in middle school and elementary school classes, too. In an elementary class, in which state and local history is usually taught, a large map of the state is laid out on the classroom floor. Various geographical features, roads, and cities may be added to enhance a lesson. At the middle school level, this type of activity could easily be adapted to a study of the Oregon Trail, railroad expansion, or acquisition of overseas territory by the United States in the late nineteenth century and early twentieth century. At the high school level, a large map of Europe showing the various territorial acquisitions of Nazi Germany between 1936 and 1939 could easily be created. Indeed, use of this type of activity is limited only by the imagination and creativity of the teacher.

PAPIER MACHE MODELS

A second type of spatial dynamics activity involves using a papier mache model. This activity requires advance teacher preparation and a large time commitment; however, the potential for student learning is extraordinary. Materials needed for this activity are cardboard, papier mache, paint, balsa wood, and newspaper. For a unit on the Civil War, the class can construct a model of the Gettysburg battlefield measuring three feet by six feet. The students outline the battlefield, including the city of Gettysburg, roads, Culp's Hill, Little Round Top, Big Round Top, Devil's Den, Cemetery Ridge, and Seminary Ridge, all according to scale.

Next, the papier mache model is created using cardboard and paint. Students can add rocks and trees, as well as buildings and cannons constructed out of balsa wood. Finally, students paint the model to add clarity and accuracy. Teachers can also use this model to stimulate student interest in other aspects of the war, such as tactics, weapons, use of geography in battles, and features of common soldiers' lives. Scenes from the movies "Gettysburg" or "Glory" or the Ken Burns PBS series "Civil War" can enrich student learning when used in conjunction with the model of the battlefield.

Using the papier mache battlefield as a focal point for a Civil War study adds detail, dimension, and substance to this topic and promotes active learning. Another papier mache model that students can make is a World War I battlefield, approximately three to four feet square, composed of the opposing trenches and "no man's land." The trench lines with their supporting trenches and barbed wire and a barren "no man's land" with a downed airplane add realism to the study of a war. The lesson can focus on the origins of the trenches in World War I, living conditions in the trenches, and the use of new technologies invented during this war.

The realism of this model can greatly enhance students' understanding of many aspects of this war. Papier mache models can be used to illustrate other topics, such as early American roads and bridges, the Erie Canal, or state and local history. For example, for a unit on state history, a teacher can use a state road map to cut an outline of the state, and the students can build a papier mache model complete with land elevations, rivers, cities, railroads, and roads.

MOLECULAR MODELING: A TOOL FOR CHEMISTRY TEACHING

Molecular Modeling has had a very important place in chemical research for quite some time now. In its early stages molecular modeling was only done by very experienced computational chemists using complicated, difficult to use programs. However, user friendly molecular modeling programs have made computational chemistry accessible to all chemists. Many organic researchers now make use of some type of molecular modeling program, but their use in teaching organic chemistry is only starting to become apparent. Programs, like Chem3D, that allow the representation of molecules in three dimensions are also very valuable teaching tools, especially for any class that discusses molecular structure.

COGNITIVE TEACHING MODELS

The field of instructional design developed in the 1960s and early 1970s at a time when behaviorism still dominated mainstream psychology. ID shared those behaviorist roots and at the time was closer to mainstream psychology in the U. S. ID theorists such as Gagné, Briggs, Merrill, and Scandura all were educational psychologists. With the cognitive revolution of the 1970s, instructional psychology differentiated itself from ID and drifted more to the cognitive mainstream, leaving ID relatively isolated with concerns of design. In a review of instructional psychology in 1981, Lauren Resnick (who only a few years earlier had developed Gagné-style learning hierarchies) observed:

> An interesting thing has happened to instructional psychology. It has become part of the mainstream of research on human cognition, learning, and development. For about 20 years the number of psychologists devoting attention to instructionally relevant questions has been gradually increasing. In the past 5 years this increase has accelerated so that it is now difficult to draw a clear line between instructional psychology and the main body of basic research on complex cognitive processes. Instructional psychology is no longer basic psychology *applied* to education. It is fundamental research *on* the processes of instruction and learning.

In her review, Resnick acknowledged that mainstream instructional psychologists had focused on issues of performance modeling and cognitive task analysis, neglecting the challenge of devising effective instructional strategies, models, and interventions. Even so, she did not look to the ID community to fill the need because "Instructional design theory..., which is directly concerned with prescribing interventions, has developed without much reference to cognitive psychology". Hence, she excluded ID theory entirely from her review. Of course, the ID community was active during this time, with even some attempt at integrating cognitive psychology into their methods —Resnick and other mainstream psychologists just weren't reading them! This polarization between ID and psychology continued through the 1980s.

In spite of efforts to move ID into the cognitive mainstream, psychologists and designers continued to move in different circles and speak somewhat different languages. Psychologists viewed designers with suspicion because of the eclectic and ad hoc nature of the ID theory base and because of the field's concern for stimulus design over cognitive processes. Likewise, the ID literature often ignored developments in cognitive theory, resulting in theory that was generally divorced from state-of-the-art learning theory.

Only recently, with the vigorous dialogue on constructivism and situated learning, have psychologists and designers resumed a substantive conversation. Psychologists such as Bransford, Perkins, Scardamalia, and Lesgold, who have taken on the challenge of design, have run up against many of the same problems addressed by traditional ID theories. At the same time, the perspectives of psychologists have stimulated reflection and renewal within the ID community. The net result of this interplay is a renewed recognition of the importance of design, as well as an array of new designs that take into account new technologies and theories of learning.

4

CHARTS

A chart is a graphical representation of some data. Charts are often used to make large quantities of data more easily understandable, and recognizable on first view. Charts can represent data in several different ways. Some of the different methods are listed below. Charts represent data in different ways depending on the type of data that is presented. For example, a customer satisfaction response may be measured in percentages - the percentage of customers satisfied, not satisfied, and unsure. In this instance, a "pie chart" may be used successfully.

A pie chart is visually appealing and allows for greatest recognition since the number of satisfaction responses can be easily compared to the number of dissatisfaction responses by comparing the size of each sector of the pie graph, which is not easily done if presented, for example, in a histogram (or bar chart). Charts can be created dynamically by computers using a charting application. Charts are not always used for mathematical purposes, but are also used in many widely differing areas.

TYPES OF CHARTS

Bar chart

A bar chart is a chart with rectangular bars of lengths usually proportional to the magnitudes or frequencies of what they represent.

— Sometimes the bars are not proportional, often because the chart didn't start at zero.

— Standards about starting a chart at zero are not universal. In some case, starting at zero will show little differences between the bars, such as for stock indexes.

— If it doesn't start at zero, that can be misleading. Mathematicians will usually signal any chart that doesn't start at zero, such as by using a squiggly line near the bottom of the y-axis.

— The bars can be horizontally or vertically oriented. Sometimes a stretched graphic is used instead of a solid bar.

Example

The following example chart is based on the results of the election for the European Parliament in 2004 and in 1999. The following table lists the number of seats allocated to each party group. The results of 1999 have been multiplied by 1.16933, to compensate for the change in number of seats between those years.

Group	Seats (2004)	Seats (1999) scaled
EUL	39	49
PES	200	210
EFA	42	56
EDD	15	19
ELDR	67	60
EPP	276	272
UEN	27	36
Other	66	29

A bar chart visualizing the above results of the 2004 election can look like this:

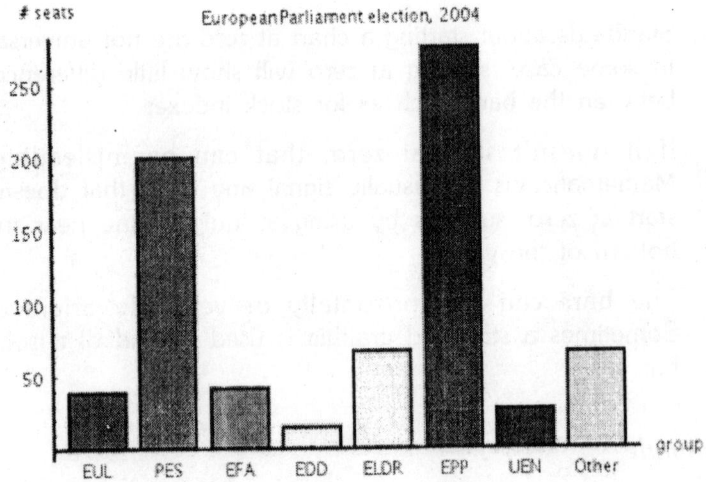

This bar chart shows both the results of 2004, and those of 1999:

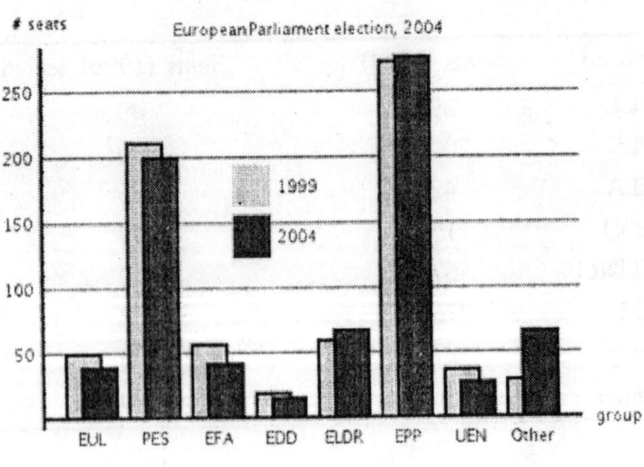

Pie chart

From Wikipedia, the free encyclopedia.

A pie chart is a circular chart divided into segments, illustrating relative magnitudes or frequencies. In a pie chart, the arc length (and consequently, the central angle and the area) of each segment, is proportional to the quantity it represents. Together, the wedges create a full disk. A chart with one or more wedge separated from the rest of the disk is called an exploded pie chart.

Example

The following example chart is based on the results of the election for the European Parliament in 2004. The following table lists the number of seats allocated to each party group, along with the percentage of the total that they each make up. The values in the last column, is the central angle of each segment, found by multiplying the percentage by 360°.

Data

Group	Seats	Percent (%)	Central angle (°)
EUL	39	5.3	19.2
PES	200	27.3	98.4
EFA	42	5.7	20.7
EDD	15	2.0	7.4
ELDR	67	9.2	33.0
EPP	276	37.7	135.7
UEN	27	3.7	13.3
Other	66	9.0	32.5

A pie chart for the above data above:

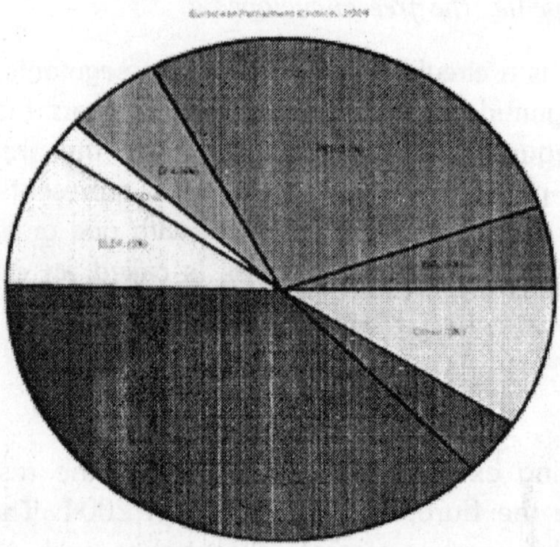

An exploded pie chart, with the largest party group exploded

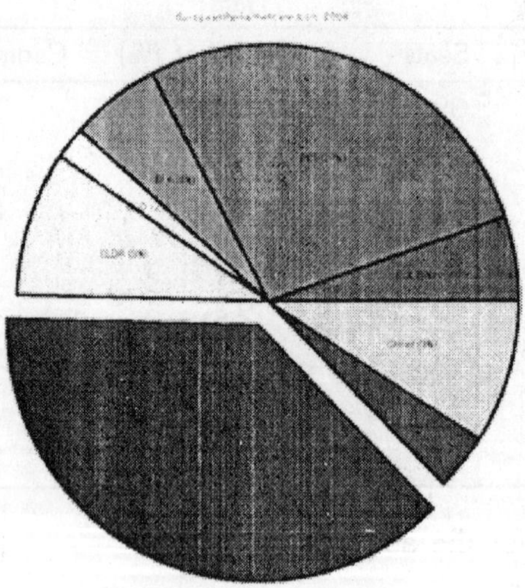

Histogram

In statistics, a histogram is a graphical display of tabulated frequencies. That is, a histogram is the graphical version of a table which shows what proportion of cases fall into each of several or many specified categories. The categories are usually specified as nonoverlapping intervals of some variable. The histogram evolved to meet the need for evaluating data that occurs at a certain frequency. This is possible because the histogram allows for a concise portrayal of information in a bar graph format.

The histogram is a powerful engineering tool when routinely and intelligently used. The histogram clearly portrays information on location, spread, and shape that enables the user to perceive subtleties regarding the functioning of the physical process that is generating the data. It can also help suggest both the nature of, and possible improvements for, the physical mechanisms at work in the process. There are different ways to display the same table, and two kinds of histograms are shown below. One shows the number of cases per unit interval, so that the area under the curve is the total number of cases. Another shows the number of cases per unit interval divided by the total number of cases, so that the area under the curve is exactly .

As an example we consider data collected by the U.S. Census Bureau on time to travel to work. The census found that there were 124 million people who work outside of their homes. People were asked how long it takes them to get to work, and their responses were divided into categories: less than 5 minutes, more than 5 minutes and less than 10, more than 10 minutes and less than 15, and so on. This table shows the numbers of people per category in thousands, so the 4,180 means 4,180,000.

Interval	Width	No. in interval	(No. in interval)/ width
0	5	4,180	836
5	5	13,687	2,737
10	5	18,618	3,723
15	5	19,634	3,926
20	5	17,981	3,596
25	5	7,190	1,438
30	5	16,369	3,273
35	5	3,212	642
40	5	4,122	824
45	15	9,200	613
60	30	6,461	215
90	60	3,435	57

The data shown in the preceding table are displayed graphically by the following diagram. The area of each bar is equal to the total number of people in that category, so the total area of all bars is equal to the total number of people in the survey (124 million).

An interesting feature of this diagram is the spike in the 30 to 35 minutes category. It seems likely that this is an artifact: half an hour is a common unit of informal time measurement, so people whose travel times were perhaps a little less than or a little greater than 30 minutes might be inclined to answer "30 minutes". Histogram of travel time, US 2000 census. Area under the curve equals the total number of cases.

Now the same data are shown in a slightly different fashion. The area of each bar is equal to the proportion of people, of all the people in the survey, who fall into that category. So the total area of all the bars is equal to 1.

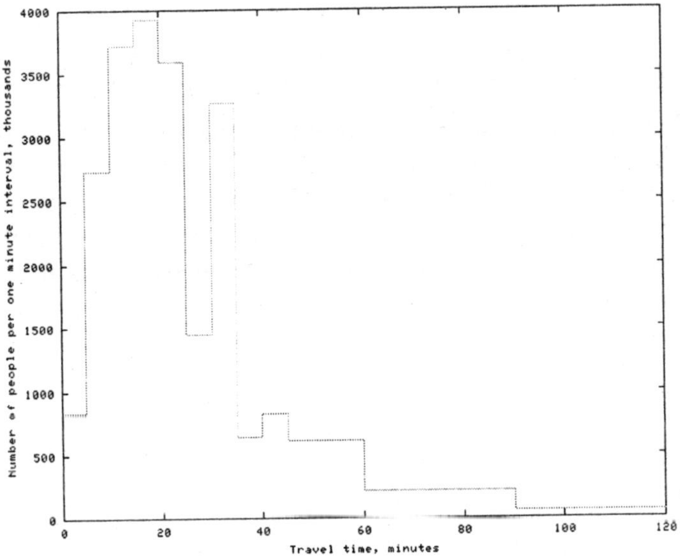

Interval	Width	No. in interval	(No. in interval) /(total no.)/width
0	5	4,180	0.0067
5	5	13,687	0.0220
10	5	18,618	0.0300
15	5	19,634	0.0316
20	5	17,981	0.0289
25	5	7,190	0.0115
30	5	16,369	0.0263
35	5	3,212	0.0051
40	5	4,122	0.0066

45	15	9,200	0.0049
60	30	6,461	0.0017
90	60	3,435	0.0004

The preceding table is displayed graphically by the following diagram. The second figure differs from the first only in the vertical scale. Which figure should be used depends on the purpose of the histogram; if the absolute numbers are important, then the first form is more useful, and the second form is more useful if proportions are important.

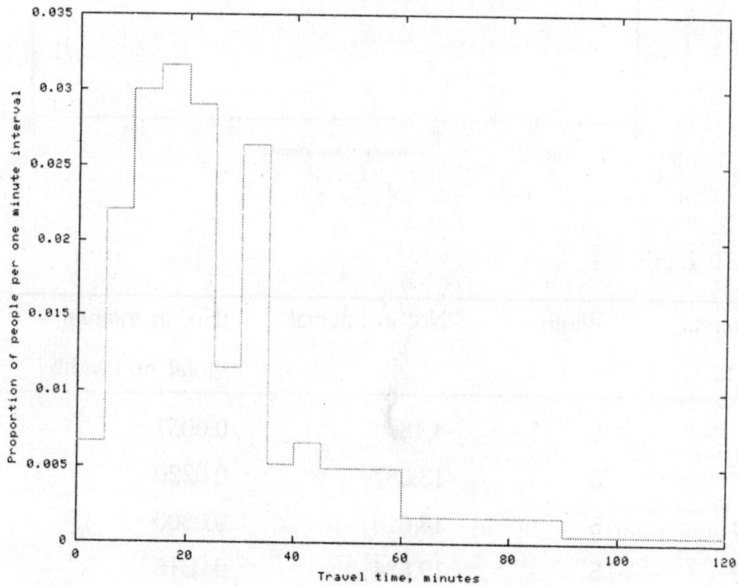

Histogram of travel time, US 2000 census. Area under the curve equals 1.

Creating a Histogram

Determine the range of the data by subtracting the smallest observed measurement from the largest and designate it as R.

Example:

Largest observed measurement = 1.1185 inches

Smallest observed measurement = 1.1030 inches

R = 1.1185 inches - 1.1030 inches =.0155 inch

Record the measurement unit (MU) used. This is usually controlled by the measuring instrument least count.

Example: MU = .0001 inch

Determine the number of classes and the class width. The number of classes, k, should be no lower than six and no higher than fifteen for practical purposes. Trial and error may be done to achieve the best distribution for analysis.

Example: k=8

Determine the class width (H) by dividing the range, R, by the preferred number of classes, k.

Example: R/k = .0155/8 = .0019375 inch

The class width selected should be an odd-numbered multiple of the measurement unit, MU. This value should be close to the H value:

MU – .0001 inch

Class width = .0019 inch or .0021 inch

Establish the class midpoints and class limits. The first class midpoint should be located near the largest observed measurement. If possible, it should also be a convenient increment. Always make the class widths equal in size, and express the class limits in terms which are one-half unit beyond the accuracy of the original measurement unit. This avoids plotting an observed measurement on a class limit.

> Example: First class midpoint = 1.1185 inches,
>
> and the class width is .0019 inch.
>
> Therefore, limits would be
>
> 1.1185 + or - .0019/2.

Determine the axes for the graph. The frequency scale on the vertical axis should slightly exceed the largest class frequency, and the measurement scale along the horizontal axis should be at regular intervals which are independent of the class width. (See example below steps.)

Draw the graph. Mark off the classes, and draw rectangles with heights corresponding to the measurement frequencies in that class. Title the histogram. Give an overall title and identify each axis.

Interpretations

When combined with the concept of the normal curve and the knowledge of a particular process, the histogram becomes an effective, practical working tool in the early stages of data analysis. A histogram may be interpreted by asking three questions:

— Is the process performing within specification limits?

— Does the process seem to exhibit wide variation?

— If action needs to be taken on the process, what action is appropriate?

The answer to these three questions lies in analyzing three characteristics of the histogram.

— How well is the histogram centered? The centering of the data provides information on the process aim about some mean or nominal value.

— How wide is the histogram? Looking at histogram width defines the variability of the process about the aim.

— What is the shape of the histogram? Remember that the data is expected to form a normal or bell-shaped curve. Any significant change or anomaly usually indicates that there is something going on in the process which is causing the quality problem.

Examples of Typical Distributions

Normal

— Depicted by a bell-shaped curve

— most frequent measurement appears as centre of distribution

— less frequent measurements taper gradually at both ends of distribution

— Indicates that a process is running normally (only common causes are present).

Bi-Model

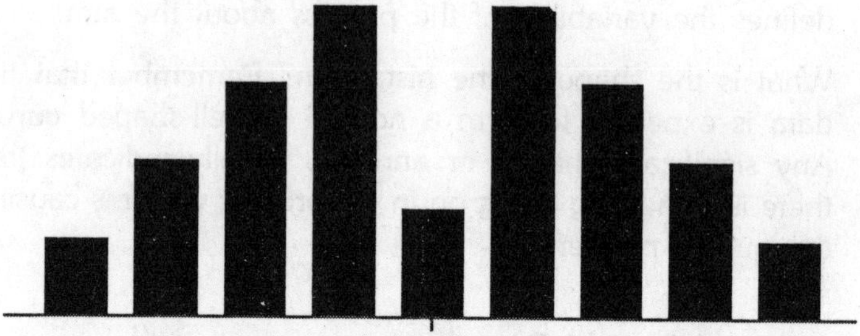

— Distribution appears to have two peaks

— May indicate that data from more than process are mixed together

— materials may come from two separate vendors

— samples may have come from two separate machines.

Cliff-Like

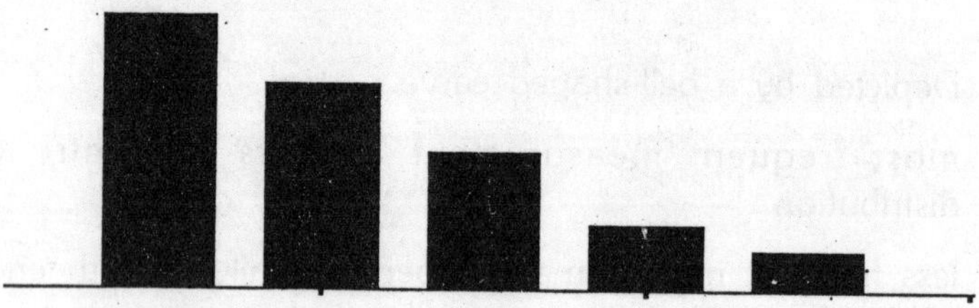

— Appears to end sharply or abruptly at one end

— Indicates possible sorting or inspection of non-conforming parts.

Saw-Toothed

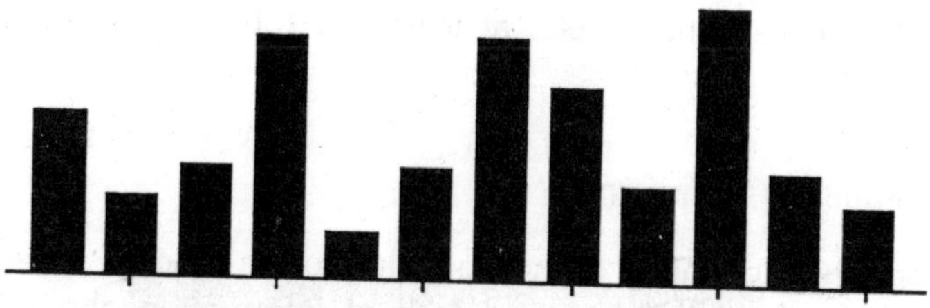

— Also commonly referred to as a comb distribution, appears as an alternating jagged pattern
— Often indicates a measuring problem
— improper gage readings
— gage not sensitive enough for readings.

Skewed

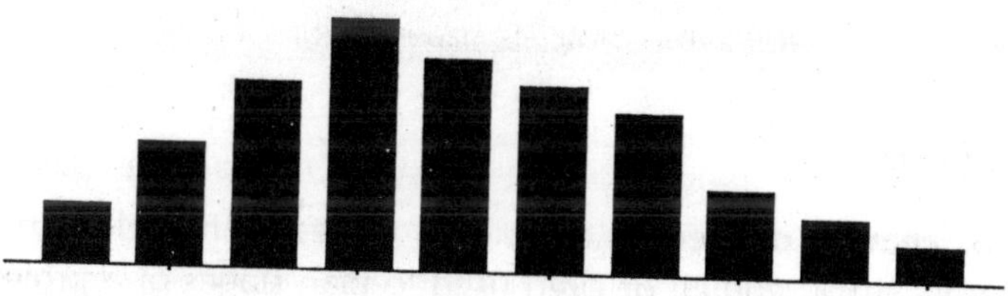

— Appears as an uneven curve, values seem to taper to one side.

It is worth mentioning again that this or any other phase of histogram analysis must be married to knowledge of the process being studied to have any real value. Knowledge of the data analysis itself does not provide sufficient insight into the quality problem.

Other Considerations

Number of samples.

For the histogram to be representative of the true process behavior, as a general rule, at least fifty (50) samples should be measured.

Limitations of technique.

Histograms are limited in their use due to the random order in which samples are taken and lack of information about the state of control of the process. Because samples are gathered without regard to order, the time-dependent or time-related trends in the process are not captured. So, what may appear to be the central tendency of the data may be deceiving. With respect to process statistical control, the histogram gives no indication whether the process was operating at its best when the data was collected. This lack of information on process control may lead to incorrect conclusions being drawn and, hence, inappropriate decisions being made. Still, with these considerations in mind, the histogram's simplicity of construction and ease of use make it an invaluable tool in the elementary stages of data analysis.

Flowchart

A flow chart is defined as a pictorial representation describing a process being studied or even used to plan stages of a project. Flow charts tend to provide people with a common language or reference point when dealing with a project or process. Four particular types of flow charts have proven useful when dealing with a process analysis: top-down flow chart, detailed flow chart, work flow diagrams, and a deployment chart. Each of the different types of flow charts tend to provide a different aspect to a process or a task. Flow charts provide an excellent form of documentation for a process, and quite often are useful when examining how various steps in a process work together.

When dealing with a process flow chart, two separate stages of the process should be considered: the finished product and the making of the product. In order to analyze the finished product or how to operate the process, flow charts tend to use simple and easily recognizable symbols. The basic flow chart symbols below are used when analyzing how to operate a process.

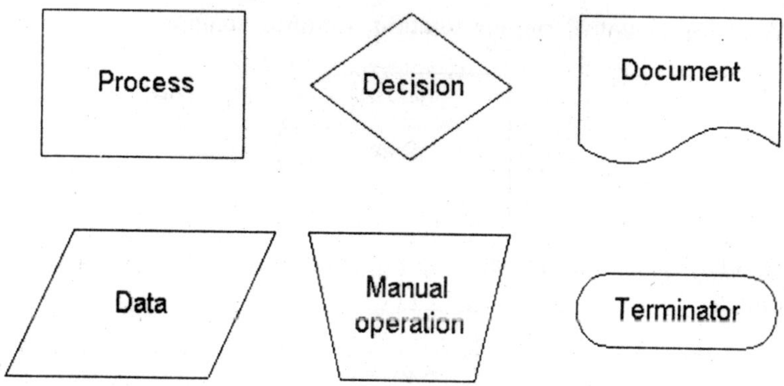

In order to analyze the second condition for a flow process chart, one should use the ANSI standard symbols. The ANSI standard symbols used most often include the following:

Drive Nail, Cement, Type Letter:

Move Material by truck, conveyor, or hand:

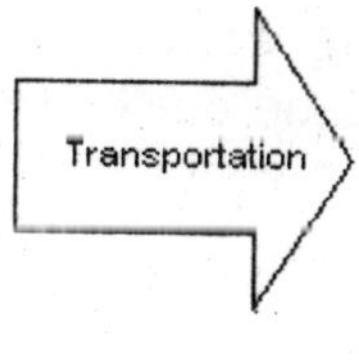

Raw Material in bins, finished product on pallets, or filed documents:

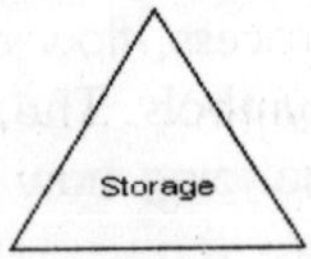

Wait for elevator, papers waiting, material waiting :

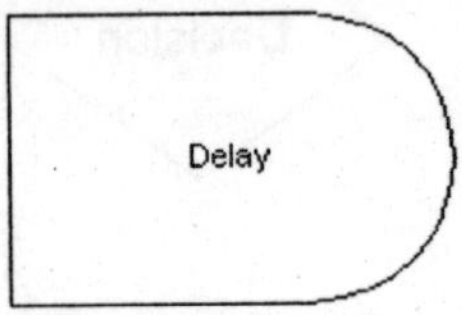

Read gages, read papers for information, or check quality of goods:

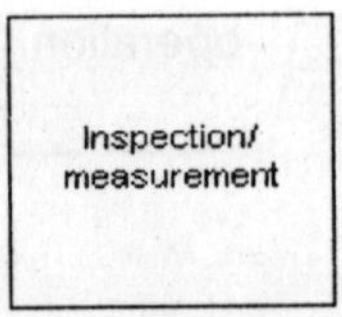

Any combination of two or more of these symbols show an understanding for a joint process:

As a whole, flow charting has been around for a very long time. In fact, flow charts have been used for so long that no one individual is specified as the "father of the flow chart". The reason for this is obvious. A flow chart can be customized to fit any need or purpose. For this reason, flow charts can be recognized as a very unique quality improvement method.

Instructions

Step-by-Step process of how to develop a flow chart.

— Gather information of how the process flows: use a) conservation, b) experience, or c) product development codes.

— Trial process flow.

— Allow other more familiar personnel to check for accuracy.

— Make changes if necessary.

— Compare final actual flow with best possible flow.

Construction/Interpretation tip for a flow chart.

— Define the boundaries of the process clearly.

— Use the simplest symbols possible.

— Make sure every feedback loop has an escape.

— There is usually only one output arrow out of a process box. Otherwise, it may require a decision diamond.

Interpretation

— Analyze flow chart of actual process.

— Analyze flow chart of best process.

— Compare both charts, looking for areas where they are different. Most of the time, the stages where differences occur is considered to be the problem area or process.

— Take appropriate in-house steps to correct the differences between the two seperate flows.

Example

Process Flow Chart- Finding the best way home

This is a simple case of processes and decisions in finding the best route home at the end of the working day.

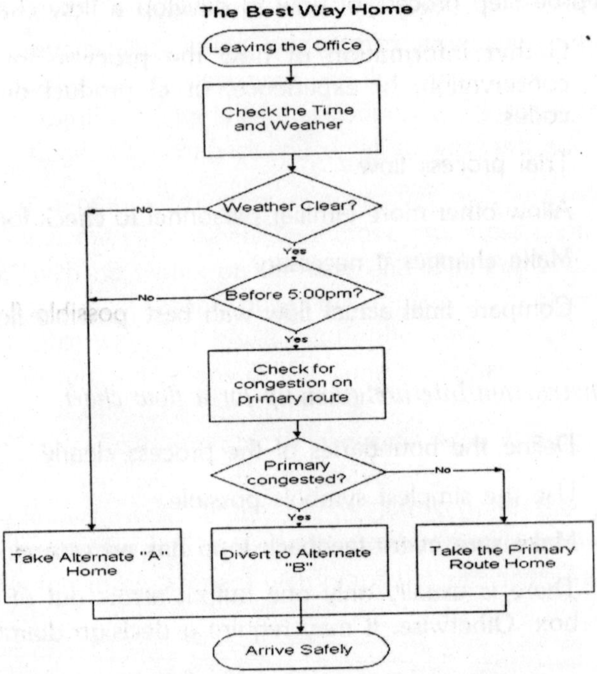

Gantt chart

A Gantt chart is a popular type of bar chart, showing the interrelationships of how projects, schedules, and other time-related systems progress over time. In project management, a Gantt chart can show when the project terminal elements start end finish, summary elements or terminal element dependencies.

Nautical chart

From Wikipedia, the free encyclopedia

A nautical chart is a graphic representation of a maritime area and adjacent coastal regions. It shows depths of water and heights of land, natural features of the seabed, details of the coastline, navigational hazards, locations of natural and man-made aids to navigation, information on tides and currents, local details of the Earth's magnetic field, and man-made structures such as harbours and bridges. It is an indispensable tool of navigation. As angles are widely used for measurement in navigation, two types of angle are shown on charts; bearings and the longitude and latitude of positions. Positions of places shown on the chart can be measured from scales on the borders of the chart, using longitude and latitude relative to a map datum such as WGS 84.

An example of a bearing is a ship's course, being the angle between the ship's heading and north. Another example is the bearing from one place to another, being the angle between the line joining the two points and the line from one of the points to the north. The Mercator projection is almost universally used in nautical charts. There are however some exceptions for very large or small scales where projections such as the gnomonic projection may be used. Since the Mercator projection is conformal, that is, bearings in the chart are identical to the corresponding angles in nature, bearings may be measured from the chart to be used at sea or plotted on the chart from measurements taken at sea.

Charts always express bearings relative to true north, at the north pole, rather than magnetic north, in northern Canada, which a magnetic compass points towards. To convert between "magnetic" and "true", the magnetic variation must be applied to the bearing. Often a compass rose on the chart provides the variation, allowing conversion of bearings between true and magnetic.

Nautical charts are based on hydrographic surveys. As surveying is laborious and time-consuming, hydrographic data for many areas of sea may be dated and not always reliable. Nautical charts are issued by the national hydrographic offices in many countries. These charts are considered "official" in contrast to those made by commercial publishers. Many hydrographic offices provide regular, sometimes weekly, manual updates of their charts through their sales agents.

Coordinated by the International Hydrographic Organization, a worldwide system of charts ("INT" chart series) is being developed with the goal of unifying as many chart systems as possible. Currently, the Admiralty Charts series issued by the United Kingdom Hydrographic Office covers almost every navigable area on earth.

Nolan chart

From Wikipedia, the free encyclopedia.

The Nolan chart is a political diagram created by the Libertarian David Nolan. He created it to illustrate the claim that libertarianism stands for both economic freedom and personal freedom (as he defined the terms), in graphic contrast to "leftist" liberalism, which advocates only personal freedom and "rightist" conservatism, which advocates only economic freedom.

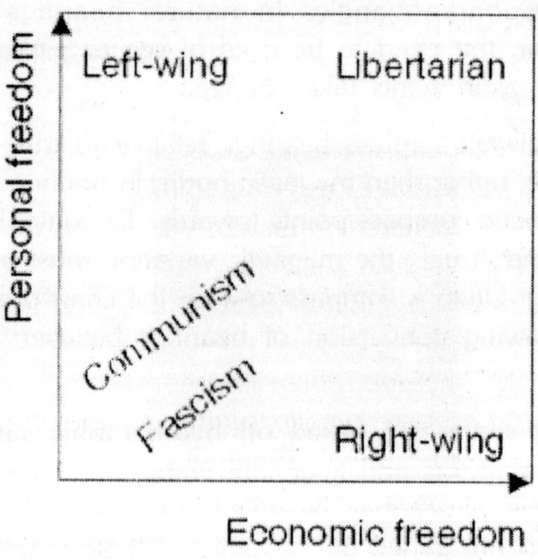

The chart further illustrates the claim that libertarianism is diametrically opposed to authoritarian control systems such as communism and fascism. Indeed, some critics have argued that one of the primary reasons behind the creation of the chart was to popularize the image of libertarianism as the "opposite" of two ideologies with a rather negative public image, thus putting libertarianism itself in a good light.

Differing from the traditional left/right distinction and other political taxonomies, the Nolan Chart in its original form has two dimensions, with a horizontal x-axis labeled "economic freedom" and a vertical y-axis labeled "personal freedom". It resembles a square divided into four quadrants. The upper left quadrant represents the political Left — favouring government that taxes more and spends more for activities such as welfare, healthcare, education, Social Security and funding for the arts and that encourages more barriers on trade and business regulations (which David Nolan labeled "low economic freedom"), but supporting personal choice in issues such as marijuana, homosexuality and the draft (which he labeled "high personal freedom"). At the bottom right is its converse, the political Right, whose coordinates place it as supporting high economic freedom and low personal freedom. Those on the Right want lower taxes and fewer social programs but support regulation by the government of cultural issues and personal behavior.

The Nolan Chart places David Nolan's own ideology, libertarianism, at the top right, corresponding with high freedom in both economic and social matters. The fourth quadrant at the bottom left represents the antithesis of libertarianism. David Nolan originally called this philosophy populism, but many later renditions of the chart have used the label authoritarianism instead. The Nolan Chart has also been rotated and visually represented in a few other ways, such as having conservatism and populism/authoritarianism at the top and libertarianism and liberalism at the bottom. In another popular portrayal, the Nolan Chart takes a rhomboid form, with left representing liberalism, right representing conservatism, down representing authoritarianism, and up representing libertarianism.

The chart is inspiration for many political self-quizzes based on these four categories—liberal, libertarian, conservative and populist/authoritarian—of political thought, many of which have been written in computer code to be taken by visitors on the Internet. The advocates and writers of these quizzes are most often libertarian, and a common remark by them about their tests is that people who are libertarians inside and didn't know it will discover their true political leanings. The detractors of the Nolan Chart are most often people who accuse people with libertarian beliefs of using it to further their agenda and gain converts to their party and political movement. One specific accusation is that libertarian "recruiters" try to convince people that, because they hold several libertarian positions, they should consider making all their positions libertarian in order to achieve consistency in advocating "liberty".

Critics of this diagram (and this kind of chart in general) claim that it represents at best a pseudoscientific illustration of a political point of view. The essential premise of the diagram is for many an oversimplified generalization; economic freedom and personal freedom are often inextricable, and both left-wing (Bakunin) and right-wing philosophers draw the same connection. Critics insist that the libertarian claim (and associated chart) rests on either the utilitarian assumption that libertarianism is a workable alternative to older, more familiar political systems or on the moral argument that it would be better only because it would leave people with more freedom, in the libertarian sense of the word. This freedom, in the extreme, may be perceived by some as tending toward anarchy, and driven by excessively self-centered or selfish motivation. In essence, they claim the "chart" exists only to distance the term "libertarianism" from the older terms of anarchism and socialism, the latter of which draws polemic connections to communism, which itself draws polemic connections to totalitarianism.

Other critics argue that the libertarian definition of economic and personal "freedom" is incorrect or flawed, and that non-libertarian ideologies actually give people more freedom than libertarianism does. One such argument is that freedom from government intervention does not assure individual freedom within the private sector, and that a strong but limited government is needed to preserve individual freedom against non-governmental powers. Nolan's usage of "populism" shows that he rejects this argument.

A few of the people who oppose the use of the Nolan Chart are strong libertarians, Objectivists or other advocates of laissez-faire capitalism who believe that the political spectrum need be portrayed only through one dimension, but not the traditional Left/Right one. They propose an axis with totalitarianism/authoritarianism (statism) at one end, and libertarianism at the other end - something similar to the first diagonal of the Nolan Chart. They insist that all types of government intervention, in any areas, are the same.

Pournelle Chart

From Wikipedia, the free encyclopedia.

The Pournelle Chart, developed by Jerry Pournelle, is a 2-dimensional coordinate system used to distinguish political ideologies. It is similar to the Nolan Chart, only that the X-axis refers to your feelings toward state and centralised government (farthest right being state worship, farthest left being the idea of a state as the "ultimate evil"), and the Y-axis referring to your belief in that problems in society will be solved once your ideology of choice is implemented (top being complete confidence that your political ideology can manage the problems in the world, bottom being mindless adherence to your ideology of choice).

"Leftist" ideologies, such as (American) liberalism, socialism and communism, tend to be placed in the upper right-hand quadrant, conservatism, fascism and Nazism are to be placed in the lower right hand quadrant, classical anarchists are in the lower left hand corner, and libertarians and Objectivists are placed in the upper lefthand corner.

Run charts

Run charts originated from control charts, which were initially designed by Walter Shewhart. Walter Shewhart was a statistician at Bell Telephone Laboratories in New York. Shewhart developed a system for bringing processes into statistical control by developing ideas which would allow for a system to be controlled using control charts. Run charts evolved from the development of these control charts, but run charts focus more on time patterns while a control chart focuses more on acceptable limits of the process. Shewhart's discoveries are the basis of what as known as SQC or Statistical Quality Control.

Instructions for Creating a Chart

Step 1 : Gathering Data: To begin any run chart, some type of process or operation must be available to take measurements for analysis. Measurements must be taken over a period of time. The data must be collected in a chronological or sequential form. You may start at any point and end at any point. For best results, at least 25 or more samples must be taken in order to get an accurate run chart.

Step 2: Organizing Data: Once the data has been placed in chronological or sequential form, it must be divided into two sets of values x and y. The values for x represent time and the values for y represent the measurements taken from the manufacturing process or operation.

Step 3: Charting Data: Plot the y values versus the x values by hand or by computer, using an appropriate scale that will make the points on the graph visible. Next, draw vertical lines for the x values to separate time intervals such as weeks. Draw horizontal lines to show where trends in the process or operation occur or will occur.

Step 4: Interpreting Data: After drawing the horizontal and vertical lines to segment data, interpret the data and draw any conclusions that will be beneficial to the process or operation. Some possible outcomes are:

— Trends in the chart

— Cyclical patterns in the data

— Observations from each time interval are consistent

Run Chart Example

Problem Scenario

You have just moved into a new area that you are not familiar with. Your desire is to arrive at work on time, but you have noticed over your first couple of weeks on the job that it doesn't take the same amount of time each day of the week. You decide to monitor the amount of time it takes to get to work over the next four weeks and construct a run chart.

Step 1: Gathering Data

Collect measurements each day over the next four weeks. Organize and record the data in chronological or sequential form.

	M	T	W	TH	F
WEEK 1	33	28	26.5	28	26
WEEK2	35	30.5	28	26	25.5
WEEK3	34.5	29	28	26	25
WEEK4	34	29.5	27	27	25.5

Step 2: Organizing Data

Determine what the values for the x (time, day of week) and day (data, minutes to work) axis will be.

	Day	Travel Time
WEEK 1	M	33
	T	28
	W	26.5
	TH	28
	F	26
WEEK 2	M	35
	T	30.5
	W	28
	TH	26
	F	25.5
WEEK 3	M	34.5
	T	29
	W	28
	TH	26
	F	25
WEEK 4	M	34
	T	29.5
	W	27
	TH	27
	F	25.5

Step 3: Charting Data

Plot the y values versus the x values by hand or by computer using the appropriate scale. Draw horizontal or vertical lines on the graph where trends or inconsistencies occur.

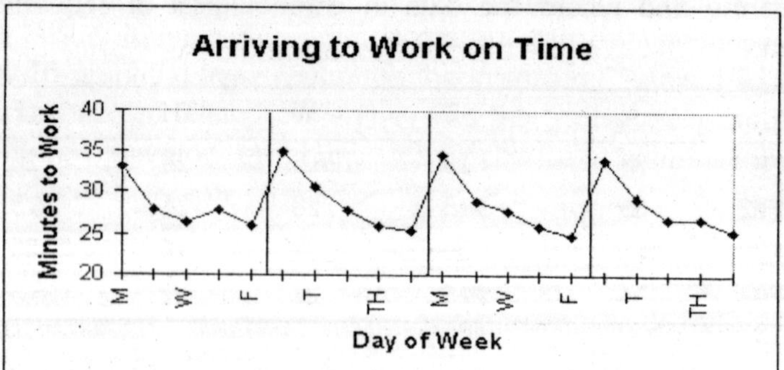

Step 4: Interpreting Data

Interpret results and draw any conclusions that are important. An overall decreasing trend occurs each week with Mondays taking the most amount of time and Fridays generally taking the least amount of time. Therefore you accordingly allow yourself more time on Mondays to arrive to work on time.

Cause-and-effect diagram

The cause-and-effect diagram is also called the Ishikawa diagram (after its creator, Kaoru Ishikawa of Japan), or the fishbone diagram (due to its shape). It was created so that all possible causes of a result could be listed in such a way as to allow a user to graphically show these possible causes. From this diagram, the user can define the most likely causes of a result.

This diagram was adopted by Dr. W. Edwards Deming as a helpful tool in improving quality. Dr. Deming has taught Total Quality Management in Japan since World War II. He has also helped develop statistical tools to be used for the census and taught the military his methods of quality management. Both Ishikawa and Deming use this diagram as one the first tools in the quality management process.

Scatter diagrams

Scatter diagrams are used to study possible relationships between two variables. Although these diagrams cannot prove that one variable causes the other, they do indicate the existance of a relationship, as well as the strength of that relationship. A scatter diagram is composed of a horizontal axis containing the measured values of one variable and a vertical axis representing the measurements of the other variable. The purpose of the scatter diagram is to display what happens to one variables when another variable is changed. The diagram is used to test a theory that the two variables are related. The type of relationship that exits is indicated by the slope of the diagram.

Key Terms

— *Variable* - a quality characteristic that can be measured and expressed as a number on some continuous scale of measurement.

— *Relationship* - Relationships between variables exist when one variable depends on the other and changing one variable will effect the other.

— *Data Sheet* - contains the measurements that were collected for plotting the diagram.

— *Correlation* - an analysis method used to decide whether there is a statistically significant relationship between two variables.

— *Regression* - an analysis method used to identify the exact nature of the relationship between two variables.

Commonly, while a cause-effect diagram has been used to describe the relationship between two variables, the histogram was used to visualize the structure of the data. However, a means of observing the kinds of relationships between variables was needed. Using the theory of linear regression which originated from studies performed by Sir Francis Galton, the scatter diagram was developed so that intuitive and qualitative conclusions could be drawn about the paired data, or variables. The concept of correlation was employed to decide whether a significant relationship existed between the paired data.

Furthermore, regression analysis was used to identify the exact nature of the relationship. The Guide to Quality Control and *The Statistical Quality Control Handbook*, written by a Japanese quality consultant named Kaoru Ishikawa are useful in providing an understanidng on how to use and interpret a scatter diagram. Ishikawa believed that there was no end to quality improvement and in 1985 suggested that seven base tools be used for collection and analysis of qualtiy data. Among the tools was the scatter diagram.

Construction of Scatter Diagrams

Collect and construct a data sheet of 50 to 100 paired samples of data, that you suspect to be related. Construct your data sheet as follows:

Car	Age(In Years)	Price(In Dollars)
1	2	4000
2	4	2500
3	1	5000
4	5	1250
—	—	—
—	—	—
—	—	—
—	—	—
100	7	1000

Draw the axes of the diagram. The first variable (the independent variable) is usually located on the horizontal axis and its values should increase as you move to the right. The vertical axis usually contains the second variable (the dependent variable) and its values should increase as you move up the axis.

Plot the data on the diagram. The resulting scatter diagram may look as follows:

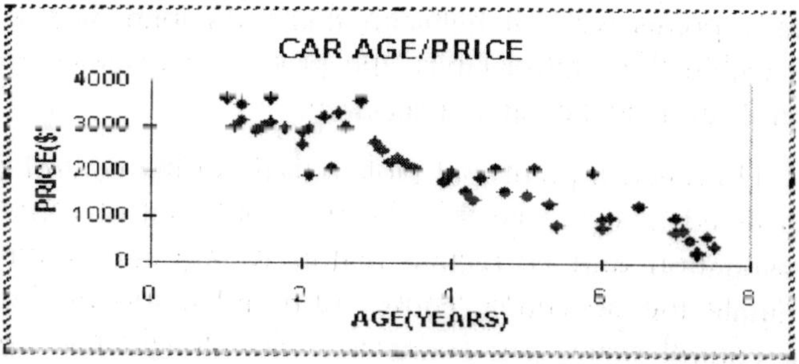

Interpretations

The scatter diagram is a useful tool for identifying a potential relationship between two variables. The shape of the scatter diagram presents valuable information about the graph. It shows the type of relationship which may be occurring between the two variables.

Control charting

Control charting is one of the tools of *Statistical Quality Control*(SQC) It is the most technically sophisticated tool of SQC. It was developed in the 1920s by Dr. Walter A. Shewhart of the Bell Telephone Labs. Dr. Shewhart developed the control charts as an statistical approach to the study of manufacturing process variation for the purpose of improving the economic effectiveness of the process. These methods are based on continuous monitoring of process variation.

Background Information

A typical control chart is a graphical display of a quality characteristic that has been measured or computed from a sample versus the sample number or time. The chart contains a centre line that represents the average value of the quality characteristic corresponding to the in-control state. Two other horizontal lines, called the upper control limit (UCL) and the lower control limit (LCL) are also drawn. These control limits are chosen so that if the process is in control, nearly all of the sample points will fall between them. As long as the points plot within the control limits, the process is assumed to be in control, and no action is necessary.

However, a point that plots outside of the control limits is interpreted as evidence that the process is out of control, and investigation and corrective action is required to find and eliminate the assignable causes responsible for this behavior. The control points are connected with straight line segments for easy visualization. Even if all the points plot inside the control limits, if they behave in a systematic or nonrandom manner, then this is an indication that the process is out of control.

Uses of Control charts

Control chart is a device for describing in a precise manner what is meant by statistical control. Its uses are

— It is a proven technique for improving productivity.

— It is effective in defect prevention.

— It prevents unnecessary process adjustments.

— It provides diagnostic information.

— It provides information about process capability.

Types of control charts

— Control charts for Attributes.

  — *p* chart

  — *c* chart

  — *u* chart

— Control charts for Variables.

  — X bar chart

  — R chart

Patterns of Control Charts

A control chart may indicate an out-of-control condition either when one or more points fall beyond the control limits, or when the plotted points exhibit some nonrandom pattern of behavior. The process is out of control if any one or more of the criteria is met. One or more points outside of the control limits. This pattern may indicate:

— A special cause of variance from a material, equipment, method, or measurement system change.

— Mismeasurement of a part or parts.

— Miscalculated or misplotted data points.

— Miscalculated or misplotted control limits.

— A run of eight points on one side of the centre line. This pattern indicates a shift in the process output from changes in the equipment, methods, or materials or a shift in the measurement system.

— Two of three consecutive points outside the 2-sigma warning limits but still inside the control limits. This may be the result of a large shift in the process in the equipment, methods, materials, or operator or a shift in the measurement system.

— Four of five consecutive points beyond the 1-sigma limits.

— An unusual or nonrandom pattern in the data.

— A trend of seven points in a row upward or downward. This may show

  — Gradual deterioration or wear in equipment.

  — Improvement or deterioration in technique.

  — Cycling of data can indicate

  — Temperature or other recurring changes in the environment.

  — Differences between operators or operator techniques.

  — Regular rotation of machines.

  — Differences in measuring or testing devices that are being used in order.

Several points near a warning or control limit.

Benefits of Charts in Classrooms

The most common mistake presenters make with visuals is overloading them, says Judith Stein, co-author of *Presentations for Decision Makers* . When using visuals, "You want the audience to look at the screen, quickly get the message, and then focus on you," she says. When viewers have to spend time reading, "you become the voice-over to a video, and lose your effectiveness as a presenter." In visual support, Stein continues, "The operative word is 'support.' Visuals are supposed to support or aid you in giving the presentation - not replace you."

Simplify Data

Stein and her partner, Marya Holcombe, train business presenters through their consulting firm, Strategic Communications, based in New Haven, Connecticut. They advise presenters that planning a presentation involves two phases:

Solving the problem.

Analyze the audience, organize the data, and decide what message to convey.

Developing the presentation.

Choose the form and substance of each visual to best communicate the message. One form is the text, or word-only, visual, which serves as a roadmap to guide the audience through a presentation. The text visual is rapidly giving way to the conceptual visual, which uses a picture or design to convey an idea. But the real workhorse of most presentations is the chart or graph that shows relationships among variables; this form enables the audience to grasp complex data at a glance.

"You create charts to help you see what's happening," Stein says. "The tendency is to grab these charts and use them in the presentation, and most of the time doing this doesn't work." Assume, for example, that you chart sales, manufacturing costs, administrative costs, operating income, and earnings for the past seven years. In the process, you discover that administrative costs have risen faster than manufacturing costs over the past three years - an important message. You should then abandon the earlier chart in favor of one that compares only the two costs in the shorter time span. "The chart you make in solving the problem may not be the best chart to convey the message," Stein says. "You have to pare the ideas down and simplify."

Make Charts Communicate

Simplifying a chart often requires changing the chart form - switching from a line graph to a horizontal bar chart, for example, because it communicates the message more effectively. How do you know when to use which chart? That depends on how well you've stated the message, says Stein.

Too often, a presenter makes the mistake of putting a label, such as 'Sales 1990-1995,' at the top of a chart. "Your heading should always tell people what you want them to look for on a chart. An action statement or message will do that for you." An action statement has a verb and is a complete sentence, such as "Sales reverse downward trend except in West."

Choosing the Chart

Once you have an action statement as a heading, look at the verbs in the statement to get an idea of the best chart to use to present your data.

Showing change over time.

Look for a key word such as "grow," "decline," or "trends." If, for example, you want to show how college entrance test scores have changed over 30 years, use a line chart. Line charts are best when a variable has more than four or five data points, and you want to emphasize continuity over several months or years. The slope of the line tells viewers in a glance the direction of the trends.

However, if you have fewer than five data points and you want to emphasize quantity at discrete times - for example, how administrative costs have risen faster than manufacturing costs over three years - use a column chart (vertical bars). Since the audience naturally associates left-to-right with the movement of time, vertical bars work better than horizontal bars for time series data.

Comparing items at one point in time.

Look for a key word such as "ranks" or "compares." If, for example, you want to show the highest profit, the lowest interest rate, or the most products sold, or you want to rank variables from largest to smallest, use a horizontal bar chart. Bar charts are often the best way to compare a set of individual items or several sets of related items. The bar's length corresponds to its ranking; the bar's label identifies the item.

Comparing parts of a whole.

Look for key words such as "percentage," "portion" or "share." If, for example, you want to show the proportion of state government budget spent on education, use a pie chart. However, the number of pie slices should not be more than five, and each slice should be easy to see and interpret. A pie chart is best when you want to highlight one part of the whole. Place this component in the 12 o'clock position and "explode" it out of the pie for emphasis.

When you want to show relative proportions of two, three, or four wholes, a segmented bar chart may work equally well or better. In this chart form, each bar represents 100 percent, and each segment a percentage. A series of vertical segmented bars shows how percentages change over time.

Comparing data by geographic location.

Look for key words such as "country" or "state." If, for example, you want to show sales by region, use a map. Distinguish among regions by using different colours, shadings, or symbols.

Other commonly used forms include the organization chart (which shows functional relationships in a group or structure), the flow chart (diagram of process), and the Gantt chart (which shows the duration of different tasks across a calendar span).

Making these simple charts - as well as more complicated forms - has become considerably easier with presentation software. With a few keystrokes, the user can change bar width, colour, type size, and other elements.

However, presenters should resist the temptation "to use every bell and whistle," says Stein. "Don't let the artistic possibilities interfere with the message."

Strategic Communications offers the following guidelines for designing visuals, regardless of whether they are overhead transparencies, slides, or computer images.

— Convey one message per chart. Make the message the heading.

— Make the chart easy to read. Label the X and Y axes and label the lines, bars, or pie wedges. Make the most important text largest, the most important data lines or sections darkest.

— Be accurate. Always start a numerical axis at zero. Compare only like variables.

— Eliminate all unnecessary details. Avoid grid lines, data points, boxes, and other devices unless they relate to the message.

— Use no more than four colours per visual.

— Avoid vibrating fill patterns, such as contrasting lines, wave patterns, and crisscrosses.

— To focus attention, use colour, shading, or images such as arrows to highlight key words or concepts.

— Write in upper and lower case. Words written in all capitals letters are hard to read.

— Make bars and columns wider than the spaces between them.

— Use presentation software sensibly. When necessary, adjust the default mode to simplify a visual.

5

GRAPHS

In mathematics and computer science, a graph is a generalization of the simple concept of a set of dots, called vertices or nodes, connected by links, edges or arcs. "Nodes" and "arcs" are old notation. Depending on the applications, edges may or may not have a direction; edges joining a vertex to itself may or may not be allowed, and vertices and/or edges may be assigned labels. A numeric label is often called a *weight*. If the edges have a direction associated with them (indicated by an arrow in the graphical representation) we have a directed graph. This means it is possible to follow a path from one vertex to another, but not in the opposite direction. If there are no directed edges, the graph is an undirected graph.

Unless otherwise indicated, the term *graph* typically is assumed to mean a simple graph, in which at most one edge exists between any two vertices (directed or undirected). If any two vertices share more than one edge, this is known as a multigraph. A multigraph that additionally allows graph loops, or edges which connect a vertex to itself, is called a pseudograph. Structures that can be represented as graphs are ubiquitous, and many problems of practical interest can be formulated as questicns about certain graphs.

DEFINITIONS

Definitions in graph theory vary in the literature. Here are the conventions used in this encyclopedia. A directed graph (also called digraph or quiver) consists of

a set V of ***vertices***, and

a set E of ***edges***, and

maps $s, t : E \to V$, where $s(e)$ is the *source* and $t(e)$ is the *target* of the directed edge e.

An ***undirected graph*** (or ***graph*** for short) is given by

a set V of ***vertices***,

a set E of ***edges***,

a function $w : E \to \underline{P}(V)$ which associates to each edge a two or one-element subset of V, interpreted as the endpoints of the edge.

Informally, it is said that a graph is a set of vertices, some pairs of which being connected by edges. Two edges of a graph are called coincident if they have a common vertex. Two vertices are called adjacent if they are the ends of the same edge. In a weighted graph or digraph, an additional function E ® R associates a value with each edge, which can be considered its "cost"; such graphs arise in optimal route problems such as the travelling salesman problem.

Normally, the vertices of a graph by their nature are undistinguishable. (Of course, they may be distinguishable by the properties of the graph itself, e.g., by the numbers of incident edges). Some branches of graph theory require to uniquely identify vertices. If each vertex is given a label, then the graph is said to be a vertex-labeled graph, whereas graphs which have labeled edges are called edge-labeled graphs. Graphs with labels attached to edges or vertices are more generally designated as labeled. Consequently, graphs without labels are called unlabelled.

PICTORIAL REPRESENTATION OF GRAPHS

Graphs are often represented pictorially as follows: draw a dot for every vertex, and for every edge draw an arc connecting its endpoints. If the graph is directed, indicate the endpoint of an edge by an arrow. Note that this graphical representation (a layout) should not be confused with the graph itself (the abstract, non-graphical structure). Very different layouts can correspond to the same graph. All that matters is which vertices are connected to which others by how many edges. This can complicate things as some graphical representations are easier to work with or easier to understand than others.

While it is usually easy to represent graphs with pictures, it will not always clarify the problems you face. For example, you may have a graph with many vertices, each one connecting many others, thus the graphical representation can look like a mess. Further, graphical representations are only useful to humans. A pictorial simplification is of no use to a computer. Thus it is necessary to come up with algorithms that can solve your problems without requiring a picture. There are different approaches to graph layout, and these are considered under a branch of graph theory termed as graph drawing.

Graph drawing

Graphs are often represented pictorially as follows: draw a dot for every vertex, and for every edge draw an arc connecting its endpoints. If the graph is directed, indicate the endpoint of an edge by an arrow. There are different approaches to graph layout and these are considered under a branch of graph theory termed as graph drawing. Note that this graphical representation (a layout) should not be confused with the graph itself (the abstract, non-graphical structure). Very different layouts can correspond to the same graph. All that matters is which vertices are connected to which others by how many edges.

Some of the well known layouts are:

- spring layout - by using an energy function that is minimized so that nodes and edges spread out by repulsion.
- orthogonal layout - layout with edges running horizontally or vertically, with approaches that reduce the number of edge crossovers and area covered. These are of great interest in the areas of VLSI and PCB layout design.
- symmetric layout - these attempt to find symmetry groups within the graph
- tree layout - these show a rooted tree-like formation, suitable for trees (ie graphs without cycles)
- hierarchical layouts - these attempt to find a source and sink within a directed graph and arrange the nodes in layers with most edges starting from the source and flowing in the direction of the sink.

GRAPH THEORY

Graph theory is the branch of mathematics that examines the properties of graphs.

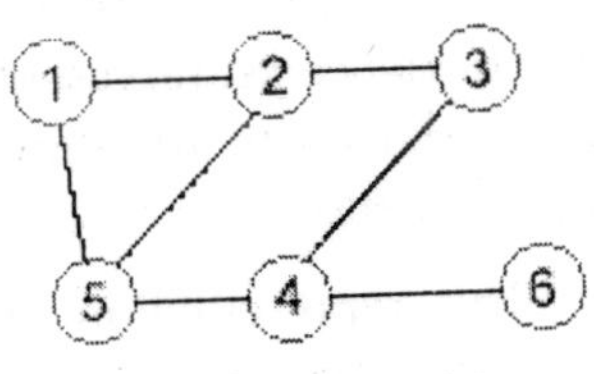

A graph with 6 vertices and 7 edges.

Informally, a graph is a set of objects called vertices (or nodes) connected by links called edges (or arcs). Typically, a graph is depicted as a set of dots (i.e., vertices) connected by lines (i.e., edges). Depending on the applications, edges may or may not have a direction; edges joining a vertex to itself may or may not be allowed, and vertices and/or edges may be assigned weights, that is, numbers. If the edges have a direction associated with them (indicated by an arrow in the graphical representation) then it is a directed graph, or digraph.

The graph with only one vertex and no edges is the trivial graph or *"the dot"*. A graph with only vertices and no edges is known as an empty graph; the graph with no vertices and no edges is the Null graph. Structures that can be represented as graphs are ubiquitous, and many problems of practical interest can be formulated as questions about certain graphs. Various networks are conveniently described by means of graphs. Directed graphs are also used to represent finite state machines. The development of algorithms to handle graphs is therefore of major interest in computer science.

Leonhard Euler's paper on *Seven Bridges of Königsberg* is considered to be the first result in graph theory. It is also regarded as one of the first topological results in geometry; that is, it does not depend on any measurements. This illustrates the deep connection between graph theory and topology.

Graph representations

In general, there are four ways to represent a graph in a computer system: The incidence list representation, the incidence matrix representation, adjacency list representation, and the adjacency matrix representation.

— *Incidence List* - This representation uses an array. Each element in the array corresponds with a single edge. Each edge contains a list of size two which corresponds to the endpoints of the edge. This can also apply to directed graphs by ensuring the first vertex be defined as the source or destination while the second should be defined as the opposite.

— *Incidence matrix* - This representation uses a matrix of M edges by N vertices. If the vertex is an endpoint to the edge, a value of 1 is assigned to their crossing, otherwise, a value of 0 is assigned. This is a terrible waste of space as every column or row represented by the edge can only have two values of 1 while the rest are labelled 0.

These two representations are most useful when information about edges is more desirable than information about vertices.

— *Adjacency list* - Much like the incidence list, each node has a list of which nodes it is adjacent to. This can sometimes result in "overkill" in an undirected graph as vertex 3 may be in the list for node 2, then node 2 must be in the list for node 3. Either the programmer may choose to use the unneeded space anyway, or he/she may choose to list the adjacency once. This representation is easier to find all the nodes which are connected to a single node, since these are explicitly listed.

— *Adjacency matrix* - there is an N by N matrix, where N is the total number of vertices in the graph. If there is an edge from some vertex x to some vertex y, then the element *Mx,y* would be 1, otherwise it would be 0. This makes it easier to find subgraphs, and to reverse graphs if needed.

These two representations are most useful when information about the vertices is more desirable than information about the edges. These two representations are also most popular since information about the vertices is often more desirable than edges in most applications.

Here are some of the special words graph theorists use tc describe what they see when they are looking at graphs:

— edge

— vertex

— degree

— size

— regular

— path
— circuit
— cycle
— hamiltonain
— eulerian
— planar
— non-planar
— distance
— diameter
— isomorphic
— complete
— neighbour
— dominating set

Edges and Vertices of Graphs

A graph is made up of dots connected by lines.

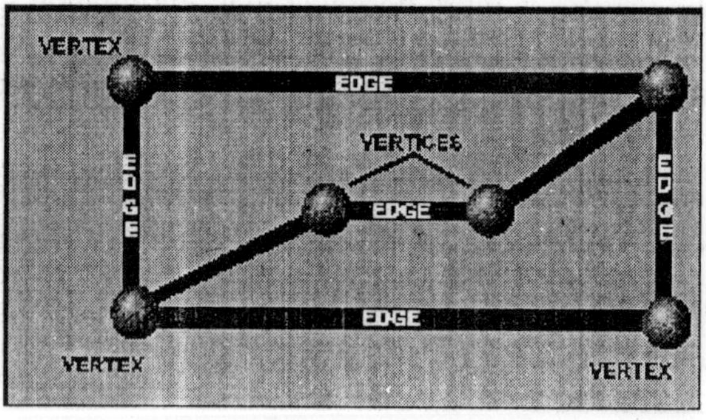

A "dot" is called a vertex. When there is more than one vertex, they are called vertices. A "line" is called an edge. (The plural is simply edges.)

The Degree of a Vertex in a Graph

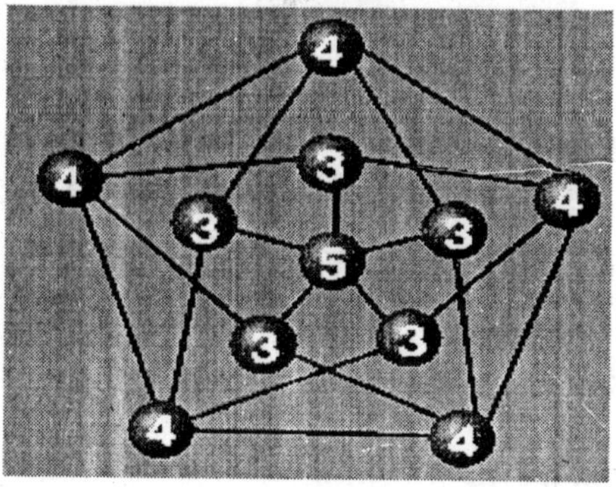

- The degree of a vertex in a graph is the number of edges that touch it.
- The number on each vertex of this graph is the degree of that vertex.

The Size of a Graph

The size of a graph is the number of vertices that it has.

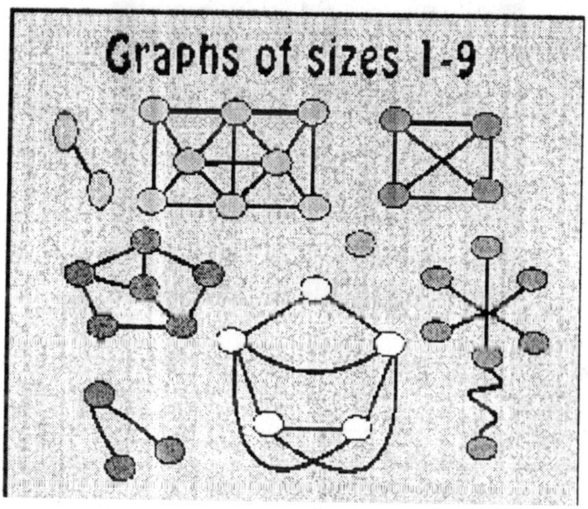

Regular graphs

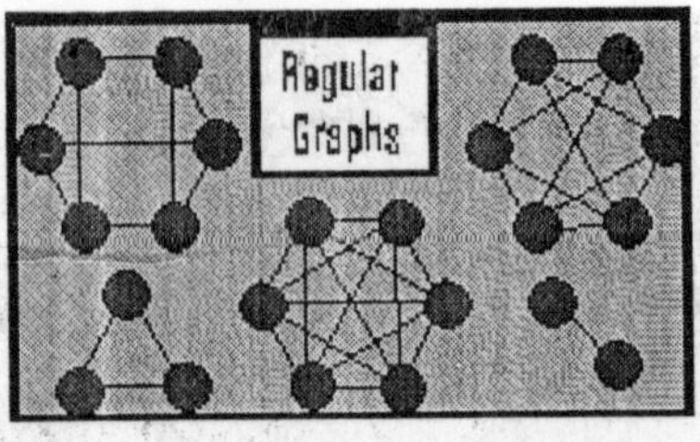

A graph is regular if every vertex has the same degree.

Paths and Cycles in a graph

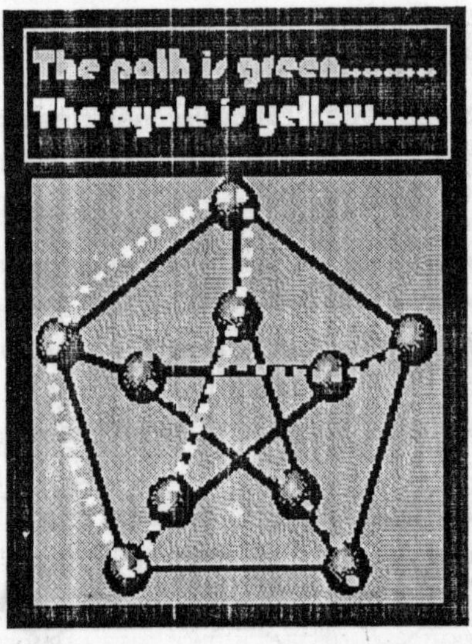

A path is a route that you travel along edges and through vertices in a graph. All of the vertices and edges in a path are connected to one another.

A cycle is a path which begins and ends on the same vertex. A cycle is sometimes called a circuit.

The number of edges in a path or a cycle is called the length of the path. Is the length of the path also the number of vertices?

A Hamiltonian Path in a Graph

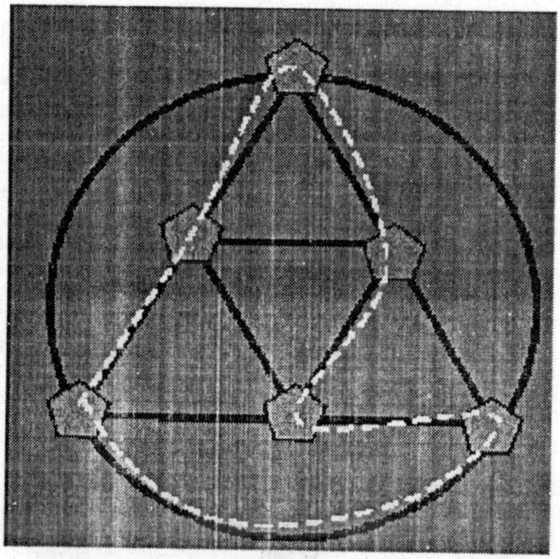

A hamiltonian path in a graph is a path that passes through every vertex in the graph exactly once. A hamiltonain path does not necessarily pass through all the edges of the graph, however. A hamiltonian path which ends in the same place in which it began is called a hamiltonian circuit or a hamiltonain cycle.

An Eulerian Path in a Graph

An eulerian path in a graph is a path that travels along every edge of the graph exactly once. An eulerian path might pass through individual vertices of the graph more than once. An eulerian path which begins and ends in the same place is called an eulerian circuit or an eulerian cycle

Planar Graphs

A planar graph is a graph that can be drawn so that the edges only touch each other where they meet at vertices.

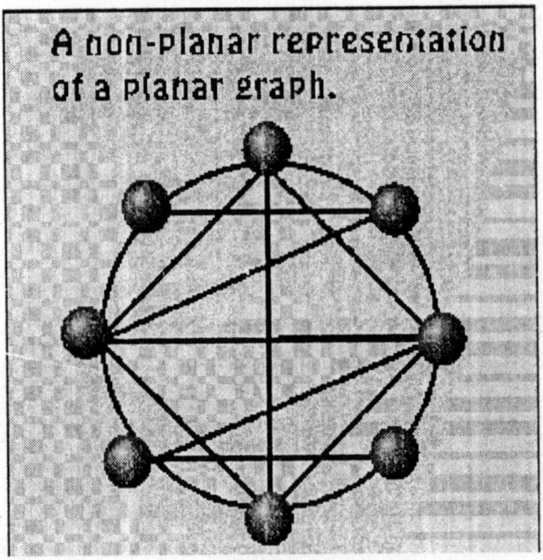

You can usually redraw a planar graph so that some of the edges cross. Even so, it is still a planar graph. When it is drawn so that the edges cross, the drawing is called a non-planar representation of a planar graph.

Non-planar Graphs

The graph above is nonplanar. No matter how you stretch the edges around, you cannot redraw the graph so that none of the edges cross each other between the vertices. A non-planar graph should not be confused with a planar graph that just happens to be drawn in such a way that two or more edged cross. The graph below is a planar graph, but it is drawn here in a nonplanar representation.

Distance in a Graph

Distance in a graph isn't measured in inches or kilmoters. This isn't surprising, because you don't do any measuring in inches or kilometers when you draw a graph in the first place. Still, when you look at a graph, you can see how it might be possible to say that some vertices are closer together then others. The distance between two vertices is a count of the number of edges along which you must travel to get from one of the verticesto the other. If there is more than one path between two vertices, the number of edges in the shortest path is the distance. The number of edges in a path is called the length of the path.

The Diameter of a Graph

The diameter of a graph is the longest distance you can find between two vertices. When you are measuring distances to determine a graph's diameter, recall that if 2 vertices have many paths of different distances connecting them, you can only count the shortest one. An interesting problem in graph theory is to draw graphs in which both the degrees of the vertices and the diameter of the graph are small. Drawing the largest graphs possible that meet these criteria is an open problem.

ISOMORPHIC GRAPHS

Two graphs are isomorphic if you can redraw one of them so that it looks exactly like the other. To redraw a graph, it helps to imagine the edges as infinitely stretchable rubber bands. You can move the vertices around and stretch the edges any way you like — as long as they don't become disconnected. Sometimes it is very hard to tell whether two graphs are isomorphic or not. In fact, no one knows a simple method for taking two graphs and determining quickly whether or not they are isomorphic.

COMPLETE GRAPHS

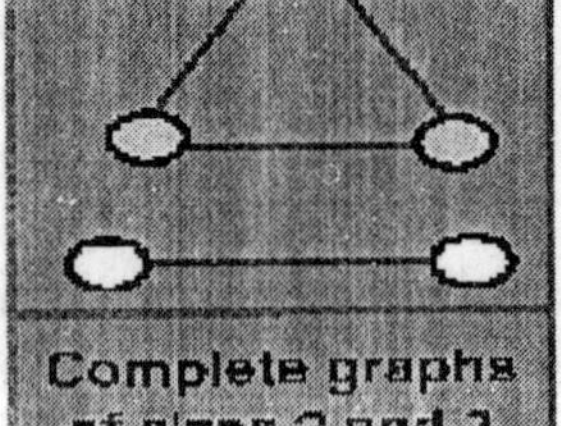

Complete graphs of sizes 2 and 3

In a complete graph, every pair of vertices is connected by an edge. It is impossible to add an edge to a complete graph because every possible edge has been drawn.

Neighbouring vertices in a graph

In a graph, the neighbours of a vertex are all the vertices which are connected to that vertex by a single edge. The distance between two vertices which are neighbours is always 1.

Dominating Sets in Graphs

In a graph, the neighbours of a vertex are all the vertices which are connected to that vertex by a single edge. A dominating set for a graph is a set of vertices whose neighbours, along with themselves, constitute all the vertices in the graph.

THE MATHEMATICS OF GRAPHS AND THEIR GAMES

When mathematicians talk about graphs, they are most likely to be thinking of the collections of dots and lines that you see in the illustrations of this section. Sometimes graphs are called *networks,* and a glance at pictures of them will show you why. The graphs of Graph Theory are not the same as the graphs which are used to plot or chart statistical information. The potential for confusion between these two very different kinds of objects that have the same name is unfortunate. When mathematicians talk about graphs, it is always clear from the context which type of graph they are considering.

The Vocabulary of Graphs

Of course there is a vocabulary of terms for talking about graphs. The following discussion of graph terminology is not a prerequisite for understanding graphs. The terms become quite useful, however, when students try to talk about their observations or their strategies for playing games. Familiarize yourself with these terms so that when students find themselves using round-about awkward constructions to try to explain something, you can supply word that are useful to describe it. Each dot is called a vertex. The plural of *vertex* is *vertices*. (Although many excited young students experiencing graph games and puzzles for the first time use the word *verticie* as the singular of vertices!) The lines that connect the vertices are called edges. Edges can connect any or all of the vertices.

Edges in a graph can cross one another without there being a vertex at the place where they cross, but edges cannot "hang loose" with no vertex on the very end. The edges of a graph can be stretched, shrunk, pulled out of place, or deformed in any imaginable way and it will still be the same graph. All of the different representations of the same graph, are said to be isomorphic to one another. Sometimes it is not so easy to tell that two graphs are isomorphic. It takes quite a bit of moving edges around to see that the graphs above are isomorphic. In fact, no one knows a reliable way to quickly determine quickly if two graphs, no matter how large they are, are isomorphic—although it is fun to experiment with graphs to see if they are isomorphic.

Mathematical Objects and their Properties

A graph is an example of a mathematical object. A *number* is the mathematical object that is probably the most familiar to everyone. Some other examples of mathematical objects are knots, maps, and finite state machines. One way mathematicians try to understand objects is in terms of their properties. The number 6, for instance, is a positive, even number divisible by 3 and less than 10. These are properties of the number 6. We could list many more. Depending on what you are trying to find out, some properties of the object you are looking at are more useful than others.

Some Properties of Graphs

Three properties of graphs that are important in many problems are size, regularity, diameter. The size of a graph is the number of vertices it has. A graph is regular if all of the vertices have the same degree. The degree of a vertex is the number of edges that touch it. Mathematicians would use the term 3-regular to describe a graph in which all the vertices were of degree 3. 4-regular graphs have vertices of degree 4, and so on. Just like the diameter of a circle measures the distance across a circle, diameter is a measure of distance between vertices in a graph.

The idea of "distance" in a graph is different from the "distance" we commonly measure with a tape measure, however, because we can stretch or shrink the edges of a graph to be any length at all. Imagine travelling from vertex to vertex along the edges of a graph. Each trip along one edge, no matter how long or short the edge happens to be, counts as one move. The distance from one vertex to another is the smallest number of moves that it takes to get there. The diameter of a circle measures the distance between two points on the circle that are farthest apart. Similarly, the diameter of a graph is the distance between the two vertices of the graph that are farthest apart.

A Real-World Problem that Uses Graphs

The connecting dots and lines of graphs make the ideas in graph theory particularly useful to people who design computer systems. On the smallest end of the scale, a graph can be used to model the way that tiny pulses of electricity flow through the silicon chips that are built into electronic devices. In the big picture, a graph can model the ways that computing systems can be interconnected, even when the computers are located all over the world and connected by telephone wires and satellites. When graphs are used to model circuits for silicon chips or large computer systems, properties like size, regularity, and distance and diameter are important.

For example, imagine that you have been given the task of deciding how to link 12 computers together. Each one of these computers will use information that is generated by all the others, so that all of them will need to exchange information with each other. Unless each computer can be connected directly to all eleven of the other ones, the computers will have to interrupt the work that they are supposed to be doing just to relay messages. It would be nice if every computer could be connected to all of the others, but that can get expensive. Suppose that each computer is made to be connected to only three others. Suppose further, that someone has figured out that the whole system can handle the traffic only if messages don't have to pass through more than two computers on their way to their destination.

If messages have to pass through three or more computers, it is likely that the whole system will get bogged down because it is doing to much work just passing messages around. How will you decide how to plug these computers together? When you try and solve such a problem, a good way to show these connections is with a graph. Draw the computers as vertices or dots and the connecting wires are edges or lines. For this problem, our will be trying to construct a graph that is 3-regular whose is not greater than three. With a little bit of experimentation, you can figure out how to connect all 12 computers so that these criteria are met.

Now suppose you are given a similar task, but instead of connecting computers, you have been asked to lay out where the electric impulses should go on a silicon chip. You are allowed to use only one side of the chip, because the other side of the chip is being used for something else. If any of your connections cross, the whole thing will short-circuit and be useless. It is quite a bit harder to find a way to draw the graph that represents the right set of connections.

This graph will be 3-regular and it's diameter will be 3, (just like the graph that you drew to connect the computers in the problem above) but it will have the additional property of being planar. That means that it can be drawn in a flat plane so that edges only touch each other at a vertex. If you can draw this graph without peeking at the the solution you should be triumphant! When you look at the solution, it is easy to verify that the graph is indeed 3-regular and planar. It may take some experimentation to verify that the diameter is also 3. Specifications about the relationship between degree and diameter in graphs occurs over and over again in questions that come up in computer system design.

Understanding Properties by Playing Games

It is difficult and confusing to pore over pictures of dots and lines and try to apply what you have memorized about graph properties to the graph that may happen to be in front of you. If you use a graph as a game board, however, and invent games with game pieces that move about it in a variety of ways, many of the properties of the graph will emerge as you develop strategies for playing the games.

Mathematics in Maps and Planning

The map of the town that is used in the activities is a collection of dots and lines that mathematicians call a graph . (Graphs are described, along with some of the terminology that is used for talking about them in Games on Graphs .) You may want to refer to that information if you are not already familiar with graphs such as these—they are made up of dots and lines, and unrelated to graphs that chart information with which you are undoubtedly familiar. The technical term for an optimal solution to the Ice Cream Stands problem is a minimum dominating set . The problem itself is probably best understood in the form of the ice cream stands story itself. If the dots are houses and the lines are roads, then what is the smallest set of locations to put the ice cream stands so no one has to walk down more than one street to get to one? A set of dots or vertices where the ice cream stands go in a solution to this problem is called the dominating set.

A dominating set for a graph is easy enough to find. But ice cream stands are expensive to build—as are warehouses, "hub" airports, electrical switching stations, etc. So it is that many situations which involve planning the location of important facilities can be modeled by a graph for which we ask the question, "What is a minimum dominating set?" We want the one with the smallest possible number of members. It turns out that for an arbitrary graph or map, there is only one reliable step-by-step procedure that you can use to find a minimum dominating set, and that is to check every possible combination of vertices to see if it is a dominating set. When you find a dominating set that might be minimal, there is not always a way to be sure it is unless you check all the possibilities for a better solution.

Is checking all the possibilities so bad? Couldn't you get a computer to do it? A computer can certainly find one possibility extremely quickly. This does not mean, however, that the computer can find and check all the possibilities in a reasonable amount of time. To know if that can be done, you have to know how many possibilities there are. The number of possibilities will vary with the size of the graph: the more vertices it has, the more possibilities there will be. But how many more? This question belongs to a branch of mathematics concerned with computatonal complexity.

The best way to try and figure out how many possibilities there might be is to look at some examples, beginning with some very small ones, and try to find some kind of trend or pattern in the way the possibilities grow with the size of the graph. A graph with only one vertex is trivial: there is one possibility. For a graph with two vertices, you could place ice cream stands on both vertices, or on one or the other, so there are three possibilities. For a graph with three vertices, you have to count the number of possibilities for each quantity of ice cream stands that is possible to use. There is only one way to arrange three ice cream stands, of course. How many ways to arrange two? One?

For a graph with four vertices, you continue in the same way, only there will be even more possibilities. It takes a lot of careful counting to begin to get a feel for how the numbers grow. Generally speaking, the number of possibilities to check grows at a much faster rate than the number of vertices in the graph. This kind of growth is called exponential . There are some problems that mathematicians and scientists would like to solve whose solutions are minimum dominating sets, but the graphs are large enough that it would take a fast computer years and years to produce a solution—longer, perhaps than the estimated age of the universe!

The fact that the Ice Cream Stands puzzle appears to be so difficult to solve allows us to use it to play with the idea of a one-way function . In the Ice Cream Stands Problem you can explore this idea by seeing how a person can create puzzles like these with the solution in mind first, but completely disguise the solution by the time the puzzle is finished. If you go from the solution to the puzzle, a good solution is always known to the maker of the puzzle. But you can't go the other way with such ease.

Of course this one-way trick isn't going to help someone who is trying to figure out where to locate the big and little computers in a large interconnected computing system, because no one created that problem with the solution already in mind! One-way functions are important, however, in cryptography , the mathematics of secret codes and secure passwords. If you had a clubhouse with a huge graph on the door, and only members knew what the minimum dominating set for the graph was, the minimum dominating set could be the password because the chances of someone else figuring it out would be slim.

GRAPHS, GAMES, AND THE NCTM STANDARDS

Mathematical Objects and Their Properties

The significant mathematical activity represented in this section is the reasoning involved in understanding mathematical objects in terms of their properties. In any branch of mathematics, the mathematical object is the "thing" under consideration. The mathematical object is defined clearly and unambiguously, and it is straightforward to verify whether something is one of those objects or not. The characteristics that an object has are its properties. Mathmatical objects can be classified and sub-classified according to the properties that they do and don't possess, and this is how much knowledge about them is gained.

The foundational four standards of the NCTM (problem solving, communcation, reasoning, and making mathematical connections) are carried out by mathematicians worldwide as they study mathematical objects in terms of their properties. When students begin to see how the study of objects and their properties is common across all branches of mathematics, and when they develop tools for doing this themselves, they can become confident that they can do any kind of mathematics, too. Seeing mathematics in this way can help them to understand how the mathematical results that they learn about may have been discovered, and to go ahead and discover things on their own rather than waiting to be "taught".

Why Graphs?

Graphs are facinating mathematical objects in the classroom because it is easy to discover things about them, yet you are unlikely to ever run out of things to discover. Because they are made of lines with dots on each end, children can draw graphs long before they can draw numbers, and they can discover many things about graphs without being able to count. The relationships between the parts of a graph are a treasure-trove for seeking patterns and relationships and for spatial reasoning.

Why Games?

There is a direct relationship between the success or failure of the strategies that one uses to play a game on a graph and the properties that the graph has. Games become easy or hard as the graphs change; certain rules become essential or irrelevant when you try the same game on different graphs. Articulating this is an essential part of communicating about the problem solving process. When games are associated with stories, the stories show how an abstract mathematical object can be connected to a situation in everyday life in the real world.

Graphing Skills of Students in Mathematics and Science Education

"Instructional programs from prekindergarten through grade 12 should enable all students to:

— create and use representations to organize, record, and communicate mathematical ideas;

— select, apply, and translate among mathematical representations to solve problems;

— use representations to model and interpret physical, social, and mathematical phenomena."

The effective use of representations in mathematics and science education has gained more importance as we enter the new millennium. National Council of Teachers of Mathematics even added, Representation, to their four process standards which "highlight ways of acquiring and using content knowledge" in their new reform document, "Principles and Standards for School Mathematics". Even though all types of representations are being encouraged in the teaching and learning of mathematics and science, graphical representations play a special role. Graphs can summarize very complex information or relationship very effectively. Although graphs are explicitly taught in mathematics classrooms as an end in themselves, many subject areas such as science or social studies utilize graphs to represent and interpret relationships.

So being able to interpret or construct graphical representations is a crucial skill for every student whether they want to pursue science or mathematics related careers. However, many researchers detected that many students lack graphing skills. Brasell and Rowe studied high school physics students' graphing skills and they concluded that "[students] do not understand the fundamental properties and functions of graphs in representing relationships among variables." Their facility with graphs was generally superficial, grounded on a few, simplistic algorithms such as plotting data points". Janvier was one of the first mathematics educators to mention the problems that students have in interpreting graphs. Mostly he argues how global meanings of graphs and interpreting graphs are left out in mathematics classrooms, while reading data and constructing and reading certain points on graphs are emphasized.

What Research Says About How to Improve Students Graphing Skills ?

In this age of technology, many researchers advocate the use of computers, calculators, Microcomputer-Based Laboratories (MBLs) or Calculator-Based Laboratories (CBLs) in improving students' graphing skills. Mokros & Tinker studied the effects of MBLs in students' understandings about graphing. The use of an MBL or CBL allows student to collect real-time physical data such as temperature, motion, light, or sound. Then these data can be transferred into a computer or a calculator to be studied through a variety of representations such as graphs or tables. They conclude that "in three-month longitudinal study of MBL, students showed a significant gain in understanding on 16 graphing items, although the instruction targeted science topics, not graphing skills". They add that "MBL may also help children develop graphing skills because it eliminates the drudgery of graph production".

Dugdale discusses the potentials for graphing software, such as Green Globs, to enhance students' understanding of functional and graphical relationships. Green Globs is a game where 13 "green globs" are randomly placed on the grid. Players earn points by entering equations that pass through as many green globs as possible. She argues that it is crucial to go beyond plotting and reading points to interpret the graphs. Sivasubramaniam compares students' graphing skills in a learning experiment with and without the use of computers. The paper concludes that "the computer group improved significantly more than the paper group in their graphing skills from the pretest to posttest."

Many educators went beyond teaching graphs as an end to themselves and used a graphing approach to teach other mathematical or scientific subjects. Oakes suggests an approach in teaching which combines the discovery method with graphing skills in science instruction which "allows students to discover the actual laws of nature rather than be given the equation and just plug in data". Hollar and Norwood use graphing calculators in teaching algebra with a graphing approach curriculum in which they could focus on real-world situations. They concluded that the students in the graphing approach curriculum showed better understanding of functions than the traditional students.

TEACHING ABOUT GRAPHS

Information Credibility

A critical component of information literacy is appraising the reliability of material. The librarian and the teacher can team to cover the variety of ways students can examine credibility and relevance both while they are searching and after they retrieve research items. Following are some of the areas that need to be covered:

— Currency of information in relation to topic focus

— Reliability of source

— Point of view

— Author's focus

— Primary or secondary source

— Opinion or fact

— Bias/prejudice

— Authority

— Intended audience

— Verifiable

— Solicited or unsolicited

— Primary/secondary information source

These skills are commonly taught in relation to text. The current move to researching CD-ROMS and the Internet, involving more and more multi-media formats, requires expanding these skills into visual literacy. The librarian has worked with audio visuals and can bring skill teaching for this area to the team. Visual literacy includes the interpretation of information from photos, pictures and other art works, graphs, charts, videos, television shows, computer-developed visuals, clip art, models, dioramas, realia, in short, anything not presented in words or sounds. Teachers and librarians can collaborate in preparing students to critique the dependability of multi-media information as carefully as they do text. An example follows, with references to specific performance indicators from the January 1996 draft of Mainés Learning Results.

Getting Information from Graphs

Purpose of the activities: Be able to distinguish between the visual impact of graphs and the information given by the numbers used on the graphs. The introduction can be done in one 45 minute class. The educator team needs to know how much experience the students have with graphing. The topic can be expanded into several lessons, with the students doing their own surveys to acquire primary source statistics. The educators would have to know what computer applications are available for students to produce their own graphs. Expansion of the introduction can also include subject area teachers for an interdisciplinary approach. The performance indicators given suggest specific areas of integration.

Visualize two line graphs - one with a fairly flat line and the second with a gradually rising line. Both graphs have the same statistics, but use different scales. The topic is dependent on what subject area teacher is teaming with the librarian. The following example chart shown is related to elections. Questions to ask for this chart: "Which graph would be used by the candidate in office to show the status of unemployment during his/her term?" "Which would be used by the opponent?" In teams, write out the actual numbers from the graph, compare and discuss. Questions to ask: What is different, what is the same between the two graphs? What impact is each candidate hoping to achieve? How is that goal reflected visually?

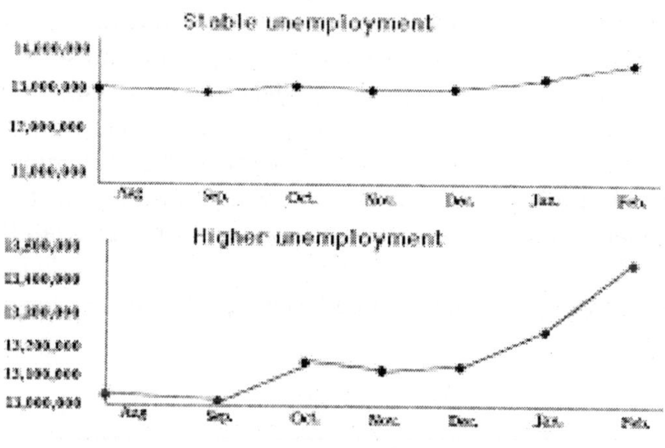

Expansion assignment

In teams of two or four with subject area dependent upon current class work. With an almanac or encyclopedia, find a set of statistics, and produce two graphs with different visual impacts. Half of the team present an argument using one graph, the other half present the opposite argument with the other graph. Whole class could vote on which graph reflects the statistics best. The type of graph will be dependent upon math class teaching - this lesson could be an excellent follow-up to math class covering how to produce all varieties of graphs.

Incorporate computers with production of the graphs - thus allowing students to "play" with, try out various visual impacts without the drudgery of hand drawings. Most computer graphing applications can flip entered statistics quickly to a variety of visuals. Long term assignment: Find graphs in current media and analyze the focus of the graph. Use the same numbers and recreate the graph to support an alternative focus.

Assessment

Any of the following areas could be appraised: the actual graph production, the visual impact of graphs, the speaking part of the presentation, the development of the persuasive argument, the use of the subject matter for the graph and presentation, the team-work involved in the project. The assessment tool shown is incomplete. As a first step, fill in the empty boxes. Now browse the visual literacy projects in the Adventure in Space chapter. Which aspect of visual literacy is a key component of each project? Choose one of them, and list measurable criteria for that component. Then complete the rubric matrix by describing three levels of achievement for each criterion.

Visual Impact of a Graph

Criteria	Adequate	Proficient	Limited
Title	At top, centered 1-2-3 words long	—	—
Colour	1 or 2 colours or shading, defining	. Distracting	Confusing
Citation	Lower left-hand corner	—	Missing

Grid	Listest line or omitted	—	—
Key - Labels block letters	Simple, readable —	—	
Bars - Lines obvious	Stand out, —	—	
Graph type	Best possible delineation	—	Ungraphable material

Performance Indicators Reflected in the Foregoing Graph Activities

- Career
  - 5-8 Impact of specific technology on issues
  - 5-8 Debates need for ethical standards in application of technology
  - 9-12 Applies experiences with tools (computergraphing) to issues of life
  - 9-12 Evaluates skills in team-designed project
- English
  - 5-8 Views in order to identify various viewpoints on a debatable issue
  - 5-8 Accurately uses oral language conventions in formal situation
  - 9-12 Uses spoken language with competency
  - 5-8 Uses a variety of resources to investigate for oral presentation
  - 9-12 Designs presentation to achieve particular rhetorical purpose

— 5-8 Adjusts viewing strategies in order to comprehend
— 5-8 Identifies bias in visual materials
— 5-8 Evaluates reliability of information from mass media
— 9-12 Identifies how bias influences peoplesÍ perceptions and formulates hypothesis about authors viewpoint

— Math
— 5-8 Graphs numerical relationships
— 3-4 Reads and interprets displays of data
— 5-8 Constructs convincing arguments based on data
— 9-12 Constructs graphs that summarize data
— 5-8 Analyses graphs to identify relationships in a practical context
— 9-12 Uses computer technology to model situations effectively
— 9-12 Analyses situations where more than one logical conclusion can be drawn from the data presented

— Social Studies
— 5-8 Develops and practices skill necessary for participatory citizenship
— 5-8 Uses information to support a point of view on a controversial historical topic
— 9-12 Analyses a variety of sources to articulate different interpretations of history
— 5-8 Uses differing points of view to examine a local environmental problem
— 9-12 Debates practices and polices to lessen the impact of population growth on earthÍs resources
— 5-8 Uses multiple points of view to analyze a contemporary geographic issue

   - 5-8 Analyze how the media characterize cultural and social groups
- Visual/performing arts
   - 3-4 Recognizes how the elements of visual arts can be manipulated to persuade
- Science
   - 3-4 Demonstrates the ability to make and use graphs
   - 9-12 Identifies a current dilemma, researches public information on, identifies points of bias, inconsistent logic
   - 9-12 Analyses situations where more than one logical conclusion can be drawn from data

Expansion assignment

In teams of two or four with subject area dependent upon current class work. With an almanac or encyclopedia, find a set of statistics, and produce two graphs with different visual impacts. Half of the team present an argument using one graph, the other half present the opposite argument with the other graph. Whole class could vote on which graph reflects the statistics best. The type of graph will be dependent upon math class teaching - this lesson could be an excellent follow-up to math class covering how to produce all varieties of graphs.

Incorporate computers with production of the graphs - thus allowing students to "play" with, try out various visual impacts without the drudgery of hand drawings. Most computer graphing applications can flip entered statistics quickly to a variety of visuals. Long term assignment: Find graphs in current media and analyze the focus of the graph. Use the same numbers and recreate the graph to support an alternative focus.

Assessment

Any of the following areas could be appraised: the actual graph production, the visual impact of graphs, the speaking part of the presentation, the development of the persuasive argument, the use of the subject matter for the graph and presentation, the team-work involved in the project. The assessment tool shown is incomplete. As a first step, fill in the empty boxes. Now browse the visual literacy projects in the Adventure in Space chapter. Which aspect of visual literacy is a key component of each project? Choose one of them, and list measurable criteria for that component. Then complete the rubric matrix by describing three levels of achievement for each criterion.

Performance Indicators Reflected in the Foregoing Graph Activities

- Career
  - 5-8 Impact of specific technology on issues
  - 5-8 Debates need for ethical standards in application of technology
  - 9-12 Applies experiences with tools (computergraphing) to issues of life
  - 9-12 Evaluates skills in team-designed project
- English
  - 5-8 Views in order to identify various viewpoints on a debatable issue
  - 5-8 Accurately uses oral language conventions in formal situation
  - 9-12 Uses spoken language with competency
  - 5-8 Uses a variety of resources to investigate for oral presentation

- 9-12 Designs presentation to achieve particular rhetorical purpose
- 5-8 Adjusts viewing strategies in order to comprehend
- 5-8 Identifies bias in visual materials
- 5-8 Evaluates reliability of information from mass media
- 9-12 Identifies how bias influences peoplesÍ perceptions and formulates hypothesis about authors viewpoint

— Math

- 5-8 Graphs numerical relationships
- 3-4 Reads and interprets displays of data
- 5-8 Constructs convincing arguments based on data
- 9-12 Constructs graphs that summarize data
- 5-8 Analyses graphs to identify relationships in a practical context
- 9-12 Uses computer technology to model situations effectively
- 9-12 Analyses situations where more than one logical conclusion can be drawn from the data presented

— Social Studies

- 5-8 Develops and practices skill necessary for participatory citizenship
- 5-8 Uses information to support a point of view on a controversial historical topic
- 9-12 Analyses a variety of sources to articulate different interpretations of history
- 5-8 Uses differing points of view to examine a local environmental problem
- 9-12 Debates practices and polices to lessen the impact of population growth on earthÍs resources

— 5-8 Uses multiple points of view to analyze a contemporary geographic issue

— 5-8 Analyze how the media characterize cultural and social groups

— Visual/performing arts

— 3-4 Recognizes how the elements of visual arts can be manipulated to persuade

— Science

— 3-4 Demonstrates the ability to make and use graphs

— 9-12 Identifies a current dilemma, researches public information on, identifies points of bias, inconsistent logic

— 9-12 Analyses situations where more than one logical conclusion can be drawn from data

6

Construction of Graphs and Charts

Charts and graphs are images that represent data symbolically. They are used to present complex information and numerical data in a simple, compact format. Some types of charts and graphs, known as pictographs, use pictures or symbols in place of the typical bars, lines, or dots of most graphs. Examples: A pie chart is a circle divided into segments with each piece of the pie representing some data. Bar and stacked charts use vertical or horizontal bars to show the relationship between numbers. Line charts use lines along a visible or invisible grid.

GENERAL PRINCIPLES OF GRAPHIC DISPLAY

A graphical chart provides a visual display of data that otherwise would be presented in a table; a table, one that would otherwise be presented in text. Ideally, a chart should be able to convey to the reader ideas about the data that would not be as readily apparent if they were displayed in a table or as text. As an example, consider one of the many disputes of the 2000 Presidential election concerned the "butterfly" ballot used in Florida's Palm Beach County. Many Democrats alleged that voters who had intended to vote for Gore were tricked by a poorly designed ballot into voting for Patrick Buchanan instead. To see what the dispute was about, consider this -- exaggerated -- interpretation of how the ballot looked to voters.

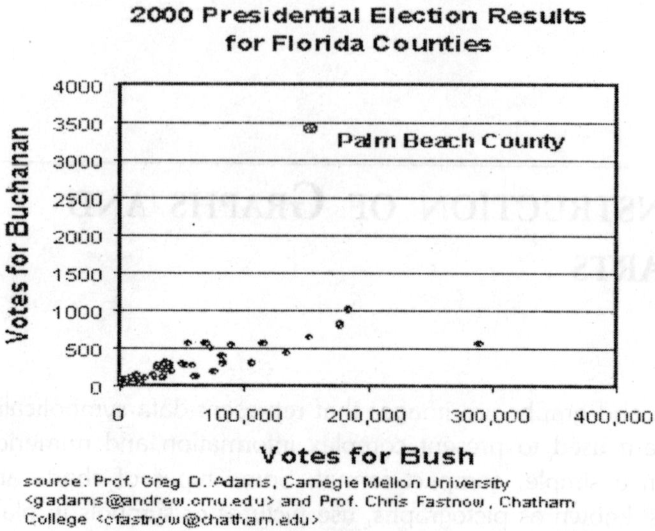

Figure 1.

One way to estimate how many votes Gore lost due to the ballot design is to try to determine how many extra votes Buchanan received. Figure 1 illustrates one of many approaches to this; each data point on the scatterplot represents the number of votes for Bush and Buchanan for each of Florida's 67 counties. Although there are problems with these data (using the percentage vote for the candidates, Buchanan's vote does not appear as exceptional), the figure makes a point that would not be readily apparent from even an extended viewing of the raw vote totals.

The three standards for tabular display of data — the efficient display of meaningful and unambiguous data — apply to charts and graphs as well. As with tables, it is crucial to good charting to choose meaningful data, to clearly define what the numbers represent, and to present the data in a manner that allows the reader to quickly grasp what the data mean. As with tabular display, data ambiguity in charts arises from the failure to precisely define just what the data represent. Every dot on a scatterplot, every point on a time series line, every bar on a bar chart represents a number (actually, in the case of a scatterplot, two numbers). It is the job of the text on the chart to tell us just what each of those numbers represents. If a number represented in a chart is, say, 33½, the text in the graph — in the title, the axis labels, the data labels, the legend, and sometimes the footnote — must answer question: "Thirty-three and a half what?"

Good graphical display, however, requires more than good tabular display as it draws on the talents of both the scientist and the artist. You have to know and understand your data; but you also need a good sense of how the reader will visualize the graphical elements of the chart. Good graphical display will tell the reader things about the data that are no apparent when the data are displayed in tabular form. Bad graphical display, on the other hand, either distorts or hides what the data would tell the reader. Data distortion occurs when the graphical elements of a chart do not give a true picture of what is going on with the data. Data distraction occurs when the graphical elements of the chart distract the readers from seeing what the data might tell them.

Data Distortion.

Before the development of spreadsheet graphing, the most common graphical mistake was the use of artist-drawn 3-D images with the height of 3-D objects representing the magnitude of the data points. In these charts, both the height and the width of the drawn object increase proportionate to the magnitude of the data points. The effect is to exaggerate the differences in magnitude as the viewer tends to perceive the area of the figures rather than just the height as representing the magnitude.

With the development of spreadsheet graphics, such visual distortions are no longer common, and the Art of Lying with graphics has become a technology rather than an art. Today, altogether new forms of bad graphical design predominate. We will consider now some of the more complicated ways of using graphical display to mislead. Figure 2 is a time series chart originally printed in a public policy textbook authored by four professors of political science employed by three public universities.

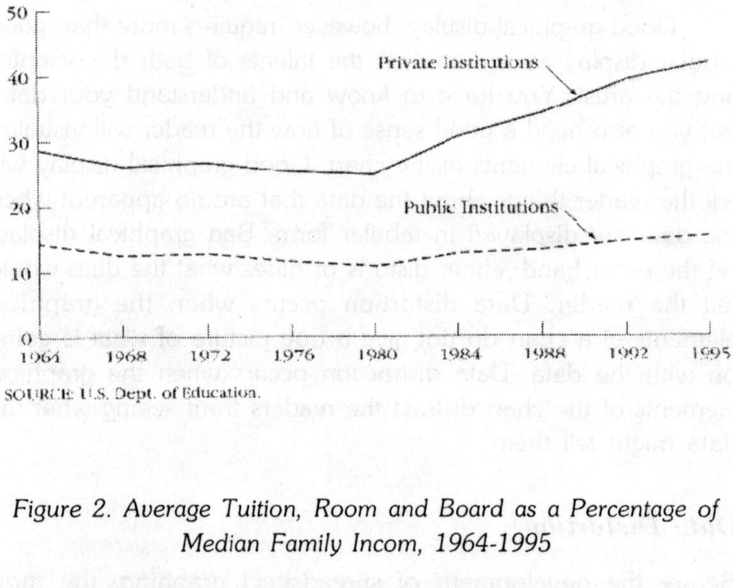

Figure 2. Average Tuition, Room and Board as a Percentage of Median Family Incom, 1964-1995

Their interpretation of the data is as follows:

> There is some evidence that the cost of higher education may not have escalated so much... Figure 2, reflect the average cost for tuition, room, and board as a percentage of median family income from 1964 to 1995. While private institutions have increased costs substantially, public university costs have remained constant. This indicates that the increased costs associated with higher education may be quite reasonable when compared to family income levels.

Note the ways in which the authors have understated the rising costs of public university education. First, the costs are "deflated" using median family income rather than the more conventional consumer price index. Especially for the years after 1982, median family income rose much faster than the consumer price index. Second, graphing both the private and public data on the same graph enlarges the scale on which the public data is displayed. It's hard to tell from the graph, but between 1980 and 1995 it appears that public university costs increased from around 11% of family income to near 15% — in effect the share of family income going to public university costs has increased by a third. The third way of minimizing the cost increases that have occurred since 1980 is to extend the time series back to 1965.

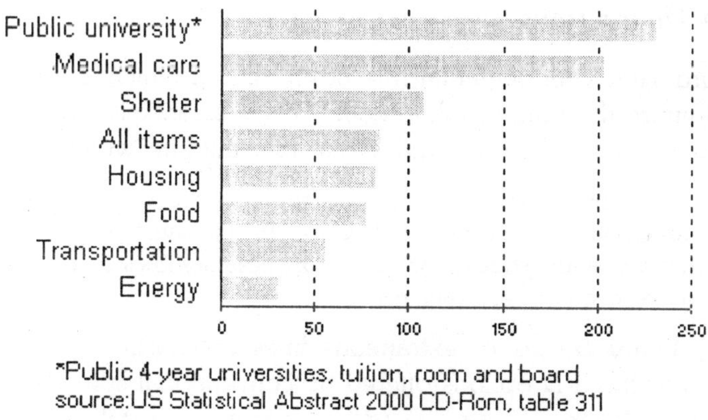

Figure 3. % Increase in Pricem by Economic Sector, 1981-1999

A completely different picture emerges if one were to compare the rate of increase in public university costs to the rate of increases in other sectors of the economy. On the left, we see that from 1981 to 1999 — over the lifetime of today's college student — public university costs have risen faster than any other sector of the economy. Faster even than rising medical care costs. In addressing the topic of health care inflation, the same authors note that: "Cost escalation in the medical field has been constant," and spend four pages of text addressing the reasons for the increases.

Examine this chart from the UNICEF that purports to demonstrate that the gap between rich and poor countries is increasing. We can see that the per capita GNP of the wealthiest countries has slightly almost doubled (from about $12,000 to about $26,000), but it is not clear that the GNP hasn't doubled or tripled among either the middle or low-income countries. Here's an example from the same source that seems to distort the data. Note the size of the two arrows, but look carefully at the first arrow — the negative $18 change is represented not by the arrow, but by the little line below it.

Data Distractions

Edward Tufte's fundamental rule of efficient graphical design is to minimize the ratio of ink-to-data. This is essentially the same advice offered by Strunk and White to would-be writers:

> "A sentence should contain no unnecessary words, a paragraph no unnecessary sentences for the same reason that a drawing should contain no unnecessary lines and a machine no unnecessary parts."

The primary causes of extraneous lines in charting graphics today are the 3-D options offered by conventional spreadsheet charting software. These 3-D options serve no useful purpose; they add only ink to the chart, and more often than not make it more difficult to estimate the values represented. Even worse are the spreadsheet options that allow one to rotate the perspective. For those who would take bad graphical display to even higher levels, the Excel spreadsheet program offers the option of doughnut, radar, cylinder, cone, bubble charts. All these are de facto violations of the Tufte's fundamental rule. As was the case with tabular display, sorting data by the most meaningful variable greatly aids in the interpretation of data. A common charting mistake is to sort the data alphabetically.

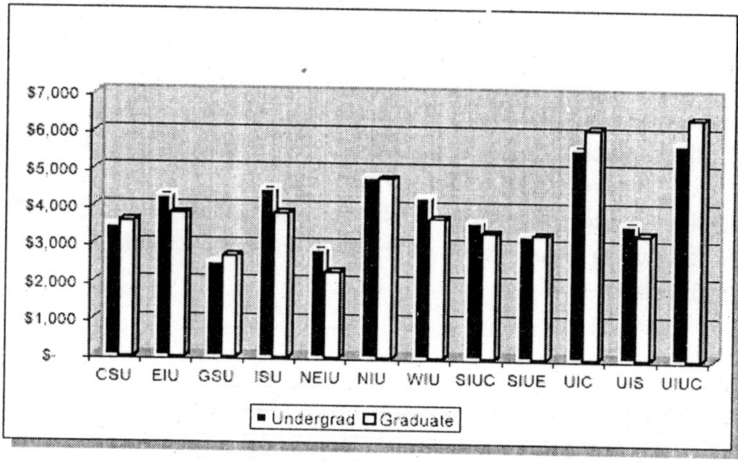

Figure 4a. Tuition and fees, public universities, 2001

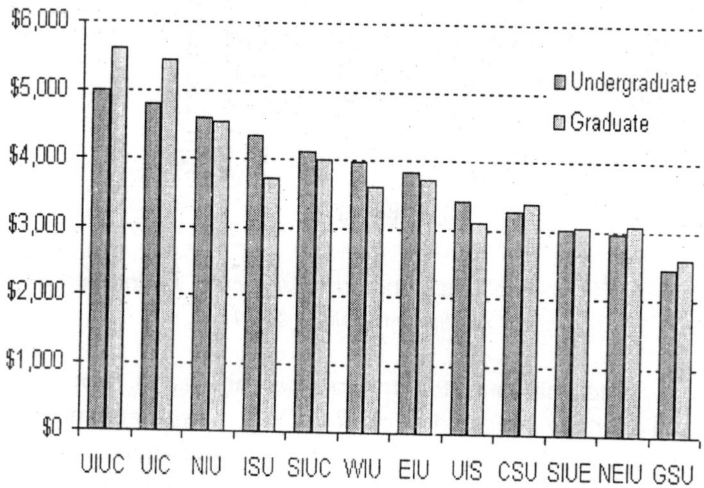

Figure 4b: Tuition and fees, public universities, 2001 (revised chart).

The corollary of Tufte's fundamental rule is "Show the Data". To often, unimportant, unnecessary, or irrelevant graphical and textual elements dominant charts, distracting from the chart's fundamental purpose of displaying data. A good chart maximizes the presentation of data and minimizes the display of non-data elements. In the preceding chart, removing the 3-D effect, placing the legend inside the plot area permits a longer Y-axis, de-emphasizing the gridlines all serve to enhance the display of the differences in the relative length of the bars. In the following chart, many of these graphical elements are over-emphasized:

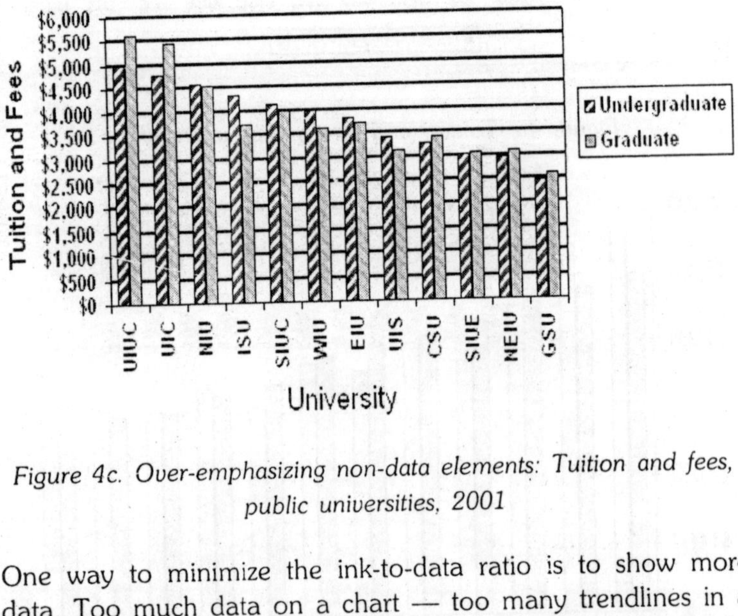

Figure 4c. Over-emphasizing non-data elements: Tuition and fees, public universities, 2001

One way to minimize the ink-to-data ratio is to show more data. Too much data on a chart — too many trendlines in a times series chart, for example — can overwhelm the data presentation, but the more common mistake is to use several charts to display data that could just as easily be displayed in one. The tuition and fee charts above could have been separated into graduate and undergraduate charts or, worse, as 12 separate charts for each university. Avoid, if at all possible, forcing the reader to make comparisons between to charts.

ChartJunk

Not content with the distractions and distortions made possible by the use of 3-D effects, charters sometimes feel the need to add all sorts of other "Chartjunk" to a graph. The extraneous features of this in this graphic.

— A completely irrelevant map of the world.

— Two entirely different kinds of 3-D charts displayed at two different perspectives.

— Country names are repeated three times.

— To display 24 numeric data points, 28 numbers are used to define the scales.

— The countries are sorted in no apparent order (not even alphabetically).

— Note the use of the letter " I " to separate the countries on the bottom chart.

While it might be possible to display these data better graphically, a table does the job quite nicely:

Pre-Tax income Distribution in Industrial Nations

	Share of Pre-tax Household Income		Ratio:
	Top income quintile	Bottom income quintile	Top to bottom shares
United States	45	4	12
Canada	42	4	9
France	47	5	9
Britain	45	6	8
W. Germany	39	8	5
Sweden	38	8	5
Netherlands	37	7	5
Japan	36	9	4

*data estimated from chart.

TYPES OF CHARTS

Most charts are a variation on one of four basic types: Scatterplot, time series chart, bar chart and pie chart; most data display charts are one of many variations or combinations of these types. Choosing the right type of chart depends on the characteristics of the data and the relationships you want displayed. With more than a few data points, Scatterplots and time series charts, can display patterns of relationship among two or more (with time series charts) variables that would not be obvious in a tabular displays. Both scatterplots and time series charts require at least two interval-level variables.

Bar charts and pie charts are used to display data for categorical variables (although a Bar chart is sometimes also used in a time series chart).

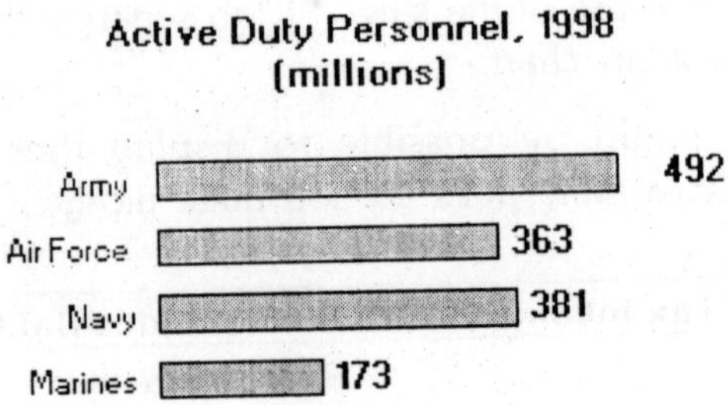

Bar charts, especially one-variable bar charts, are generally not an efficient means of displaying data. The bar chart on the left, for example, contains an absolute minimum amount of ink; the gridlines, plot area frame, and axes have all be removed. Still, the bars themselves are unnecessary — serving only to provide a graphical representation of the size of the four numbers. Because the size of each bar in a bar chart represents a number that would otherwise be displayed in a table, one could justify the use of bar charts only if one assumes that the reader would more easily discern the relative size of two or more number if they are represented graphically.

Pie charts are even worse in this respect than bar charts. Any data that can be displayed in a pie chart can also be displayed in a bar chart.

Times Series Charts

The annual time series chart is one of the most efficient means of displaying large amounts of data in ways that provide for meaningful analysis.

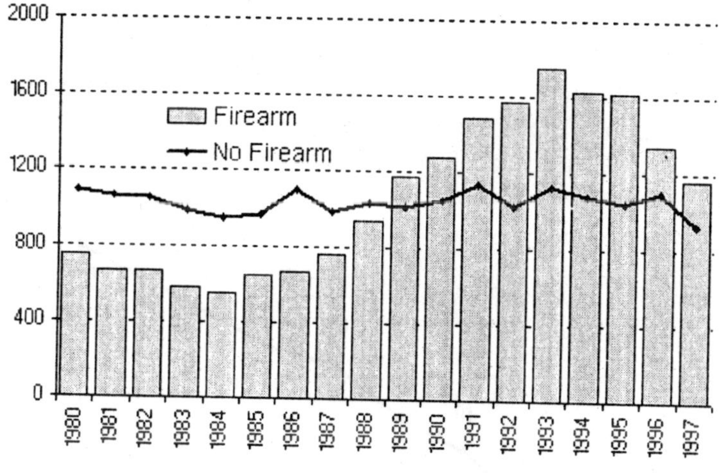

Figure 5. Juvenile homicide victims by firearm involvement

Standards for Times Series Charts:

— Time is almost always displayed on the X-axis from left to right.

— Display as much data with as little ink as possible.

— Avoid clutter

— In bar charts using time as a category variable on the X-axis, always display the time points on adjacent bars.

— Make sure the reader can clearly distinguish the lines for separate variables.

— When displaying fiscal or monetary data over-time, it is often best to use deflated (i.e. adjusted for inflation, per capita or "as a percent of GNP") measurements.

Problems with Time Series charts

Scaling: When two variables with numbers of different magnitudes are graphed on the same chart, the variable with the large scale will generally appear to have a greater degree of variation; the smaller-scale variable will appear relatively "flat" even though the percentage change is the same. In figure 6, XYZCompany's stock seems to be growing much faster than ABCorp's, yet the rate of increase is identical.

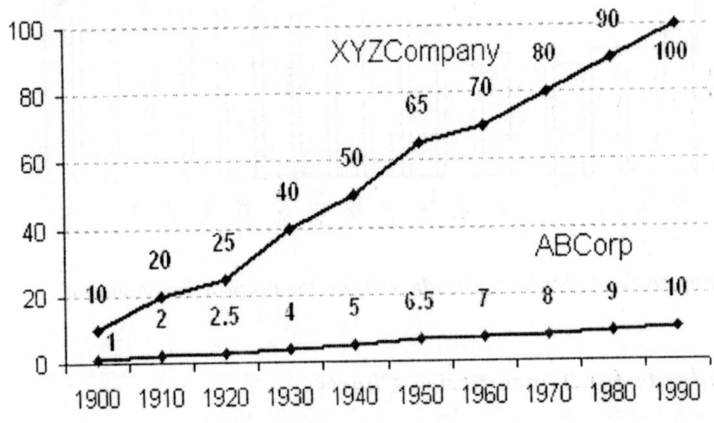

Figure 6. Stock Prices: Two Hypothetical Companies

When the differences in scale are so great as to eliminate most of the perceived variation in the smaller-scale variable, using a second scale (displayed on the right-hand side) is sometimes preferable, although this makes the interpretation of the graph more complicated. In figure 7a and 7b, the difference in scales for the poverty and unemployment are almost, or perhaps no quite, great enough to justify a second axis scale.

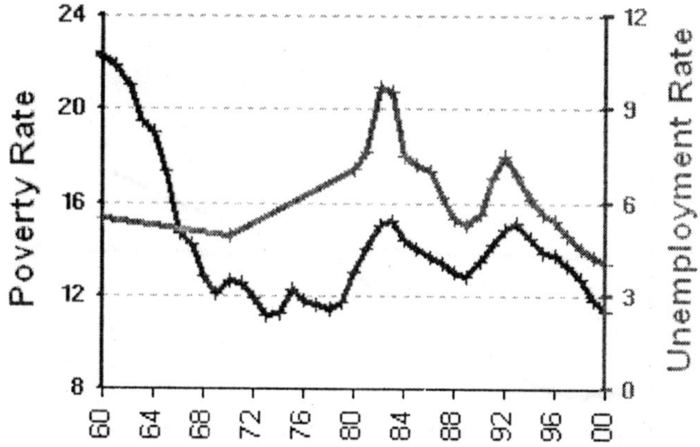

Figure 7a. Poverty and Unemployment 1959-00

Figure 7b. Poverty and Unemployment 1959-00

Many who have written about graphical distortion condemn the use of two-scale charts because the relative size of the two scales is completely arbitrary. This is true. Increasing the size of either scale in figure 7 will make the corresponding line appear flatter. One the other hand, using the same scale to measure variables of different magnitudes, as we saw in figure 5, has problems too.

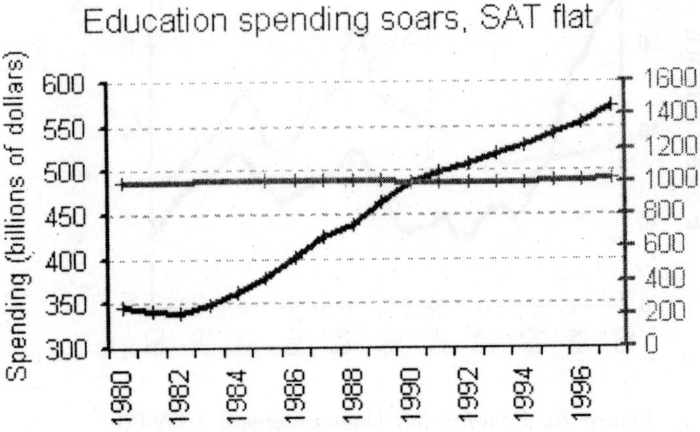

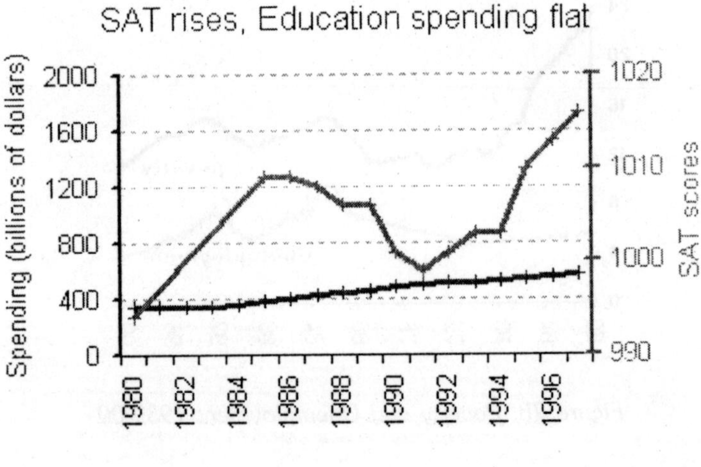

Another solution is to rescale the variables. This is often done with price or other monetary data by setting the initial year values of both variables equal to 100. Multiply each variable by the 100 times the inverse of the value for the base year.

Crossing lines. When several times series lines are printed in black and white, it is sometimes difficult to separate out the different tend lines. Mixing solid, dotted, and dashed lines for each variable may solve this problem, although it is sometimes difficult to distinguish between dotted and dashed lines. Here's an example of a published chart with ambiguous lines.

Scatterplots

The two-dimensional scatterplot is the most efficient medium for the graphical display of data. A simple scatterplot will tell you more about the relationship between two interval-level variables than any other method of presenting or summarizing such data.

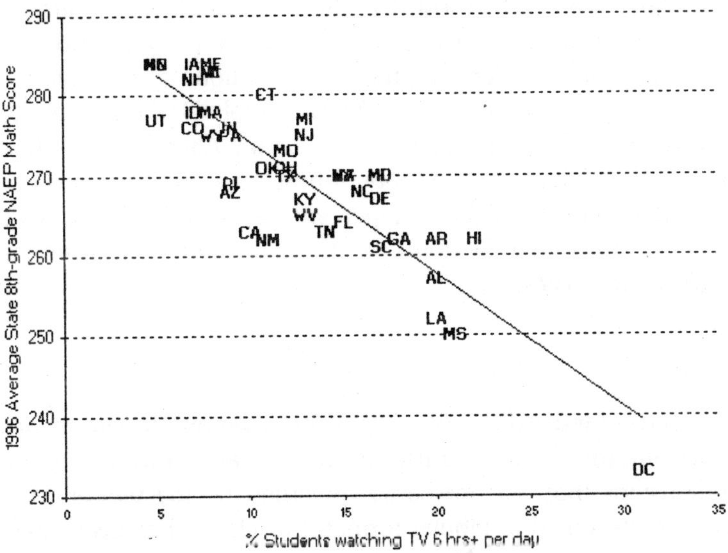

Figure 8. State Math Scores and Students TV Viewing Habits

With good labeling of the variables and cases and common sense scaling of the X and Y axes, there's not a lot that can go wrong with a scatterplot.

Basic rules of Scatterplotting:

— Have two interval-level variables.

— Use the titles and axis labels to clearly define the variables.

— Be sure to define the cases (e.g., indicate whether the data points represent persons, cities, or countries).

— Scale each axis to each variable's full data range.

— If there is an implied causal relationship between the variables, the independent variable (the one that causes the other) should be on the X-axis and the dependent variable (the one that may be caused by the other) should be on the Y-axis.

In the "Math and TV viewing" chart, above, TV viewing is the independent variable. (If you were trying to predict which types of students watch the most TV, the axes would be reversed.) The scatterplot contains two optional plotting features: a regression trendline denoting the linear relationship between the two variables and the use of State postal ID data labels to indicate each state's position on the chart. Although the chart suffers from overlapping data labels, the interpretation is straightforward; the higher the percentage of students in a state watching more than 6 hours of TV each day, the lower the state's math scores.

Bar Charts

Time series (and scatterplot) graphs are often an efficient means of displaying lots of data in little space and depicting relationships that are not easily discerned by the viewer were the data presented in tabular format. Bar charts, however, often contain little data, a lot of ink, and rarely reveal ideas that cannot be presented much more simply in a table. Minimizing the ink-to-data ratio is especially important in the case of bar charts.

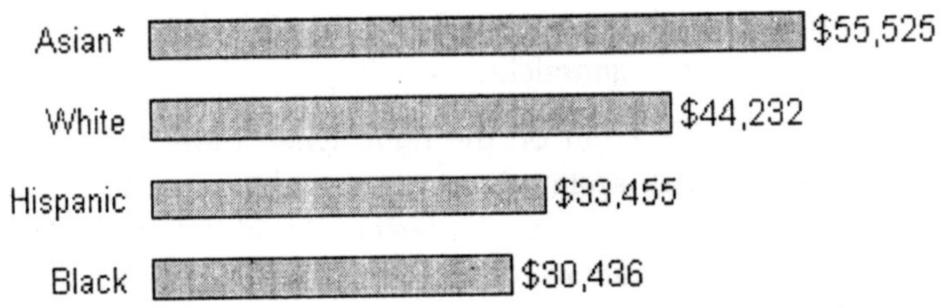

*Asan or Pacific Islander
Bureau of Labor Statistics:
http://www.bls.census.gov/cps/ads/2001/susenote.htm

Figure 9. Median Household Income, by Race and Ethnicity: 1999

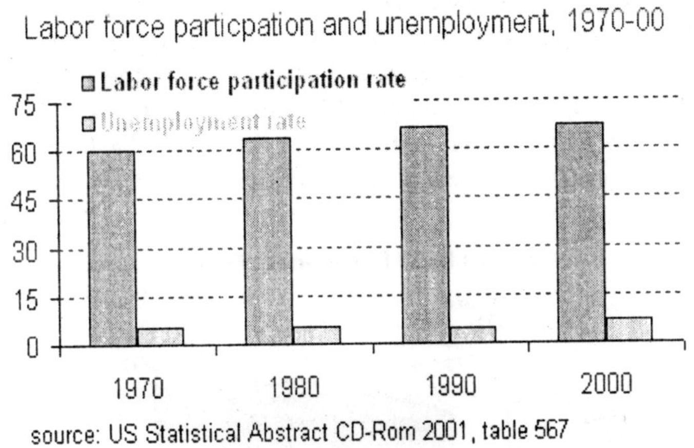

Figure 10.

The chart on the left features the absolute minimal amount of ink while still retaining both the bar chart format and a good definition of the data. Never use a 3-D bar chart. Keep the gridlines faint. Display no less than four or more than six numbers on the y-axis scale. If there are fewer than five bars, consider using data labels rather than a y-axis scale; it doesn't make sense to use a five-numbered scale when the exact values can be shown with four numbers. Microsoft Excel does allow stacked and stretched images on bars, this too falls into the category of distraction gimmicks.

As we see in the chart on the right, when more than one variable is bar-charted, scaling is as big a problem as it is with times series charts. Colour is of greater consideration in bar charts than in line or scatterplots. Softer colours are better than primary colours.

Pie Charts

Pie charts should rarely be used. Pie charts usually contain more ink than data and provide for a poor representation of the magnitude of the data points. It is more difficult for the eye to discern the relative size of pie slices than it is to assess relative bar length. With pies, it is difficult to figure out whether the Navy or Air Force is larger without looking at the numbers; from the bar charts it is obvious. 3-D pie charts are even worse, as they also add a visual distortion (in this case, the thick 3-D band exaggerates the size of the undergraduate slice).

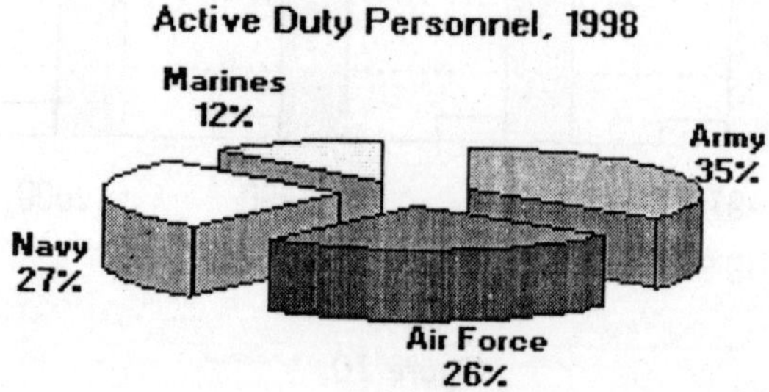

Figures 11a. 3-D Pie chart, exploded

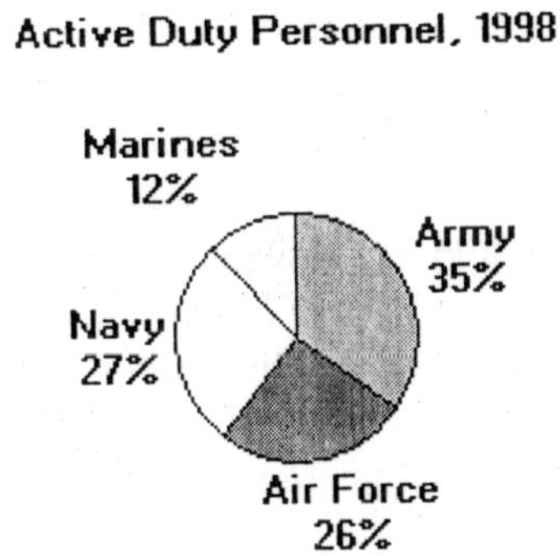

11b. 2-D Pie

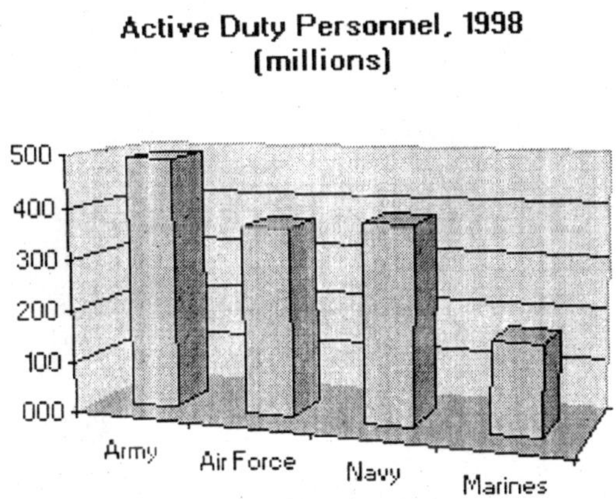

11c. 3-D Column Bar

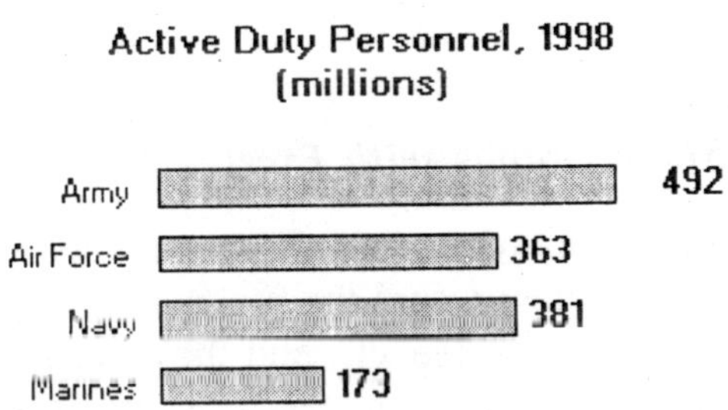

11d. Simple 2-D Bar

Note how much less ink the 2-D bar charts uses compared to the 3-D bar. Using data labels rather than a y-axis scale in this case reduces the number of numbers displayed from 6 to 4, and adds precision as well. Normally, the sorted data here, so that the Navy would be between the Army and Air Force, but since the Marines are a part of the Navy (and the Air Force, originally, a part of the Army), this order made more sense. A strict application of the ink-to-data in this case, however, would eliminate the bars altogether and simply present the data as a table.

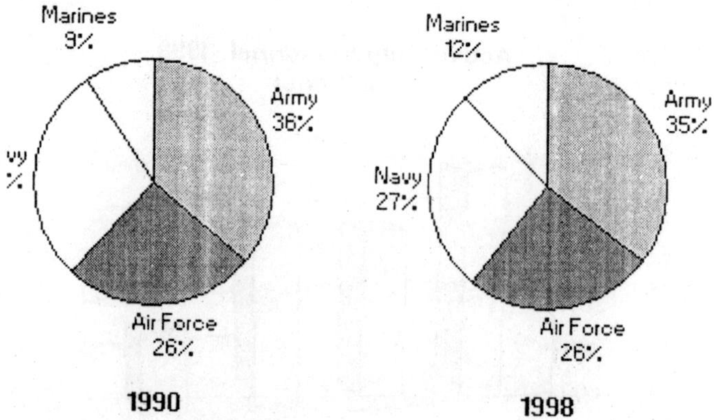

Two Pies are worse than one: Pies are even less effective when an additional variable is added and comparisons between pies are required (sometimes by adjusting the relative size of the pies).

How to Make Graphs with Excel

Numbers appear all around us. They trace the rise and fall of the stock market, they record the progress of our students, they list the distances to the planets, and they weigh the guinea pig in the back of the classroom. Students spend a good deal of their time in school learning to work with numbers, and to understand how numbers help explain how the world works. Computers need numbers in order to operate, and in fact in the early days of computing you needed to feed the machine numbers - it did not understand text, nor images nor sound.

Collections of numbers, like the results of an election, or the batting averages of a team, or the growth of a population over the years, are often used to communicate important ideas in school and in public communication. But it takes a lot of work on the part of the viewer to interpret these numbers to understand what they mean. It's often more efficient to use a graph to show the "story behind the numbers." And in most math curricula, the making and understanding of graphs is an important skill. This week's article gets you and your students started making graphs from collections of numbers.

The instructions here refer to Microsoft Excel, which is the program most people use to organize their numbers and to create graphs quickly. Other spreadsheet programs, such as AppleWorks, that might be found in a school operate in similar ways and will require few modifications to the steps listed here. Feel free to copy these instructions for your students or modify them as needed for a particular assignment.

How Tall?

The best way to learn to make graphs with a spreadsheet is to build a small collection of numbers, and then experiment with various graphs. So take the browser window in which you are reading this article, and make it smaller, so that it covers about half the screen to the right. Then open your spreadsheet program and create a new blank document. Narrow this window toward the left of your screen so that you can see both the spreadsheet and this article at the same time.

Into the spreadsheet enter the names of the members of a family (real or imaginary) and their heights. Your collection of data should look something like this:

A	B	C
1	Height	
2	Molly	49
3	Jimmy	68
4	Kathi	64
5	Annie	66
6	Ben	73
7		

In this example, the numbers that represent height are called values, and the words that represent names are called labels. Each label and value is entered in one cell of the spreadsheet. The label Jimmy, for instance, is in cell A3 - column A, row 3 - while the value 73 is in B6. And cell C7 is empty. (Of course you may use any kind of data you like for this exercise, but keep it small and simple to begin with using short labels and straightforward values.)

Make a Graph

The process of making a graph from data like these takes four steps:

— *Select some data*. Click and drag the mouse to select the numbers and words that you want to include in the graph. In this example we will graph all of the data, but in many situations you won't want to include all the information in the graph. Select only what you need, in this case selecting the area from A1 to B6.

— *Create a chart*. From the menubar choose Insert - Chart. Then choose the type of chart you want (column, bar, line, pie, and so forth). Then click the Finish button. (Notice that Excel refers to what you are making as a chart, while most teachers would call this a graph. Don't let the terms fool you.)

— *Examine your graph*. Excel will construct your graph automatically, but not always in exactly the way that you might wish. Does it appear as you had planned? Does it include all the necessary information? Will it make sense to the audience? Does it include any extraneous or distracting elements? Make a note of what needs changing.

— *Modify the graph*. For a simple graph like this, you may not need to change anything. But if you do, simply double-click the item you want to change, and you will get a dialog box that lets you change it. To get rid of an item on the graph, you simply select it (one click) and press the delete or backspace key.

For displaying the comparative heights of the members of a family, a column graph is appropriate, because the vertical columns in the chart appear similar to people standing up next to each other. If we were graphing the distances to various cities, we might best show it as a horizontal bar graph, because we move horizontally when we travel to them. A pie graph is best used when we are showing the parts of a whole, such as the proportions of a population with various colours of eyes. A line graph might best represent data that shows a continuous trend or flow over time, such as air temperature.

To change a graph from one type to another, select the graph, and then from the menubar choose Chart - Chart type... Notice that Excel provides two levels of choice here, a general graph type on the left, and a specific format on the right. The best way to understand how this works is to make a graph of your own, and then try changing the type to see the results. Avoid the tendency to make the graph too fancy. Excel provides many formats, some of which are over decorated and make your graph hard to understand. Choose the simpler formats and your graph will do better job communicating to its audience.

Complex Graphs: To make a more complex graph, you would add more columns of values to your spreadsheet, and then show them all in one graph. For instance, in the example shown above you might add a column for weight and another for girth. But be careful - a graph that compares widely different measures is hard to make sense of. In this case, you would avoid including a column that showed the annual income of each person on the list, because the numbers would be way off the scale and the comparisons with height and weight irrelevant.

To make a graph from a spreadsheet with multiple columns, carefully select all the data that you need, and then from the menubar choose Insert - Graph. All of the selected data will be shown in the graph, each column of numbers with its own line or box. Sometimes the values of the various measurements are out of proportion to each other, such as heights that range from 50 to 70 inches next to weights that range from 150 to 300 pounds. The graph produced by such data might not be easy to interpret if both measurements are plotted on the same scale. Excel lets you construct a graph with two different axes, each with its own scale of values. To create such a graph, choose the Custom Types tab in the Chart Wizard window, and then scroll down to the Line-Column on 2 axes type. This will scale the heights from 0 to 80 on the left axis, and the weights from 0 to 300 on the right.

Saving Graphs: When you save an Excel document, the graph is saved with it, and whenever it is opened the graph will appear where you left it. You can also save the table of numbers and the graph as a web page, by choosing Save as Web Page from the File menu. You can also copy the graph alone by selecting it, and then choosing Copy from the Edit menu. From here it can be pasted into any document, such as a report in Microsoft Word or an image in Adobe Photoshop.

Printing Graphs: To print the graph along with the table of numbers on the same page, first deselect the graph (this is best done by clicking the mouse in one of the cells of the spreadsheet), and then choose Print from the File menu. To print only the graph, select it by clicking once on the graph, and then choose Print from the File menu. Students and teachers both can find many ways to use graphs for teaching and learning. The best way to get started is to experiment with your own collections of numbers, graphing them every chance you get, and trying different types and formats until you find the ones that work best.

7

OHP

The Overhead Projector, or "OHP" is one of the most frequently used (and misused) tools in education and training today. It may be facing a challenge from the data projector, but it is still more flexible and useful for all except uninterrupted, rehearsed presentations.

USE OF OHP

The use of the OHP sends a message: "This has been prepared." This is in contrast to using the whiteboard or flip-chart, which sends "This is spontaneous". There is a case for both kinds of message, of course, under different circumstances.

OHP vs. Data Projector

Data projectors are becoming increasingly popular, although still (in 2003) very expensive. If you have the choice, consider these factors:

OHP	Data Projector
Not much to go wrong: and if it does, you can often fix it yourself	Requires a computer as well, and a link: there's a lot of temperamental hardware.

Restricted in the range of media it can use: OHTs and a few transparent or silhouetted objects	Can use static or animated graphics, sound and even movie clips, with a sufficiently powerful machine
Can easily take OHTs out of sequence, to re-cap or jump ahead to respond to a question.	Needs a dual-monitor set up, if students are not to see the nuts and bolts of the set-up when you want to select a slide out of order
OHTs are bulky and rather fragile	You can put an entire lecture sequence's material on one floppy—your entire teaching career's output on CD or DVD.
Temptation to use badly-designed OHTs: pages of books copied onto transparencies, for example.	Your presentation package makes it harder to produce a bad show than a good one.
You can write on and otherwise amend OHTs on the fly.	On the whole you are stuck with what you have prepared,
Students can use write-on OHTs for reporting back from groups, etcm	Not really practicable

The essence of the OHP

In order to put the following tips into context, consider a few points about the OHP in the classroom:

1 The OHP is usually under the control of the teacher: this means that it is by default an instrument of teacher-centred instruction. This is not necessarily a bad thing, and teachers can develop its use as a tool of session management. Switching it on, for example, is likely to send the message, "Now get ready for some input from me", and can be used to curtail discussions which are veering off the point. Similarly, switching it off when a discussion starts is a way of acknowledging that the class group is making the running.

2 It presents a series of images in sequence: the timing and ordering is again controlled by the teacher. Indeed, having a series of OHTs can readily substitute for the teacher having to have her own notes, and free her up to pay more attention to the class, and to expound the material more spontaneously.

But the fact that each image is shown for a limited period of time means that its content needs to be digestible within that period. So apart from sheer legibility issues, there should not be too much on any one OHT.

3 It is, of course, a visual medium: this requires attention to the needs of students who may not find it accessible. These include not only students with visual impairments, but also dyslexic students. There is some evidence to suggest that the high contrast of the screen, which is a help to many students, can hinder the reading of those who have some forms of dyslexia. Students with hearing impairment may find it difficult to follow the lips of a lecturer and look at the screen at the same time.

Conventional text is linear: we all know it takes time to read. Graphics, including some non-conventional text such as mind-maps, and labelled diagrams, are perceived at once as a whole, and then "read" in unpredictable orders by different students. This comes more naturally to some students than others. You have two channels of communication going at the same time, assuming that you are talking at the same time. You need to consider how they interact.

— Are they parallel? Do the two channels carry the same information, with the one reinforcing the other? That may be useful on occasion, but if you are reduced to reading out verbatim the contents of the OHT (except when it is for the benefit of students with difficulties), the redundancy level may be too high.

— Are they complementary? Do the two channels carry different information? This is often the case when the

OHT is used for graphics. More visually-oriented students may find it difficult to pay attention to what is being said when concentrating on the screen: more aurally-oriented students may find their natural tendency to listen to the voice hinders their ability to make sense of the image. Give the students a few moments to digest what they are seeing before commenting on it.

4 You are requiring the students to look: when they are looking at the screen, most of them will not be able to make notes, so a lecture or class which uses a lot of OHTs may also require handouts, if it is the kind of session which calls for notes. Remember, too, that copying diagrams or charts from a screen takes much longer than making text notes. Keep graphics simple. Be explicit about what is worth noting and what not. However, if leaving time for copying breaks up the session too much, think again about providing the information in other ways, too. If your material was prepared in one of the standard presentation packages, it could be exported directly to an intranet or Virtual Learning Environment (VLE), for example, for consultation after the session. (Presentation packages may provide an automatic "Export as Web Page" facility).

Tips for use

1 It's sucking eggs time again! Get the OHP set up for optimum image size, focused, etc. before the class starts. Make sure everyone can see.

2 Once you are sure of the above, you have no need to look at the screen. You can concentrate on the class. Needless (?) to say, don't get in their way.

3 So do not point to material on the screen itself. Use a pen or other pointer on the stage of the OHP. If your hand is at all shaky, lay the pointer down on the OHP stage.

Standing in front of the screen to point out salient topics:

— means that you are tempted to talk to the screen and not the class

— means that some of the image is projected onto you, and there is a large obscuring shadow on the screen

4 The only exception is when you are projecting onto a whiteboard, and writing/drawing on the board to elaborate on the image. (This is also the only occasion when you should project onto a whiteboard, which will also reflect back the light source, and may well form a "hot-spot" obscuring the image for some students.) Even this can usually be dealt with more effectively by writing on an overlaid transparency on the OHP stage.

5 Do not leave an old OHT showing when you have moved on to talk about something else. Switch off between OHTs, or at least between sequences.

OHP Hardware

The OHP is a simple machine: it has a lamp in the base (although there are portable versions which project a lamp downwards from the lens housing onto a reflective stage), usually cooled by a fan. The lamp may have high and low settings, and a "fringing" control to position it centrally. Some machines have a slide device to change bulbs semi-automatically if one blows. There will be a cut-out system which switches off the power automatically if you open the base.

The light is distributed by a fresnel screen to illuminate the stage evenly, and then focused by a lens and mirror arrangement (often enclosed), onto the screen. The focus knob moves the lens assembly up and down a column.

The OHP needs to be square to the screen: otherwise the image will be distorted. Note, too, that the reflectivity of screens may fall off rapidly as the viewer moves to the side. Providing a good view necessitates attention to seating arrangements.

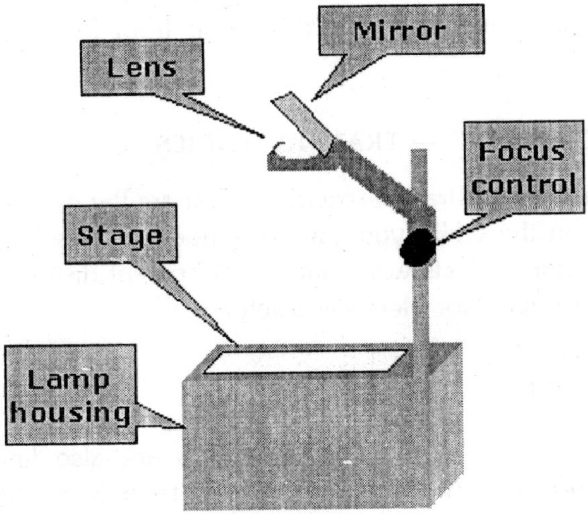

On older machines, the lens can move from being parallel with the stage, resulting in selective lack of focus which cannot be cured with the focus control. Loosen the holding screw and adjust it, or use discreet brute force (which is probably how it got misaligned in the first place — and not many teachers routinely carry a screwdriver). If something like the image on the right appears, it is because the lamp is misaligned under its condenser lens.

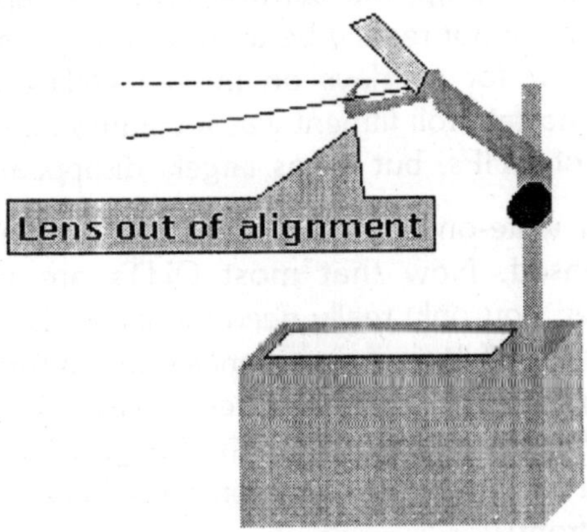

Some machines have a slide or knob control on the front to

cope with this: if not, call the technician! Re-alignment is not difficult, but something of a distraction from the business of the class.

OHP "SOFTWARE" — TRANSPARENCIES

Although prepared transparencies (OHTs) are the most common medium on the OHP, you can get silhouettes of solid objects, and interesting effects with shallow transparent dishes of liquid (with due regard for electrical safety)

Kinds of OHT

There are three kinds of OHT: OHTs are also known as "transparencies" (risking confusion with 5x5cm slides) or "viewfoils"

— *Write-on film*: the old-fashioned "acetate". You can also write on the other kinds, but you cannot do anything *but* write or draw on this kind. In particular, never try to put it through a photocopier or a laser printer: it will melt and gum up the works very expensively. Nowadays, acetates are chiefly used when students need to prepare OHTs in class (such as writing up the results of syndicate discussions: it has advantages over flip-charts in that it is easier to take away and type up, but because only one report is shown at once it cannot readily be used for comparisons between reports), or for overlays on printed OHTs. A few years ago, an acetate roll fitment was a common and very useful feature of OHPs, but it has largely disappeared.

  Pens for write-on film come in two kinds: permanent and water-based. Now that most OHTs are prepared on computer, you only really need the latter. Their marks can be washed off laser transparencies for re-use, but not of course off ink-jet transparencies (unless, like mine, your printer has the facility to flip the image when printing, so that you can print the image onto the back, and still write on the front).

— *Laser transparencies*: also used for photocopying. These are thicker and heat-resistant, and often come with a backing sheet. Printing on them generates large amounts of static. Most prints (unless you are really well-heeled) are black only. Make sure you tune your printer-driver to give the best rendition it can of half-tones. When highly magnified, grey-scales often appear like old "dotty" newspaper photos.

— *Ink-jet transparencies*: still the most expensive (50p per sheet retail, about half that through institutions) but the best for colour. One side of this transparency has a slightly "gritty" covering: that is the only side which will take the ink, so make sure it faces the print-head. They can take a long time (15 mins +) to dry, and a fast printer may deposit a new sheet on top of one which is still tacky, often with unfortunate results. So do not leave your printer unattended, and remove each sheet as it emerges. Do not try to put this kind of transparency through a photocopier or laser printer. Note that using a template from a computer package which gives you a tinted background will greatly increase the printing time, and usage of ink. Again, explore the printer-driver options for best quality: most printers allow you to specify that you are using transparencies.

Designing OHTs

1 Conceive of your OHTs as a sequence, rather than as "one-offs". Do not try to cram too much on each one. See notes on using the OHP, and on the reveal technique, below.

2 KISS: Keep It Simple, Stupid.

3 If at all possible, use a presentation package to prepare them. They feature in all the major office suites on all platforms, and they almost impose good practice on you.

If you must use a word-processor:

— Use landscape rather than portrait format, with wide left and right margins (12 pica, 5cm, 2 inch). This stops the line getting too long, so the eye has difficulty in following it, and also ensures that the border of the OHP stage do not cut off the edges of your OHT. Landscape rather than portrait makes it less likely that you will try to cram too much in.

— Use a minimum text size of 18pt: this is recommended for legibility. Dedicated packages will encourage large sizes by default.

4 Use both UPPER and lower case for your text: this shows the shape of the word more clearly and greatly enhances legibility. PRINTING may be clearer for poor handwriting, but that is not an issue with computer-prepared OHTs.

5 Three or four points per OHT is generally enough—certainly no more than six.

6 Use bullet points and paragraph spacing to distinguish the points: all packages encourage you to use a hierarchy of bullet points to show the relative importance of the topics

7 You can also use bold face and larger sizes or both (and colour) to emphasise key words or phrases. Do not use underlining: it interferes with the shape of the word.

8 On the other hand, be selective about what you emphasise: too many competing emphases interfere with comprehension. Putting everything in bold does not necessarily help legibility.

9 Better still, use graphics. All packages have simple but adequate drawing tools, and an hour's playing with them will pay great dividends.

10 If you use pictures, use vector graphics if possible (broadly speaking, the products of "drawing" rather than "painting"

applications). They can be re-sized without loss of definition, so that you can fill your OHT with them, and they look better when projected.

(Photographs and other figurative pictures are "bitmaps", made up of pixel dots, which get chunkier if you enlarge them, or run into each other if you reduce them: unfortunately, all but the most sophisticated Web graphics at the time of writing are bitmaps—although all my diagrams started life as vector graphics—so don't expect too much if you put Web pictures onto your OHTs.)

11 In particular, use mind-mapping to give an overview of your session. You can keep returning to the mind-map OHT to help students keep track of what has been covered. You can also give it to them as a handout to help them to structure their own notes, or as an aide-memoire. There are free or evaluation copies of mind-mapping software available from here and (occasionally) here

12 A popular technique for using OHTs is that of the "reveal". You start with the OHT concealed by a piece of paper, which you withdraw paragraph or point by point, as you talk about them.

- If you are still using the reveal technique, you probably have too much on each OHT
- It does have the advantage of keeping previous points on screen as you proceed...
- but it is usually clumsily done, and the paper falls off as you reach the bottom of the OHT, revealing the final points—ready or not!
- Instead, why not use the facility to copy content in your presentation package, to build up a sequence of slides, in which the earlier points have been de-emphasised by making them smaller, or greying them out, so that they do not compete with the current point?

— If you must use it, put the cover paper *under* the transparency: it stops it falling off until you reach the very bottom.

13 In particular, there is no excuse for photocopying blocks of text from a book onto an OHT. If you need direct quotations, scan them and use an Optical Character Recognition (OCR) program to convert them to text so you can format them properly.

8

AUDIO

AUDIO TOOLS IN EDUCATION

Why Sound Quality is Important

Popular media such as compact discs, movies, and music videos have helped to raise our standards for what qualifies as "good sound." Unfortunately, the sound quality in distance learning classrooms often leaves much to be desired. Poor sound quality will make it more difficult for students to understand the material being presented. It may also reduce their level of interest and participation in the class. Classroom audio systems that are poorly designed or implemented will inhibit interaction between students at different class sites, because they will not always be willing to make the effort required to overcome technology barriers which prevent them from being heard.

Complaints from instructors and students about classroom sound typically run along these lines:

— "It sounds like the person speaking is at the bottom of a barrel."

— "When someone talks, the first couple of words get cut off."

— "We can't turn it up loud enough to hear without getting feedback or howling."

— "When we talk, we hear an echo of our own words."

The technical and operational causes of these problems are rarely apparent to someone who does not have specific audio training. Fortunately, an understanding of just a few basic audio concepts can help the designer, installer, or user of a distance learning audio system to achieve very good sound quality in the classroom environment.

What it Takes to Make a Distance Learning Classroom Work

There are four main parts which make up a distance learning classroom:

— the classroom itself,

— an audio system,

— a video system, and

— a link to a transmission network.

THE CLASSROOM

Room Acoustics vs. the Audio System

The sound that is sent out of the classroom to other sites begins with the classroom itself. The acoustics of the room - that is, the way in which the room affects sound waves - are determined by physical characteristics, such as the size of the room and what materials are used to construct and cover *surfaces such* as walls and floors. If the acoustics of the room are poor, the sound picked up by the audio system and transmitted to other sites will be unclear and fatiguing to listen to. In extreme cases, voices may be nearly unintelligible, or interaction may be so difficult that teaching cannot take place.

The classroom and the audio system both have a major impact on sound quality. For sound that is crystal-clear, and for the audio system to be as cosmetically appealing and "user-friendly" as possible, both the acoustics of the classroom and the design of the audio system must be optimized. In many instances, however, certain restrictions may force compromises in one area, which must be offset by optimization in the other area. For instance, if circumstances dictate the use of a classroom with poor acoustics, then there will be little room for compromise in the design of the audio system. Similarly, if budgetary constraints or user preferences force compromises in the design of the audio system, it becomes critical that the acoustics of the classroom be very good. When a poor audio system is combined with poor room acoustics, results are usually so unsatisfactory that instructors and students prefer not to use the system at all.

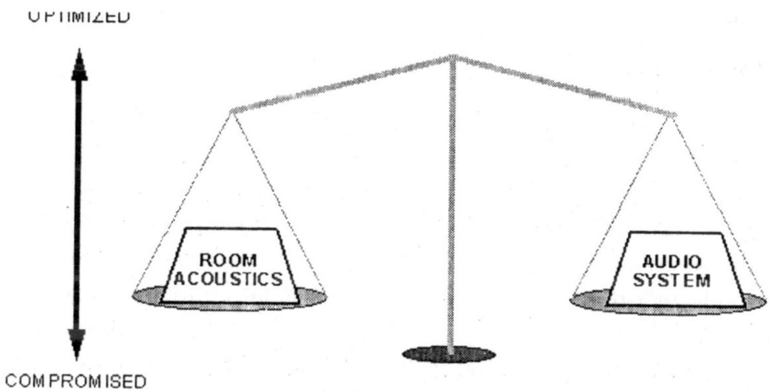

Room acoustics vs. audio system: if one must be compromised, the other must be optimized in order to maintain acceptable sound quality.

When you are present in the same room as a person talking, your brain makes use of both the aural information supplied by your ears and the visual information supplied by your eyes. This combination of sight, sound, and brain power allows you to "ignore" or "filter out" some of the noise and undesired sound, and to concentrate on the desired sound (the talker.) A microphone does not have this ability, so it must be able to "hear better" than a human listener would in order to pick up clear and intelligible speech. But what makes one room sound good, and another sound poor? And is it possible to know in advance whether a particular room is a good choice - from an acoustic standpoint - for distance learning?

How to Tell if a Classroom is Acoustically Suitable for Distance Learning

Room acoustics is a broad term comprised of many components. For our purposes, there are two acoustic variables which have a major impact on the sound of a classroom: *decay time* and *background noise level.*

Decay Time

Sound waves emanate from a talker in all directions. Some travel directly from the talker to the microphone, while others take a roundabout route, bouncing off of the walls, ceiling, or floor. The reflected sound reaches the microphone later than the direct sound, and blends with it to become audible as a continuation or "smearing" of the original sound. *Decay time* is how long it takes for this reflected sound to weaken or "decay" to the point that it can no longer be heard. The decay time of a room is determined by its size, shape, and construction.

The decay time in a large marble cathedral might be as much as 5 seconds; in a classroom with concrete block walls and tile floor it might be 1 or 2 seconds; in a conference room with thick carpeting and heavy drapes it might be 1/2 second. If a room is too reflective, speech that is picked up by a microphone in that room will usually sound as if the talker is "at the bottom of a barrel" or "at the end of a long hallway." This is in spite of the fact that the sound may be perfectly acceptable to a live listener in the room. In general, the longer the decay time is, the worse the sound will be.

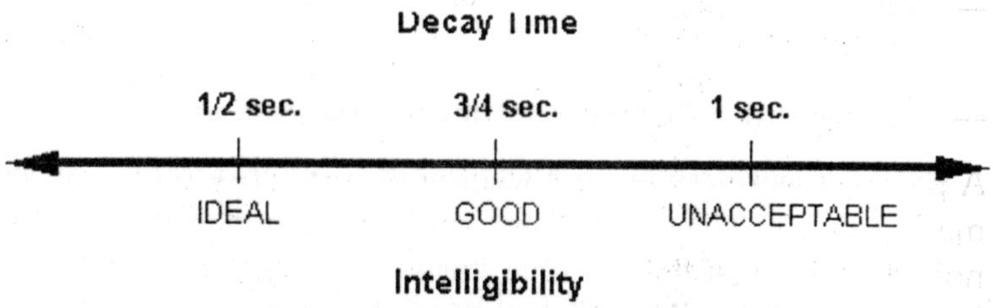

Guidelines for acceptable decay time in a distance learning classroom.

Decay time is measured with special test equipment which generates a burst of "white" or "pink" noise, and then measures how long sound persists after the noise has ceased. The measurement is typically made by a professional sound system installer or acoustic consultant in the process of evaluating a classroom for distance learning use.

Background Noise Level

Simply put, "noise" is any sound that the listener does not want or need to hear. Low levels of background noise can sometimes be suppressed or "tuned out" by the brain for a few minutes, but this quickly causes listening fatigue. As the level of noise increases compared to the level of speech, intelligibility suffers and listeners begin to miss words. Typical sources of background noise that make listening more difficult in a classroom include:

— cooling fans in computers or overhead projectors

— air ducts that vibrate or rumble

— air vents that produce an audible "rush" as air moves through them

— people walking or talking in hallways outside the classroom

— equipment rooms located next to, above, or below the classroom

— fluorescent light fixtures that hum or buzz

A precise measurement of background noise in a room can be made using a device called an *audio spectrum analyser*. The noise level is measured in units called decibels, abbreviated dB. Because sounds with different tonal characteristics affect the human ear differently, measurements are made at many points across the audible spectrum. The resulting data are then compared to standardized Noise Criteria or "NC" curves to determine the acceptability of the room for a given purpose. Rooms used for distance learning, teleconferencing, and similar activities should have an NC rating of 35 or less (which is very quiet.)

Another device, called a *sound level meter* or *SPL meter*, provides an average reading of the noise level in a room. Be aware, however, that the sound level meters sold at neighbourhood electronics stores are usually not capable of detecting low frequency noise (such as the rumbling of an air duct) and therefore may not provide an accurate and useful measurement of the noise level in a classroom.

How Room Acoustics Can Be Improved

In most classrooms, some improvement to the acoustics of the room will need to be made. The most common need is for a reduction in the decay time of the room, which is usually accomplished by covering some of the surfaces (walls, floor, ceiling, and windows) with commercially-available materials or panels designed to absorb, rather than reflect, sound waves. A reduction in background noise is typically addressed by repair or replacement of light fixtures, and adjustment of or modification to air conditioning vents and ducts. Noise coming from outside the classroom is usually more difficult to control, however.

Footsteps in a hallway might be silenced simply through the addition of carpeting, while reduction of noise from highway traffic or nearby equipment rooms might require major reconstruction of walls, ceilings, or floors. Reducing the transmission of noise *into* the room from outside sources can be very expensive, and should not be attempted without the help of an experienced acoustic consultant. In some cases, it may be wise to consider an alternate location for the classroom.

COMPONENTS OF THE AUDIO SYSTEM

The particular equipment that makes up a distance learning audio system varies depending on class size, seating arrangement, the subject being taught, the available budget, and other factors. Certain fundamental pieces of audio equipment are common to nearly all systems, however:

— a wireless microphone for the instructor

— desk- or table-mounted microphones for the students

— a microphone mixer to control, balance, and combine the signals from the microphones

— an amplifier and one or more loudspeakers to distribute the audio from other classroom sites throughout the room

Specific information about different types of microphones and wireless microphone systems, how they work, and how to choose the best type for a particular application is included in *Guide to Better Audio*, a complimentary booklet available from Shure Brothers Incorporated. Specific information about amplifiers and loudspeakers is available from manufacturers and vendors of those products.

Thanks to popular spy movies such as the James Bond series and "Sneakers," many people are under the impression that commonly available audio equipment can perform miracles, such as picking up intelligible speech from a mile away, or with a microphone hidden in an air duct. While it is probably

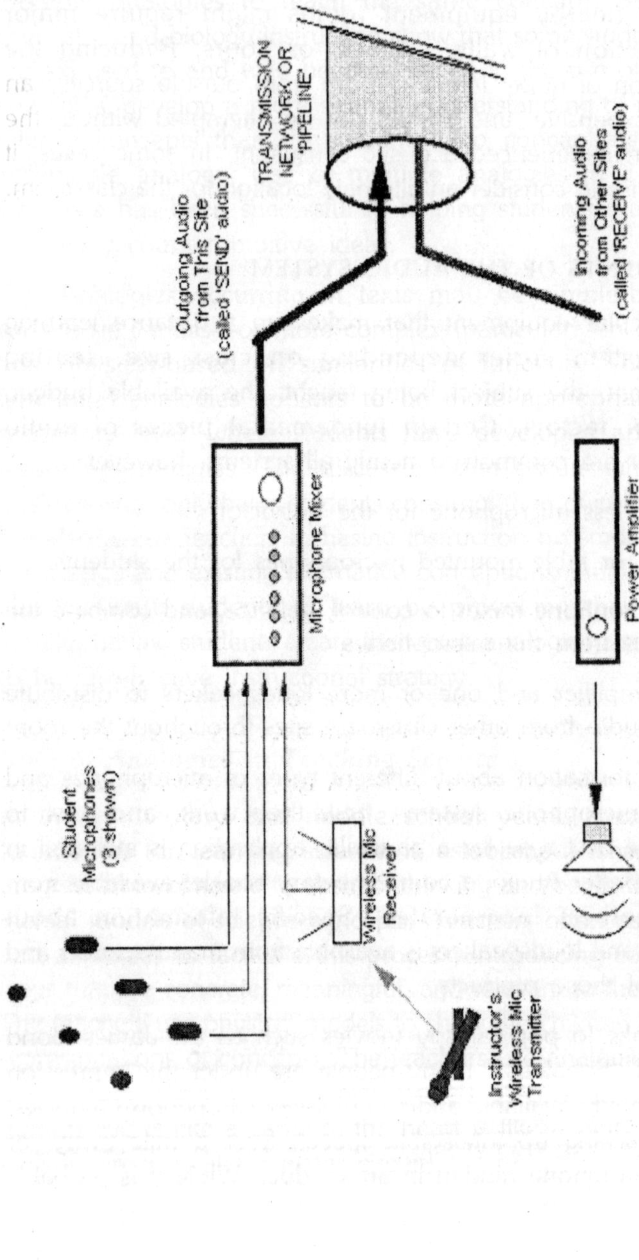

Flow diagram of a basic distance learning audio system.

true that a team of acoustic experts working for months with powerful computers could extract intelligible dialogue from a recording made that way, such feats are not possible during a live program or within the typical school system's budget. Modern audio systems can perform well under a wide range of conditions, but they cannot compensate for having poor sound fed into them.

Noise and reflected sound are impossible to remove once they are picked up and combined with speech.

Fortunately, there are time-tested "rules" for designing audio systems that can minimize the effects of less-than-ideal acoustic conditions. Three of these are so important that, if they are ignored, there is almost no hope of achieving satisfactory sound quality no matter how much time, money, or effort is spent.

Audio System that "Make or Break" Sound Quality

1. Talker-to-microphone distance

One of the most significant factors in determining the performance of an audio system is the distance from the talker to the nearest microphone. As the microphone is positioned farther away from the talker, the loudness of the speech reaching the microphone decreases, so the microphone's sensitivity to sound - its ability to "hear" - must be increased to compensate. This causes the microphone to pick up more of the desired sound (speech), but also to pick up more of everything else - background noise, reflections, sound from the loudspeakers, etc. The farther away the microphone is from the talker, the more hollow and noisy the sound will be.

So, when it comes to microphone placement, how far is "too far"? It so happens that there is a certain distance from the microphone beyond which a talker will sound hollow and difficult to understand, regardless of what type of microphone is used or which way it is pointed. This is called the *Critical*

Distance, abbreviated Dc. The Critical Distance is different for every room, and is determined primarily by the volume of the room (in cubic feet) and the decay time.

In a typical classroom, microphones should be located less than two feet from talkers.

Those talkers who are at or beyond the Critical Distance from the nearest microphone will be difficult to understand, no matter what type of equipment is added to the audio system or how it is adjusted. Given that most classrooms have a Critical Distance of from two to five feet, the following guidelines should be used for determining acceptable distance from the talker to the nearest microphone:

— less than 2 feet is ideal

— between 2 and 3 feet is good

— between 3 and 5 feet is marginal

— x more than 5 feet is unacceptable

When in doubt, always place the microphones nearer to rather than farther from talkers. Moving microphones closer to talkers is the single most significant improvement that can be made to most classroom audio systems.

The Best Places To Locate Microphones In a Classroom

We've discussed just how important it is to place microphones close to talkers, but where exactly should microphones be located to pick up students' questions? The answers depend on how the classroom is used and on the seating arrangement. What subjects are taught in the classroom? If the schedule includes foreign language classes, or advanced courses that include lots of technical terms, intelligibility is critical. In this case, microphones should probably be placed on the student desks so that they are less than two feet from the talkers. Lecture-type classes that do not rely on heavy student interaction may permit slightly longer talker-to-microphone distances.

If it is likely that students will be spreading out books and papers on the desks, flat surface microphones may be inadvertently covered up, resulting in muffled sound or pickup of rustling noises. Slim, flexible "gooseneck" microphones solve this problem by elevating the sensitive part of the microphone above the surface of the desk - away from the noise and closer to the talker. The toughest situation is when the room layout must be changed regularly.

If microphones cannot be mounted on student desks or tables, the only remaining option is usually to suspend microphones from the ceiling. The longer talker-to-mic distances required for adequate head clearance when students are entering and leaving the classroom represent a significant compromise in the audio system design - one that usually cannot be completely compensated for. Excellent room acoustics are absolutely essential in classrooms which utilize suspended microphones. If room acoustics are poor or merely average, then suspended microphones should never be considered.

The Case Against Ceiling Microphones

For appearance and security reasons, it is always tempting to place microphones directly on the ceiling of the classroom, where they are out of sight and out of reach. This is absolutely the worst location for microphones, however, and virtually guarantees that sound quality will be terrible in all but the quietest and most acoustically-perfect rooms.

First of all, ceiling microphones are far beyond the Critical Distance for most rooms, making voices sound hollow and distant. Second, ceilings almost always contain air vents which produce noise, and air ducts which cause the ceiling to rumble and vibrate. Ceiling microphones are closer to these undesired sounds than they are to the students - exactly the opposite of the way things should be for intelligible voice pickup. Finally, students do not talk up toward the ceiling; if anything, they talk down at the desk or the floor!

Number of open microphones

An often-overlooked factor in audio system performance is the *number of open microphones*, abbreviated *NOM*. This is the number of microphones which are "live" or "open" at any moment, meaning that the sound that they pick up is being recorded on tape or heard by other sites on the network. Only those microphones which are "open" affect sound quality; mics that are turned off by a switch or turned down all the way by a volume control do not. While you might expect that using several microphones to pick up the sound of a talker would sound better or louder than a single microphone, in reality it sounds much worse. This is because each additional microphone picks up some of the background noise and reflected sound in the room, even though it is not picking up the words of the talker.

Having four microphones turned up when only one person is speaking results in audio that is nearly 90% noise and reflected sound being transmitted to other sites. So, if only one person is speaking and four microphones are open, the audio system is fed four times as much background noise and reflected sound as with just one open microphone, but no additional speech (because the additional three microphones are probably too far away to clearly pick up the talker.) What this means is that only the microphone nearest to the talker should be turned up. If you want to hear what a difference this can make, make a tape recording of one person talking in a room, first with several open microphones and then with only one open microphone. The improvement in sound quality that results from turning off the unneeded microphones is dramatic.

What can you do to keep unneeded microphones turned off in the classroom? There are really only three options: have a designated operator turn the microphones on and off as needed; have the students operate their own microphones; or have an automatic microphone mixer do it. If a trained person is available to operate the sound system during every class, that person could be responsible for turning the appropriate microphones on and off when students speak. This is usually a poor choice, however, because even the best operator cannot react to a talker until a few words have already been missed - and a student's question may only consist of a few words. Another option is to require the students to control their own microphones. This is done using Push-to-Talk or "PTT" microphones, which require the student to push and hold a button to be heard. This can be effective if the students remember to push the button when they want to talk.

Depending on the age and interest level of the students, this may or may not be a reasonable expectation. Some instructors feel that forcing students to make such an effort before they can speak creates a barrier to interactivity, while others (especially those who teach several remote sites at once) appreciate the "shield" from unwanted distractions and interruptions which manually-operated microphones can provide for the instructor. An additional concern is that the students who are in the same room as the instructor usually do not feel compelled to activate their microphones when they talk, with the result that students at other sites cannot hear them.

A third solution to the problem of keeping unneeded microphones turned off is to use an automatic or "voice-activated" microphone mixer. This is a microphone mixer which automatically turns individual microphones on and off in response to the presence of sound at the microphone. Basic automatic mixers use a simple "fixed threshold" method to decide when to activate microphones. With this method, the sound level at any microphone must exceed a preset minimum (called the "threshold") before the microphone will be turned on and the talker will be heard. Proper adjustment of fixed threshold models is critical, because background noise levels within the classroom usually change from day to evening or even from hour to hour, and speaking levels vary significantly between individuals.

For instance, if the threshold is set low enough so that a quiet talker can activate the microphone, then the system may be overly sensitive to background noise, and microphones may activate every time the air conditioning turns on, or when the hallway fills with students during a passing period. Conversely, if the threshold is set high enough to prevent such incidences of false activation, then quiet talkers may not be heard. More sophisticated automatic mixers are available which constantly adapt to changes in background noise level. These units feature a "floating threshold" which is referenced to the level of noise in the room. Talkers need only speak slightly louder than the background noise level to activate a microphone. These systems are generally easy to set up and require almost no fine-tuning, since they adjust themselves to changing conditions in the room.

Microphone pickup pattern

Directional microphones (also called *unidirectional*) favour sounds from the direction in which the microphone is aimed, and reject sounds coming from behind the microphone. This trait offers two very important benefits which make directional microphones especially suitable for use in distance learning classrooms.

First, they can be aimed toward a desired sound source (the students), and away from an undesired sound source (the loudspeakers.) This helps to prevent the sound from other sites (coming out of the loudspeakers) from being picked up by the microphones. This loudspeaker audio would otherwise be retransmitted, which could cause annoying echoes or howling.

Second, most directional microphones pick up only one-third as much background sound as non-directional types, making them far less sensitive to the ambient noise and reflected sound present in the room. With less noise and reflected sound mixed in with the audio, speech is clearer and more intelligible.

Note that a directional microphone begins to lose its effectiveness as the distance from the talker increases. The further it is from the talker, the less improvement in sound quality it can offer over a non-directional model. In fact, when placed near (or beyond) the room's Critical Distance, a directional microphone will sound just as poor as a non-directional type.

Common Problems with Distance Learning Audio Systems and What You Can Do About Them

A live, two-way interactive communications link is more complicated than a regular audio system used for public address or recording. The three major audio problems which plague distance learning classrooms are feedback, transmission echo, and reflected or "hollow" sound. While feedback and reflected sound are commonly encountered in many sound reinforcement systems, echo is unique to two-way communications.

Feedback

Feedback is the howling or squealing that is heard when sound from a loudspeaker is picked up by a microphone and reamplified. Feedback can easily occur between audio systems located in different rooms, if the microphones in each room pick up too much of the sound from the nearby loudspeakers and retransmit it to other sites, where it can be picked up by microphones and transmitted back again.

Leakage from loudspeakers into microphones, causing feedback or echo.

There are many factors which can contribute to microphone-to-loudspeaker leakage, so there are many possible solutions which may work in a given classroom. Here are the corrective measures which are most successful at eliminating feedback in a distance learning network:

— Change the positioning and/or proximity of the microphones and loudspeakers relative to each other. For best results, loudspeakers should be positioned *behind* (not above) typical directional microphones, which are less sensitive to sounds arriving from the rear than to those arriving from the front.

— Turn the loudspeaker volume down in the room. Lower volume levels, while making it more difficult for people to hear, reduce the tendency of the audio system to how.

— Reduce the number of open microphones (NOM), through the action of a live operator, or the use of Push-to-Talk microphones, or an automatic mixer. Reducing the number of open microphones has the same effect as turning down the overall volume of the audio system (but without the penalty of lower listening levels), thereby reducing the incidence of feedback.

— Make the surfaces in the room less reflective by adding sound absorbent panels or coverings. In rooms with less-than-optimal acoustics, microphone-to-loudspeaker coupling may occur even though there is no direct path between the two. In this case, sound leaves the loudspeaker and is reflected off of the walls, ceiling, or floor, reaching the microphones indirectly.

Transmission Echo

Some types of transmission networks slightly delay the audio and video signals before or during transmission. This may be due to the time required for satellite transmission or the action of a device called a *codec*, which compresses the signal so that it can fit into a smaller (and less expensive) amount of space on the transmission line. When distance learning sites are connected over a network which induces some signal delay, the sound from the loudspeakers at the remote site can leak into microphones there, which causes an echo to be returned to the originating site. In other words, a talker in Classroom A speaks, his or her voice comes out of a loudspeaker in Classroom B and leaks into a microphone there, and that signal is transmitted back to Classroom A, where the talker hears an echo of his or her own words 1/4 to 1 second after having said them.

If the leakage problem in Classroom B is not severe, the returned echo may be low enough in volume to be tolerable, but in almost all cases it is so annoying that conversation is impossible. Various methods of dealing with echo have been devised; most of these were intended to minimize echo in long distance telephone lines. One type of device, called an *echo canceller*, monitors the incoming (or 'Receive') audio from other sites, and compares it to the signal that is about to be transmitted (the 'Send' signal). If the echo canceller detects the presence of the incoming audio in the outgoing signal, it creates a replica of the incoming audio and electronically subtracts it from the outgoing signal. This reduces the amount of echo, but does not completely "cancel" it. Notice that the echo canceller attempts to prevent the incoming audio from other sites from being sent back to them, but it does not do anything about the echoes that other sites may be sending to *your* site.

For this reason, if *one* site on a network requires echo cancellation equipment, *all* of the sites on that network will almost certainly need it.

There are two general types of echo cancellers. The first, called a *line echo canceller*, is designed to remove electronic echoes from telephone lines; most long distance telephone circuits employ these devices. Line echo cancellers cannot significantly reduce the complex echoes which result from loudspeaker-to-microphone leakage in a classroom. The second type, called an *acoustic echo canceller*, is designed to reduce the chance of an echo being produced due to this leakage. Acoustic echo cancellers are commonly mistaken to be capable of removing the hollow sound associated with a room that is too reflective; no electronic device can do that. In fact, excess reflected sound makes it more difficult for the echo canceller to work properly, and reduces the degree to which it can reduce transmission echo.

Acoustic echo cancellers take time (1/10 of a second or more) to "learn" how to reduce echo in a particular room, and they have to go through this learning process whenever the path from loudspeaker to microphone changes. This might be caused by a wireless microphone user moving around the room, or microphones being turned on and off by an automatic mixer. During these "learning" periods, echoes will not be reduced. Echo cancellers are expensive, and are not an alternative to good room acoustics and proper audio system design. At best, they can improve the sound quality of a distance learning network that suffers from echo problems, but they cannot make a classroom that has poor acoustics sound good.

Reflected or "Hollow" Sound

One of the most persistent and annoying problems with distance learning audio systems is the hollow sound - as if the talker is "at the bottom of a barrel" - caused by a room that is too reflective. Unfortunately, reflected sound cannot be removed by any type of electronic device; it must be kept out of the microphones in the first place. The obvious solution, of course, is to make the room less reflective by covering surfaces with specially designed sound-absorptive materials.

If changes to the room acoustics do not provide a sufficient improvement, the number of simultaneous open microphones (each of which adds a measure of reflected sound and background noise to the audio signal) must be reduced. Directional microphones can also reduce pickup of reflected sound, but only if they are positioned at less than the Critical Distance from the talker. Beyond the Critical Distance for the room, directional microphones offer minimal benefit. Finally, microphones can simply be moved closer to the talkers. Because the speech reaching the microphones will then be louder, the sensitivity of the microphone can be turned down at the microphone mixer, thereby decreasing its sensitivity to reflected sound and background noise as well.

The Broadcaster's Secrets

Television news shows routinely feature live interviews by satellite with leaders around the world. Somehow, they never seem to experience any of the audio problems that plague many distance learning networks. What do broadcast engineers do that allows them to dodge the effects of feedback, echo, and reverberation? Here are three "audio commandments" that broadcasters live by:

— Place the microphones as close to the talker as practical. In the studio, news anchors always wear a very small microphone (called a "lavalier" type) clipped to the necktie or jacket. In the field, reporters may wear a lavalier or use a standard handheld microphone. Because the camera shot is usually a tight close-up the microphone may not be visible, but rest assured that it's no more than a foot or so away from the talker's mouth. In situations where the talker cannot wear or hold a microphone, a long "shotgun" type microphone is mounted on a pole and held by a technician above and in front of the talker, just outside of the camera's field of view. While effective for recording, shotgun microphones offer little advantage when used in a classroom. They, too, sound poor when used indoors at or beyond the Critical Distance of the room.

— Use an ear piece. Broadcasters hear each other, the guests, the director, the commercials, and everything else through a small flesh-coloured earphone worn in one ear. In high-noise environments such as sports events, the commentator wears a tight-fitting headset (to block out noise) with a boom microphone positioned just an inch or so from the mouth (for clear speech with minimal noise pickup.) Loudspeakers are rarely used, so loudspeaker-to-microphone leakage is eliminated. No leakage means no problems with feedback or echo. This is especially critical, given that remote interviews by satellite - which are subject to significant signal delays - often must be set up on a moment's notice.

— Use as few open microphones as possible. Fewer microphones pick up less noise, and require less time to set up and plug in. To optimize sound quality, an engineer constantly adjusts or "rides" the settings at the microphone mixer. You will rarely see more than four microphones being used at one time on television, but when more microphones are required than the engineer can keep up with, automatic mixers are frequently used.

Install the Audio System in Your Classroom

Hopefully, you are beginning to have a better understanding of the technical issues which must be dealt with in the design, installation, and use of a distance learning audio system. These may require more time or technical expertise than you can commit to the project. In any case, one of the following three options should help you to get a distance learning classroom installed at your institution:

- Work with a qualified A/V consultant or sound system contractor. An acoustic or A/V consultant designs systems and writes what is known as a spec, or specification, of the equipment and room modifications required foı the project. The consultant does not actually sell or install the equipment, however. A sound system contractor, working from the consultant's design, sells, installs, and services the equipment. In some cases, the contractor both designs and installs the system. It is very important to work with firms that have experience with two-way interactive systems, such as teleconferencing or videoconferencing rooms or distance learning classrooms, because of the unique problems which arise in them as opposed to more typical public address systems found in churches or auditoria.
- Purchase a pre-packaged system from a turnkey system provider. Companies which offer certain key elements of a distance learning system, such as fiber optic transmission equipment or service, sometimes "bundle" their own products or services together with those of companies that make the other equipment necessary (such as cameras, monitors, etc.) They are then able to market a complete distance learning system package for one price. In most cases, the actual installation of hardware is handled by a local sound system contractor.
- Do it yourself. Institutions that have qualified technical people on staff with a knowledge of audio, video, and room acoustics, may be able to configure, install, and service a distance learning system without assistance. This may be a viable option if the system is a simple one - meaning that class sizes are small, echo is not a problem, and necessary modifications to the room acoustics are minimal.

RADIOS IN THE CLASSROOM: CURRICULUM INTEGRATION AND COMMUNICATION SKILLS

Teachers have explored the use of radio in the classroom almost since radio technology entered into the mainstream of society, yet radio remains a relatively unused mode of instruction.

Teaching The History of Communication

Students may begin their study of communications technology by reading about some early devices and their inventors. Radios and telegraphs are part of early communications technology history, and Samuel Morse, Guglielmo Marconi, Lee DeForest, Philo Farnsworth, and David Sarnoff were communications pioneers. The first popular radios were called crystal radios because they used crystals to receive the broadcast signals. Building a crystal radio, either from a kit or from parts, is an engaging, hands-on science activity.

In addition to building the crystal radio, earth science and chemistry teachers might consider making the galena crystals that receive the signals. Many early crystal radio listeners made their own galena crystals before radios were sold in stores. Teachers can also use radio assembly projects to help students learn about electricity, wave energy, the electromagnetic spectrum, the earth's atmosphere, and the sun's effects on the earth's atmosphere. Many popular electronics stores have a full range of reasonably priced, easy to assemble electronics and radio kits.

AM-FM Radio: Hands-On Geography and Language Arts Activities

Depending upon your geographic location, you may hear many AM-FM radio stations from Canada, Mexico, Central America, and the Caribbean. If you are near those regions, you will hear broadcasts by English, French, and Spanish native speakers-a special opportunity for foreign language learners. Some AM-FM stations now maintain Web sites and offer their listeners real-time programming and audio archives. Listening to online audio resources requires computer software such as RealAudio, a sound card, and speakers.

Many U.S. AM stations may be heard across the country. Listening to broadcasts from other U.S. locations makes an excellent activity for learning U.S. geography. The term DX means long-distance, so listening to faraway stations is known as "DXing" among radio hobbyists. In the evening, AM radio broadcasts are heard over great distances because atmospheric conditions allow AM radio waves to bounce between the atmosphere and the earth. Students might hear AM broadcasts from several hundred miles away if they listen to AM stations after dark.

International Shortwave Broadcasts: Hearing the World on a Radio

Just as an AM-FM radio is a tool for students learning about local and regional geography, a shortwave radio is a good tool for learning about world geography. Every country in the world has shortwave radio broadcast stations, and most stations have programming in English, as well as their native language. Beginning with 6th-grade social studies curriculum, the study of geography may be enhanced by listening to international shortwave broadcasts. Students will hear news and cultural programming that will enhance the information found in books, encyclopedias, and on the Internet. Topics such as latitude and longitude, time zones, continents, hemispheres, and the tropics may all be highlighted through radio listening activities.

Writing letters to international stations to give listener reports is a long-standing shortwave listening hobby activity. The writing assignment combines listening and language arts skills. Stations usually reply with letters or special postcards, brochures, posters, key chains, and bumper stickers. Teachers may use these items to prepare interesting displays in a classroom learning centre.

NOAA National Weather Service Broadcasts

Many people listen to a radio to hear weather reports; however, in a classroom it's not always convenient to wait for a radio station's weather report. With a weather radio, you don't have to wait. Weather radios are tuned to the NOAA (National Oceanic and Atmospheric Administration), weather channels that provide broadcasts 24 hours a day. Most NOAA broadcasts range about 50 miles from their main location. Many AM-FM radios, scanner radios, and CB radios include NOAA channels for listeners' convenience and safety.

NOAA also coordinates a national program for trained volunteer weather watchers called Skywarn. Teachers may wish to consider Skywarn training for a class weather project or for individual science projects. A scanner radio will bring the world of work into the classroom. These high-speed scanning receivers monitor government, businesses, and nonprofit organization's frequencies in your local community. Unlike the shortwave radio, a scanner radio receives local FM communications and broadcasts within a range of about 50 miles.

Since the conversations you hear on a scanner radio are between people, there is no way to know when they will occur. A scanner radio scans through many frequencies and stops when a transmission signal is detected. The listener will hear many transmissions, and it is important to program the scanner radio to listen to the public service agencies desired. Some occupations that use scanner radios include: police, fire, hospitals, ambulances, aircraft, schools, universities, factories, warehouses, boats, taxis, city buses, delivery trucks, utility companies, TV and radio news crews, the FBI, mall security, hotels, and construction crews.

Amateur Radio: Practicing Hands-On Communication Skills

Many students today build their own web pages; however, students in the 1950s and 60s, built stereos and radios with kits from companies like Heathkit. Many students earned amateur radio licenses from the Federal Communications

Commission (FCC) and built their own ham radio stations. Today, most ham radio operators buy ready-made radio equipment, and many enthusiasts listen to packet radio (connections between radios and computers) or participate in ham satellite communications. Other ham radio operators communicate with the NASA Space Shuttle and the Mir Space Station via amateur radio. Not long ago, the FCC eased the requirements for the entry-level ham license by eliminating the Morse code requirement.

Students and teachers can now become No-Code Technician Class operators by passing two multiple-choice exams. Study guides for these exams include the entire FCC question pool, as well as full explanations for each answer. Kindergarten-age students have earned licenses, however most young hams are in the middle and high school grades. Many schools across the country and around the world have amateur radio stations. Students can practice speaking, interviewing, listening, and writing skills in an amateur radio school club or classroom activity. Some teachers use the amateur radio as the communications link for school-to-school projects. Real-time radio conversations allow students to practice listening and speaking skills-a valuable experience that is not found with an e-mail connection.

OPTICAL DISK FORMATS

The first optical disks that became commercially available, around 1982, were compact audio disks. Since then, and during a particularly active marketing period from 1984 to 1986, at least a dozen other optical formats have emerged or are under development. The rapid proliferation of formats has led, understandably, to some confusion. Optical disks go by many names—OD, laser disk, and disc among them—all of which are acceptable. At first glance, they bear some resemblance to floppy disks: they may be about the same size, store information in digital form, and be used with microcomputers. But where information is encoded on floppy disks in the form of magnetic charges, it is encoded on optical disks in the form of microscopic pits. These pits are created and read with laser (light) technology.

The optical disks that are sold are actually "pressed," or molded from a glass master disk, in somewhat the same way as phonograph records. The copies are composed of clear hard plastic with a reflective metal backing, and protected by a tough lacquer. As the disk spins in the optical disk player (reader, drive), a reader head projects a beam from a low-power laser through the plastic onto the pitted data surface and interprets the reflected light. Optical disk players can stand alone, like portable tape players, or be connected to stereos, televisions, or microcomputers. Optical disks lack the erasability and access speed of floppies, but these disadvantages are offset by their huge storage capacity, higher level of accuracy, and greater durability.

Optical disk formats are described by capability, information form, and disk size. The most familiar capabilities are:

— Read Only Memory (ROM, RO): permanent, unalterable storage, currently the only firmly established format.

— Write Once, Read Many (WORM, WO): new data can be written to the disk, but existing data cannot be altered or erased. The drive head contains two lasers: one for reading, and a more powerful laser for etching new data pits. WORM capability may reduce storage capacity by a third. Both 5.25- and 12-inch versions were marketed around 1985.

— Interactive (I): stores information in any or all forms, along with interactive programming that allows flexible access, animates visuals, runs games, etc.; similar to the capabilities of microcomputer software.

— Erasable (E): information can be deleted and overwritten. This format requires complex technology and is still being developed.

These capabilities may or may not be available on disks containing different forms of information—audio, text or data, video or graphics, or a combination. And various forms of information can be found on different sizes of disk, most often 12 or 4.72 inches in diameter. Some 12-inch formats are:

— Optical Digital Data Disk (OD3, ODD): contains digitized information (bits), usually text, sometimes images, and used primarily in business and research settings. The disk may have ROM or WORM capabilities.

— Video Disk (videodisc, laser video disk, LV, reflective optical video disk): carries sound and moving images—movies—as analog (continuous) signals. The disk itself may be silvery, reflecting colours for a rainbow effect.

— Digital Video Disk (digitally encoded video disk) contains digital video, audio, and/or text. Still video is more common than motion video because it is more economical to store and easier to access. Digital motion video must be converted to analog signals for playing on standard home televisions. The disk may also include some interactivity programming.

— Interactive Video Disk (IVD): stores 54,000 still frames or 30 minutes of full-motion video with audio. A microcomputer interface allows IVD to gain some interactive capability, although interactivity is hampered by the analog video signal. This format has applications in education, business and industrial training, public information terminals, and games and other entertainment.

Most compact disks (CDs) are 4.72 inches across; a few are 5.25 inches. Audio, text, and still video are stored on CDs. The first two formats below are the most commercially successful to date:

— Compact Audio Disk (digital audio disk; CD-audio): contains digital stereo audio signals, generally 75 minutes of high-fidelity, static-free music.

— Compact Disk-Read Only Memory (CD-ROM): has tremendous storage capacity, used to store text databases such as bibliographic indexes. One compact disk holds 550 MB of data, the equivalent of 1,500 floppy disks. This amounts to 275,000 pages of information or 200 pounds of paper. Audio or still video may be integrated with text. This format is marketed for library, academic, and professional applications.

— Compact Disk-Write Once, Read Many (CD-WORM): often contains text or text with still images. Several 5.25-inch formats with write and possibly erase capabilities are also under development.

The next wave of optical disk formats is about to break. This year or next we are likely to see:

— HDTV Video Disk: a digital format that is readable by high-definition television, with more than double the number of lines per screen.

— Compact Disk-Interactive (CD-I): a writable, very adaptable format that will store text, multichannel audio at several quality levels, still or motion video with low- or high-definition, and animated graphics. Signals may be all digital or include some analog video. CD-I players can stand alone or link to home entertainment systems. This disk and a similar product, compact disk video (CD-video, CD-V), are targeted for mass-market education and entertainment.

— Digital Video Interactive (DVI): similar to CD-I, but a highly integrated system that promises more. Compressed digital signals allow the storage capacity of CD-ROM and more motion video than CD-I and IVD: up to an hour of video, with multitrack audio. This disk also has the interactive graphics capabilities of a microcomputer program. Applications include simulations, video paint, special effects, sales tools, and scientific imaging. DVI's release is slated for 1990 or later.

— Compact Disk-Erasable Magneto Optic (CD-EMO): combines optic and magnetic technologies in a format that is expected to be easily erasable and reusable for 10 years. Like WORM, EMO requires a drive head with separate read and write lasers. In writing, heat from the laser works in conjunction with a change in magnetic polarity to change the shape of the pit. The erasable disk should also appear within two years.

Audio Teleconferencing in Education

Teleconferencing is electronic communication between two or more people at a distance. Today, teleconferencing may connect multiple locations and can be divided into three major types: audio, video, and computer. These types can be combined for an almost endless set of applications. College and university users have discovered that teleconferencing enables them to extend the budget dollar; extend educational opportunities to distant locations; accommodate a variety of classes, from college credit courses to continuing education and public service programs; and provide a flexible format for meetings.

Audio conferencing is actually telephone conferencing because telephone technology makes up the network that interconnects the conferees. Although audio conferencing is not entirely suitable for such tasks as resolving conflicts and interviewing, the medium's advantages include the following:

— Use of familiar technology—the telephone

— Accessibility (400,000,000 telephones worldwide)

— Ability to set up conferences on short notice

— Comparative low cost

To make audio conferencing more comfortable, speaker phones are available to permit callers physical flexibility. These work satisfactorily for up to eight or ten participants. More sophisticated speakers are available for larger groups. Costs for dial-up conferencing vary; telco or meet-me usually will cost

$20 to $40 per location per hour. The following audio teleconferencing options are available:

Dedicated Conference Networks : A dedicated conference network permanently wires preselected locations together. To conference, callers need only to pick up the phone at each location. These systems can be very large. The University of Wisconsin, for example, uses a network of more than 200 locations throughout the state to disseminate information and teach classes. Dedicated networks generally have better sound quality than dial-up networks and are cost-effective when usage is high.

Dial-Up Networks : Dial-up networks use the public switched telephone network. In the telco operator-assisted mode, the operator calls and connects all participants. This system works well for a few locations, but difficulties occur when numbers increase.

Meet-Me Conferencing : To overcome these difficulties, several private telephone conferencing companies have formed to offer a new type of service, "Meet Me" Conferencing, in which each participant calls the conferencing centre from any convenient location. If everyone is prompt, a large number of locations can be interconnected for conferences in five minutes or less. The sound quality is superior to that of telco conferencing and is generally unaffected by numbers of participants. Telephones anywhere can be connected, in contrast to limited locations in dedicated networks. Meet-me systems are now available for in-house installation where usage makes them cost-effective.

Direct Dial Conferencing Systems : Direct Dial Conferencing System is an innovation that makes it possible for one caller to set up a telephone conference with up to six additional participants by using a touch tone phone.

Blending video and audio conferencing characteristics, "audiographics" refers to the transmission of print and graphic information over telephone lines to complement voice communication with visuals. Audiographics systems include a variety of devices: electronic pens, blackboards, and tablets, as well as computer systems, slow scan television, microfiche, telewriters, and facsimile machines. Although not widely used, a potentially useful educational device is the electronic blackboard. The blackboard converts writing to audible tones which are transmitted over telephone lines, received at one or more locations, and displayed upon a television screen. Tariffs vary but cost is about $800 per month per location for both send and receive capabilities.

Video Teleconferencing

Video teleconferencing combines the audio and visual media to provide interactive voice communications and television pictures. The images include anything that can be captured by a television camera. Though full motion video (such as that transmitted on home television) is the most familiar technology, a number of options exist, including freeze-frame television, compressed video systems, and full motion video systems. Costs vary for these three systems; freeze frame is the least and full motion video the most expensive. A single full motion video conference of several hours, linking as many as ten locations, could run between $150,000 and $225,000.

Although most educational institutions use economical audio teleconferencing, several pioneer videoconferencing systems (including satellite systems) are available. Many video systems used in higher education are dedicated networks used on a local, regional, or statewide basis. Most use one-way video and two-way audio networks for point-to-multipoint education programming. Some programs are directed toward health professionals, others to continuing education courses, university credit courses, and administrative meetings. Several full motion educational video systems connect as many as 30 locations. The largest freeze frame video system, operated by the University of Wisconsin Extension, connects 26 locations.

Freeze-Frame Television: Freeze-frame, or Slow Scan Television, uses the narrowband telephone system to transmit data, voice, and still video images. Transmission time may vary from a few seconds to more than a minute.

Compressed Video Systems: A Compressed Video System also uses a telephone data circuit. It compresses the video signal to eliminate redundant electronic information with a picture processor, or codec. The video picture appears instantly but there may be some jerkiness or blurring of fast movements.

Full Motion Video Systems: A Full Motion Video System uses wideband channels to send video, voice, and data. Because of the large channel capacity, it transmits a full video picture with continuous motion instantly, using cable, microwave, or satellites.

The advantage of full motion teleconferencing is high quality and natural conferencing format. The major disadvantages of full motion video are its high cost and limitations in linking multiple locations. Unlike the systems that use telephone channels, wideband video cannot readily link multiple sites for two-way video.

Computer conferencing

Computer conferencing permits two or more people to communicate with each other via computer terminals in a non-real-time mode. It is like "electronic mail" because the user can put a message into the computer and have it retrieved and answered later. But conferencing technology goes further. Specific software programs have been developed that permit members of a conference to interact with each other and to access a wide variety of stored information relevant to their objectives. Computer conferencing adapts to course teaching, student counseling, and informed information exchange. The University of Michigan is the educational leader in this field.

9

VIDEO

INSTRUCTIONAL TELEVISION

Instructional television (ITV), is an effective distance education delivery system that can be integrated into the curriculum at three basic levels:

— *Single lesson* - Programs address one specific topic or concept, providing a lesson introduction, overview, or summary.

— *Selected unit* - A series of programs providing the content foundation for a learning unit in the course curriculum.

— *Full course* - Programs from one or more ITV series may be integrated into a full semester course typically in conjunction with instructional print materials.

ITV may be either passive or interactive. Passive ITV typically involves pre-produced programs which are distributed by video cassette or by video-based technologies such as broadcast, cable, or satellite. In contrast, interactive ITV provides opportunities for viewer interaction, either with a live instructor or a participating student site. For example, two-way television with two-way audio allows all students to view and interact with the teacher. At the same time, cameras at remote sites allow the teacher to view all participating students. It is also possible to configure the system so that all student sites may view one another.

Advantages

— Since most people have watched television, the medium is familiar.

— Motion and visuals can be combined in a single format so that complex or abstract concepts can be illustrated through visual simulation. The old cliche "a picture is worth a thousand words" rings true.

— Instructional television is an effective way to take students to new environments (the moon, a foreign country, or through the lens of a microscope).

— Time and space can be collapsed, so that events can be captured and relayed as they happen.

— It is very effective for introducing, summarizing, and reviewing concepts.

— It can be used effectively as a motivational tool.

Limitations

— Broadcast quality ITV is expensive to create.

— Video production is time consuming and can be technically demanding, often requiring relatively sophisticated production facilities and equipment.

— Sites choosing to interactively participate in an ITV program may require specialized equipment, facilities, and staffing.

— Most prepackaged ITV courses use a mass media approach to instruction aimed at the average student. As a result, they can be ineffective in serving students with special needs.

— When used passively, without interaction, its instructional effectiveness can be limited.

— Unless professionally produced, completed ITV programs often look amateurish.

— Once completed, ITV programs can be difficult to revise and update.

Designing Instruction for ITV

In designing instruction for ITV, the challenge is to think in visual terms. Taking advantage of the visual imagery of ITV can counter an over-reliance on lecturing. Carefully planning ways to show instead of tell may improve the instructional effectiveness of ITV. It may be helpful to visually represent:

— Outlines or lists

— Key points

— Complex material in a step-by-step fashion

— Relationships

— Information that needs to be summarized for retention and recall

Make use of:

— Pictures — to show what things look like.

— Diagrams — to illustrate conceptual relationships, organizations, and structure of content material.

— Maps — to show spatial relationships.

— Graphs, tables, and charts -- to summarize information.

Take advantage of video's ability to show movement to:

— Demonstrate the operation of tools and equipment.

— Demonstrate skills that learners are expected to emulate.

— Conduct experiments in which the processes must be observed.

— Analyse change over time using animation, slow motion, or time lapse photography.

— Reveal the spatial, three dimensional qualities of an object or structure.

— Transport learners to places or situations not otherwise in their experience.

— Present primary source materials for analysis, such as film of historical events or naturally occurring situations.

Conducting ITV Lessons

Because teachers and students are physically separated by a distance, the teacher's challenge is to psychologically reduce the gap not only through the appropriate use of technology but also through the use of effective teaching practices. Good teaching ensures that a rapport develops between students and teacher. Once basic teaching methods are considered, try employing the following three step strategy for conducting ITV lessons:

Set the Stage

— Remember that it takes longer to deliver instruction at a distance than in a traditional face-to-face setting. Plan lessons accordingly.

— Practice in front of a live camera prior to class. If possible, have a colleague, a few target students, or a media technician view your presentation and on-camera presence, offering suggestions for improvement.

— Organize all class materials and visuals before the start of the class. It is best to have a trial run with technical staff so that all participants know the role they are expected to play.

— If using an overhead camera to electronically project visuals, understand its operation and limitations prior to the start of the class.

— Prepare viewers for new terminology to be used in the program, and answer any questions regarding the technical equipment being used, such as cameras, television monitors, audio equipment, etc..

— Inform students if there will be camera operators or technicians in the classroom. Although the students may be initially curious, this will fade as the class progresses. In-class technicians are trained to be as unobtrusive as possible.

— Students should have the necessary background materials to make the best use of televised lessons. Consider the use of study questions to assist in focusing discussions.

— Consider team teaching to maintain viewer interest with a change of voice, image, and presentation style. If using guest speakers, give students necessary background information prior to the class. Do the same for the guest speakers. Let them know the specific purpose of their session, what is expected of them, and the general background of participating students.

During the ITV Session

— Vary facial expressions, tone of voice, body movements, and eye contact with the camera to enhance verbal communication.

— Engage students by using humour, asking questions, involving students, and praising student contributions.

— Maintain energy and dynamism to attract and hold the distant learners' attention. Remember, enthusiasm is contagious. So is boredom.

— Present content in five to ten minute blocks interspersed with discussion. Alternate between instruction and interaction.

— Keep lecture sessions simple and clear. To help focus viewing, indicate key points to look for.

— Do not read material.

— Maintain a moderate speaking pace.

— Do not digress — keep students on track.

— Include different kinds of student involvement— watching, reading, writing, and talking.

— Vary the centre of focus for activities from the on-camera presenter to a receive site group or individual.

— Incorporate timely breaks as a respite from the television monitor.

— Motivate peer learning and support by encouraging students to work together both in and out of class.

— Review the concepts discussed in the program and clarify any misunderstandings by asking focused questions.

— Integrate activities to reinforce the content presentation. These activities might include quizzes, worksheets, role-playing, and experiments.

Make sure opportunities are included to enhance student interaction by:

— Planning a block of time for interaction and then letting students know in advance that interaction is anticipated. Initiating an interaction within the first twenty minutes will get students motivated to participate in learning rather than lulling them into just watching.

— Designating students at distant sites to lead discussions or survey the room for questions.

— Clearly defining discussion topics or questions and then allowing time for students to prepare responses. Assigning discussion questions in advance of the television session will help students prepare for the interaction. Have the questions appear in writing on the screen so students see and hear the questions.

— Encouraging student-to-student interaction by asking an in-class student or a student from a distant site to respond to questions. The instructor does not always have to answer questions.

— Functioning as content facilitator not just content provider.

Following the Session

— Review the taped recordings of the presentation, either with technical staff, a colleague, or by yourself. Take notes for improving presentation, style, and delivery methos.

— Seek student feedback on the strengths and weaknesses of the instructional materials and the teaching strategies being used.

— Be open to new ideas and delivery techniques for improving instructional effectiveness.

INTERACTIVE VIDEOCONFERENCING IN DISTANCE EDUCATION

Interactive Videoconferencing (IV) is an effective tool that may be used in distance education settings. This system can be integrated into the distance education program with minimal adaptation to the curriculum and course and is designed to support two-way video and audio communication between multiple locations.

The Technology of IV

Most IV systems utilize compressed digital video for the transmission of motion images over data networks such as high capacity Integrated Services Digital Networks (ISDN). The video compression process decreases the amount of data transmitted over the lines by transmitting only the changes in the picture. By minimizing the bandwidth required to transmit the images, video compression also reduces the transmission cost. Interactive videoconferences are often transmitted on dedicated T-1 phone lines.

These high speed lines are very effective for videoconferencing, but they are typically leased circuits with an expensive monthly cost. The fixed monthly charge is usually based on distance, not usage. Therefore, the cost effectiveness of IV systems increases with use. Interactive videoconferencing systems can operate at different data rates, at various fractions of T-1 capacity, enabling the transmission of multiple simultaneous videoconferences over the same T-1 circuit. An IV system can also share a T-1 circuit with other digital data uses such as Internet transmissions or file transfers.

Point-to-point

Interactive videoconferencing is commonly used to connect two locations using sophisticated computer technology. The core of IV is the codec (coder/decoder). This is the electronic device that transmits and receives the video signals that the class members will see on their television monitors. It may be easier to think of the codec as an extremely sophisticated modem. A modem takes digital data and transmits it over regular phone lines. The codec takes analog signals, compresses and digitizes them, and transmits the signals over digital phone lines. Other types of equipment, such as television monitors, are needed to make IV successful. In addition, various forms of instructional technology can be incorporated into IV, including video cassette recorders/players, microphones, cameras, and computers .

Point-to-Multipoint

Some systems are also capable of simultaneously connecting more than two sites through the use of a multi-point control unit, or MCU. Multi-point conferencing can be effective although the scheduling, technical, and logistical dimensions of MCU conferences can be imposing.

Dial Out Capability

A relatively new "dial out" feature, allows the use of multiple telephone lines to connect two or more sites in the same conference. Simultaneously accessing multiple lines may be difficult in small areas. In addition, the cost of the telephone line usage may be prohibitive since the cost of the call would be multiplied by the number of lines utilized in the conference.

Advantages of Interactive Video

Interactive video can be effective because it:

— Allows "real time" visual contact between students and the instructor or among students at different sites.

— Supports the use of diverse media. Blackboards, handwritten documents, and videos may be incorporated at all sites.

— Enables connection with experts in other geographical locations.

— Can provide access to at-risk or special needs students.

— Provides additional access to students at remote sites.

Limitations of Interactive Video

As with any technology, interactive video has its limitations:

— The initial cost of the equipment and leasing the lines to transmit conferences may be prohibitive.

— Companies which produce codecs have each developed unique methods of compression which are incompatible, although protocols have been established to allow communication among brand names. However, this "universal standard" compromises resolution and quality to a certain degree.

— Unless a strong effort is made by the instructor, students not located with the instructor may remain uninvolved in the course.

— If visuals, like handwritten or copied materials, are not properly prepared, students may have a difficult time reading them.

— If the "pipe" that carries the transmission among sites is not large enough, the students may observe "ghost images" when rapid movement occurs in "real time".

— If the system is not properly configured, class members may observe an audio "echo" effect. The result is audio interference that detracts from the learning environment.

Types of Videoconferencing Systems

— Small room videoconferencing. This system is designed primarily for small groups (1-12 participants) at all sites seated around a conference table.

— Classroom videoconferencing. This type of system usually uses high quality AV components, codecs, and an interface that allows all participants to be seen on the monitors.

— Desktop videoconferencing. This system utilizes a personal computer and videoconferencing software. These systems are less expensive, but offer limited resolution. They are most effective for individual and small group use.

Designing Instruction for Interactive Video

When designing instruction to be delivered over IV, the instructor should focus attention on all students, not just those at the "home" site. Lessons should incorporate a variety of activities for all students at the various sites. Use small group activities, student presentations, and an occasional break to add variety to the lesson. As a rule of thumb, instructors should change instruction methods every 10-15 minutes. In other words, switch from lecture to question-answer to small group activity on a regular basis.

It is often helpful to bring guest lecturers into the classroom. It may also be helpful to have guest speakers at one or more of the distant sites. This will encourage involvement of the distant students, as well as allowing the students at the origination site to "see what it is like" to have the teacher at another location. When preparing class visuals, keep in mind that small fonts and light colours do not show up well over the monitors. A variety of formatting will also assist in maintaining student interest and attention. When formatting visuals, be sure that they will fit on the television monitor.

Instructional Strategies

Establish Class Expectations: In the distance education classroom, some students may adopt the "TV" attitude, expecting the course to be entertaining, not educational. Address this attitude through well planned and focused presentations with emphasis on teacher-student interaction.

Reduce Distractions: Students should also be forewarned to minimize extraneous noise and activity. Both detract from the quality of the course. Use Variety and interaction. The instructor should begin the course by preparing the learners for an active experience. Interactive videoconferencing is interactive, unlike regular television, and students can make the class much more interesting by being actively involved.

Encourage Dialogue: By asking questions and noting body language, instructors can ascertain the interest and comprehension of the students at both all sites. This kind of attention will make all students feel more comfortable.

Training for Instructors and Students: It is important that an instructor be taught how to use all features of the equipment. A short session (30 minutes) should be sufficient to give the instructor a "hands-on" overview of the equipment features. It would also be helpful to provide the instructor with a quick reference sheet outlining major functions.

Some of the critical operations that an instructor should be capable of performing are:

— Turning on the codec and the monitors.

— Dialing the distant site(s) to establish a link.

— Controlling camera focus and field at the origination site and at the distant site(s).

— Adjusting the volume to an acceptable level.

— Dialing out to a remote location.

— Selecting the appropriate data rate.

— Re-setting "echo canceling" capability.

— Switching to and from the document camera.

— Switching to and from the computer output.

— Utilizing a computer to generate and display multimedia presentations.

— Using the VCR to broadcast a video for all locations.

— Terminating the link with the distant site(s).

— Shutting down the equipment.

Some institutions have technicians who will assist the instructor in setting up or monitoring the videoconference. However, the instructor should still be aware of the process because the technician may not always be available. Student training may also be critical since they may be called upon to operate the equipment if the instructor is at another site, is unavailable, or if a guest speaker needs assistance. Interactive videoconferencing can be an effective instructional tool for the distance educator. As with other technologies, its usefulness is directly related to the instructor's understanding of its benefits, limitations, and utilization strategies.

MASS MEDIA USE IN THE CLASSROOM

In its 75th anniversary issue the education journal "Clearing House" reprinted an article originally published in 1930. Entitled "Educating the Twentieth-Century Youth," the article argued that 20th-century youth should be taught using 20th-century methods and went on to discuss the use of the stereograph, the stereopticon slide, the radio, and the motion picture. The first two media named are museum pieces today, while radio is the home of talk shows and disk jockeys, but the motion picture is still going strong, joined by television and videotapes. A well designed course of instruction can utilize these mass media to channel a student's enthusiasm and route it to an academically useful goal.

What do Films and Television Offer to Educators?

Film communication offers links between classrooms and society. Motion pictures can help explore cultural context, may be integrated easily into the curriculum, are entertaining, and allow flexibility of materials and teaching techniques. Motion pictures can also be related to students' personal experiences, act as a focus for teacher-student interaction, and can be used to promote awareness of the interrelationship between modes (picture, movement, language, sound, captions). TV and video are also highly valuable as teaching tools, and seen as especially effective for reaching visual learners and special populations. According to a recent wide-ranging survey, TV and video are being used more deliberately than ever before and are being more fully integrated into the curricula.

Teachers look for quality programming, programs of appropriate structure and length, and advance information to allow them to preview and tape. The survey found that students and teachers are becoming more media savvy and are increasingly using camcorders and other video production equipment. It also found that the focus on computer acquisition and use has not replaced television in the classroom. Or, as one educator has stated: "Because students live in a media-oriented world, they consider sight and sound as 'user-friendly'".

Potential Applications in Language Arts

Even before the ease of using the VCR, the "introduction to film course" had become a staple in American colleges and universities. What has become apparent over the years is that film can be used as an adjunct to almost any discipline, most especially the language arts. Lovell notes that in addition to encouraging the use and development of communication skills, film can be used to establish a social context for English as a second language and to provide visual "texts" for deaf students. Indeed, movies can be considered as a form of text. They are controllable teaching instruments, and offer a great variety of subject, communicative language, language environment, and cultural content.

Post contends that videotapes of literary classics can become powerful allies of the teacher in the English classroom if used effectively. She adds that films allow the teaching of longer works that might otherwise be omitted or the teaching of controversial works that might be excluded from the curriculum. The example she gives is of Tennessee Williams's "Cat on a Hot Tin Roof." Although the film is definitely an adult film, the screenplay contains none of the potentially objectionable material or language that appears in the original play. If videotapes of historical and literature-based films are going to be used as shortcuts to learning, then teachers should structure videotapes into the curriculum and classroom experience to teach students how to intelligently evaluate what they are watching and to compare the visual with the originally published work.

In teaching Nathaniel Hawthorne's "The Scarlet Letter," teachers should encourage students to read the book and watch the recent film and then write a research paper for which they: (1) read articles about the movie; (2) identify places in the film and book that contradict each other (for example, the film has a contrived "happy ending," a plot change which astounded and bothered American literature teachers); (3) write a compare and contrast paper that will explain the significance of these differences and how they change the meaning of the original work; (4) conduct research to explain why the director/script writers made these changes; (5) conduct research to determine whether the book and the film accurately portray the historical period; and (6) analyze how the alteration of history or literature by the film affects the public view. Another way to examine the artistic choices made by actors, writers, and directors would be to use short clips from different film versions of classic literature-Laurence Olivier's "Hamlet" and Kenneth Branagh's "Hamlet," for example.

What are some other Applications?

Science fiction has long been the favoured recreational reading genre for adolescent boys. Librarians and teachers could use a wide range of science fiction materials as teaching tools. From Mark Twain and H.G. Wells to Anne McCaffrey and Isaac Asimov, novels and short stories can provide the grist for discussion in such subjects as psychology, history, sociology, anthropology, and science. There are many movie and television versions of science fiction tales which can be used for reading motivation and for stimulating the imagination. Science fiction films can especially engage students and encourage greater enthusiasm and interest in science. Even a "fun" movie such as "Jurassic Park" can be used as a vehicle for science comprehension.

In addition, television networks such as PBS and CNN provide classroom guides for educational materials-PBS for their many documentaries and CNN to accompany their daily broadcasts. A look at CNN's Guide for October 1998 shows the following topics related to science: scientists find trace fossil; the evidence of billion-year-old worms; John Glenn's return to space sparks a renewed interest in Space Camp, and a NASA invention helps one young woman win her battle with cancer. These segments could be viewed in the classroom to spark discussion among students.

How can Films and Television Target and Motivate Writing?

Jeremiah outlines an instructional model for using television news and documentaries for writing instruction in the secondary and postsecondary classroom. He believes that the structure and content of news presentations mirror the practice of essay writing, and thus can serve as a writing project that effectively serves instruction. A step-by-step examination of a selected TV program can be undertaken in a single class period, using the following strategies: (1) as a warm-up mechanism, the teacher introduces the writing skill (for example, to inform or to persuade); (2) students are allowed time for questions and comments; (3) the news segment or documentary is shown; (4) students produce an outline for the news report they will write in response to the stimulus; and (5) the outlines are assessed for organization.

The outlines are collected at the end of the class period to minimize any external influences; and the students produce a full-length essay during the next class period, after their outlines have been returned. Another approach from Boyd and Robitaille suggests using the popular mass media to generate topics for a composition workshop designed for the college writer but adaptable for secondary-level writers. This approach concentrates on advertising images but also uses movies, monthly magazines, and television series to help foster critical thinking while writing. The workshop is built around a sequence of analogies between what the students already know experientially as film and television viewers and what they need to know as essay writers.

Moss uses the lowly, elemental daytime soap opera as a vehicle for teaching remedial writing in the SEEK program in New York City colleges. Utilizing a VCR and videotape so that everyone can watch the episode at the same time, Moss begins by asking the students to write on the most elementary level. The assignment is intended to tap into their passionate devotion to "the soaps"-which characters do they like the best, the least, and why? Then the class members discuss the acting and begin to impose critical criteria on the material. A short lesson on genres establishes appropriate aesthetic categories, and the students can begin to dissect the narrative in a composition.

CLOSED CAPTIONED TELEVISION FOR ADULT LITERACY LEARNERS

Closed captioning is the process by which audio portions of television programs are transcribed into written words that appear on the television screen at the same time as the program. Captions are similar to the subtitles used for foreign language films, but differ in that they can be received only through the use of an electronic decoder, or "black box." In addition, live programs, such as the evening news and sports events, can be simultaneously captioned. Closed captioning technology was originally devised for the benefit of the deaf, but there has been recent interest on the part of reading and literacy specialists in the use of closed captioned television (CCTV) with hearing audiences as well.

A wide variety of public and commercial television programs of potential use in reading instruction are closed captioned, including news, documentaries, dramas, movies, sitcoms, and advertisements. The major networks (ABC, CBS, NBC, PBS, and the Fox Television Network) offer more than 400 hours of captioned television per week. Almost 100 percent of all major network primetime programs are closed captioned, as are a large percentage of sports and children's programs. Thus, educators may choose from an abundant supply of programs of potential use with language learners of all ages and interests. According to guidelines approved by Congress in 1981, non-profit educational institutions are permitted to record and use television programs for instructional purposes so long as certain conditions are met:

— Only public and commercial programs may be used;
— Individual teachers (not media librarians or other support personnel) must initiate the recording;
— Recordings must carry the copyright notice;
— Recordings may be used for instructional purposes only;
— Recordings must be used within ten consecutive school days of the time the recording was made;
— Recordings may be shown only once within this ten-day period although the showing may be repeated once if required for instructional purposes;
— Parts of programs may be shown, but these may not be edited to produce anthologies; and
— Tapes must be erased within 45 days of the original recording.

Educational Uses of Closed Captioned Television

Educators have begun to investigate the use of CCTV as a language and literacy learning tool. Studies to investigate the potential uses of CCTV in teaching reading to members of the hearing community have been commissioned by organizations such as the National Captioning Institute (NCI) in Falls Church, VA, and the Caption Centre in Boston, MA. These studies have focused on students learning English as a second language (ESL), students in remedial reading programs, students who are learning disabled, and adults who are functionally illiterate. Probably the most widely used educational application of CCTV is with students learning English as a second language.

In many school districts, ESL students are taught in special classes until their test scores indicate their potential to succeed in the regular classroom. Educators are seeking innovative approaches that will enable ESL students to participate in mainstream content classes while continuing to develop their English language skills. Video technology provides just such an innovation. People of all ages and educational backgrounds seem to be attracted to television, and numerous captioned television programs and tapes can be used in conjunction with specific curriculum topics and objectives. For example, CCTV has been found to improve the sight vocabulary of adult literacy students, and to provide reinforcement for new vocabulary in the second language class by providing a context for its use.

CCTV has also been shown to facilitate listening comprehension and the acquisition of native-English speech patterns in ESL learners. Studies also report the motivating influence of captioned television, and extremely positive attitudes on the part of students toward this medium. The use of closed captioned primetime television programs with high school ESL students and students in remedial reading programs increased the students' motivation, and resulted in an improvement in their English vocabulary, reading comprehension, and word analysis skills. Other studies that cite the benefits of captioned programming and films for nonnative English speaking and remedial students are Maginnis; Parlato; Koskinen, Wilson, and Jensema; and Huffman.

CCTV for ESL Elementary Students

A study conducted with fourth- through sixth-grade ESL students in Prince George's County, MD, revealed a variety of potential benefits of CCTV:

— CCTV provides speech, writing, and supportive visual context simultaneously, making lessons accessible to students who use different types of learning strategies.

— Second language learners generally like CCTV and demonstrate a strong sense of achievement when they are able to comprehend the information presented through CCTV.

— CCTV can be used with heterogeneous groups of students. Less proficient students may be able to understand individual words from either the audio or visual track, while more proficient students may be able to process language from both tracks, perhaps even noticing discrepancies between the two, and thereby becoming more conscious of language use and form.

— Language use in CCTV classrooms is rich in terms of the variety of speech acts generated by the students. One observer noticed, for example, that students were eager to initiate questions and comments about the CCTV instruction.

Classroom teachers involved in the study identified a number of other advantages provided by CCTV, including the following:

— a variety of language and literacy activities;

— increased opportunity for students to read;

— visual reinforcement of word/image associations;

— a challenge to read quickly and to pick out key words;

— an opportunity for auditory discrimination through comparison of captions and audio;

— an opportunity to study the correspondence between spoken and written language;

— a means of checking or reinforcing listening comprehension; and

— novelty, which serves as a motivator.

Evidence of the effectiveness of CCTV instruction with the students included the following:

— increased oral participation on the part of the students;

— increased awareness of language as evidenced by requests for clarification; and

— the regular use by students of expressions learned from the videos, such as "Get out of here!" and "Happy landing!" from Sesame Street episodes.

Closed Captioned Television for Adult ESL Learners

A recent action research project conducted by Smith investigated how CCTV could be used to help teach ESL to adults enrolled at the Arlington County, VA, Refugee Education and Employment Program. This program serves students from all over the world who speak a wide variety of native languages. They provide a remarkably diverse laboratory for investigating the effects of any educational innovation focusing on adult learners of English. Smith found corroboration of many of the findings of the elementary school study discussed above. She found that students were immediately attracted to the CCTV technology. They paid rapt attention to the screen and worked hard to decipher the language. They spontaneously wrote down the unknown words they saw on the screen.

The captions enabled students to identify the written forms of familiar vocabulary, and reinforced the meaning in an audio and video format. Students often repeated phrases from the captions over and over to themselves while watching. On subsequent viewing of a program, they paid greater attention to the captions, anticipating the spoken text by saying the phrase aloud as soon as it appeared on the screen, even before it was spoken on the audio track. In addition, students used vocabulary from the program in follow-up discussions and written exercises. Smith hypothesized that seeing and hearing the words used repeatedly in the context of a coherent story with video cues made them appear more real—words students could actually use in everyday conversations.

Smith concluded that CCTV has great potential for teaching adult ESL students. Captioning transforms the seductive medium of television into a literacy and language learning tool and helps introduce newcomers to an important conveyor of culture and information. Smith warns, however, that care must be taken in identifying suitable programming. Students approach programs with varying degrees of linguistic proficiency and familiarity with the cultural contexts involved.

Identifying, Selecting, and Adapting CCTV Materials for use with Adult ESL Literacy Learners

Parks urges that teachers exercise care in the selection of CCTV programs for classroom use. Both suitability and familiarity of subject matter need to be considered, and the level of difficulty of both the captions and the audio must be taken into account. In developing exercises and lesson plans, Parks recommends that the teacher do the following:

- Prepare manageable tasks that match students' ability levels;
- Promote active and full participation of students;
- Control the length of the lesson to ensure maximum concentration and interest;
- Provide for student control of the presentation by giving students opportunities to operate the television and VCR; and
- Give students ample opportunities to review.

Koskinen, Wilson, and Jensema provide ideas for developing reading lessons using captioned materials with adults, with lesson outlines and sample lesson plans. Ideas for lesson plans are also provided by Parks and Parlato. The Caption Centre has developed CC Writer, for creating closed captions and subtitles, and CC Jr., which produces open captions using an ordinary videocassette recorder, an IBM PC, a standard word processor, and a specially-modified adapter. These products make it possible to develop tailor-made texts for video programs, matched to the specific proficiency levels and needs of particular groups of students.

VIOLENCE IN AUDIO-VISUAL MEDIA

Over the past 20 years there have been numerous studies and frequent warnings about violent television programs and movies arousing young people to act violently. Of course, other social factors can increase the likelihood of violence by youth: lack of interaction with parents, brutality in home life, exposure to violence in neighbourhoods, and easy access to guns. Nevertheless, researchers have pointed to many hours of viewing excessive violence as a potential contributor to violent behaviour by youngsters.

TV Shows, Movies and Video Games in American Households

Nearly 100 percent of households have television, and the total number of sets is increasing; 87 percent of households have two or more television sets. Over 60 percent of 12- to 17-year-olds have a television set in their bedroom. Cable TV is found in about 77 percent of American homes, greatly increasing the number of channels and programs available. Children readily learn the TV-viewing lifestyle from the adults around them. Within households viewing time may total up to 59 hours a week. In addition to extensive viewing of programs and movies on television, children at home have access to other on-screen entertainment, including video games and the Internet.

Stanger and Gridina found that 67 percent of homes with children had video game equipment. Slightly over 68 percent of homes with children have computers and 41 percent have access to the Internet. Boys are more than twice as likely than girls to play video games and are more likely than girls to use the Internet. While Internet use is increasing widely throughout society, television is still the main source of entertainment and news for the majority of Americans.

The Extent of Violence in Television Programs

Recent studies indicate extensive violence in television programs. The National Television Violence Study, for example, found that 57 percent of programs contained violence, usually numerous acts of violence in a single program. In approximately 75 percent of these programs, the violence seemed to be sanctioned, with no punishment of the perpetrators. Violence was depicted as humorous in more than a third of the programs. Only 4 percent of the violent programs offered a strong anti-violence message. Premium cable programs, often showing movies, had the highest percentage of violence.

A study of children's programs showed that they were 10 percent more violent than adult programs. For over three years, the UCLA Centre for Communications Policy conducted studies monitoring violent content of TV programs and other home media. The UCLA studies point to specific programs and video games in which persistent acts of violence are portrayed, including "The X-Files," the "Duke Nukem 3D" video game, and the kind of "sinister combat violence" found in Saturday morning programs for children. There has been some improvement in recent years, especially in the television networks. But youngsters are still seeing and hearing a great deal of violent behaviour during their usual viewing hours, and there is evidence that increasingly they are watching programs during later hours and seeing more graphic shows that combine sex and brutality.

Effects of Viewing Violence

Attraction to violent action is a cumulative effect of many hours and years of viewing violence on television and in movies by young people who have not developed critical resistance. According to the American Academy of Pediatrics, by age 18 the average adolescent will have viewed 200,000 acts of violence on television alone. Researchers observed that while a young viewer might see three to five violent acts in an hour of prime-time television viewing, Saturday morning cartoons contain 20 to 25 violent acts per hour. Pediatricians warn that media violence can be especially damaging to children under age 8 because they cannot readily tell the difference between real life and fantasy.

Analysis of research reveals that while viewing violence can have serious long-term effects, making some young people comfortable with physical aggression and even arousing them to violent action, it can make others increasingly fearful of being victims. The negative influences are related to (a) frequent viewing of excessive violence in movies, TV programs, cartoons, and video games; (b) lack of interaction with family members or peers who provide mediating influences; and the need for critical study of the media in education.

Instructional Responses

What can educators do in response to the adverse effects of violence in audio-visual media on children and adolescents? Staying informed about research on the topic is an obvious first step. Until recently, such research has been difficult for educators to obtain. Textbooks and training programs used in the education of social studies teachers are just beginning to include mass media literacy studies and the skills needed to build a critical defence against the effects of violence in the entertainment that is so pervasive in the lives of American children. Pioneering curriculum and instruction are needed to bring media awareness and media literacy into courses for both teachers and students. Law-related education and citizenship/civic education programs are strong promoters of critical thinking.

Therefore, lessons about media violence are well-suited to teacher training and classroom activities in these subjects. Because young people are already highly interested in TV viewing and video games, teachers readily can lead students into structured evaluation and critical thinking. Six types of instructional activities, including appropriate questions and resources, are recommended for teaching about violence in the media.

1. Review the First Amendment rights of freedom of expression and discuss laws that limit broadcasts during specific hours and that regulate distribution of video games in order to protect children.

2. Examine the rationale for the television program rating system, the V-Chip in new TV sets, and the feasibility of parental review and application of V-Chip technology.
3. Provide consumer education for home media consumption.
4. Conduct discussions and surveys involving the community to highlight the problem of violence in mass media and to generate practical solutions to the problem.

LITERACY INSTRUCTION THROUGH COMMUNICATIVE AND VISUAL ARTS.

According to Flood, Heath, and Lapp, visual arts includes everything from dramatic performances, comic books, to television viewing. The communicative arts, such as reading, writing, and speaking, exist as integrated elements in the visual arts. These authors argued that using visual arts in literacy instruction motivates students to become involved in the communicative arts. By taking visual arts away from the communicative arts in the classroom, schools would grow away from the fundamental skills that adults need to function in society.

Television and Multiple Media as Instructional Tools

Television viewing occupies a significant portion of students' lives. Starting from preschool, American children spend more time watching television than any other activity. Despite various negative effects associated with television viewing, several studies demonstrate that TV can be an effective tool in literacy instruction. For very young children, some studies suggest there is an overlap between children's pre-reading television viewing and their later reading skills. The results reveal that children who were good at comprehending materials presented via TV were also good at comprehending materials presented aurally. Research also showed that viewing educational television programs may be beneficial to young children's literacy learning.

The evaluation of the television series "Between the Lions" on Public Broadcasting Service (PBS) indicated that the kindergarteners who watched this series significantly outperformed their non-viewing peers on the tasks of word knowledge, concepts of print, phonemic awareness, and letter-sound knowledge. For older students, incorporating TV into reading instruction may motivate reluctant readers and result in improved reading fluency. Koskinen, Wilson, and Jensema used closed-captioned television programs with 35 second through sixth grade remedial readers in an exploratory study. The anecdotal evidence indicated that closed-captioned programs were effective in promoting the learners' reading fluency. In Goldman and Goldman's study, the audio portion of TV programs were turned off and the high school remedial students were motivated to read the captions in order to understand the story.

Two recent studies show that multimedia can also be an effective instructional tool in the language arts classroom. One fourth grade teacher used television/videos in conjunction with texts, using computers for information and writing, and other reading/writing instruction (e.g., book clubs) to engage students in a language arts unit. Students' reading comprehension and attention span increased, content knowledge was reinforced, and students had more aesthetic responses. Jester incorporated reading, writing, and grammar lessons with multimedia for a book report presentation in a sixth grade language arts classroom. The multimedia presentation helped students organize ideas more clearly, provided students with easier methods for revision and editing, allowed students to differentiate between words and ideas through the use of colour and fonts, and sustained students' attention longer than traditional media.

Using dramatic activities in Language Arts Classroom

Using dramatic activities as an instructional tool in the language arts classroom is based on the principle that drama directly involved the child, and an involved child would be interested in learning . The following studies document the effectiveness of incorporating dramatic activities into the language arts curriculum. McMaster reviewed research studies regarding the use of drama in literacy education and found that drama is an effective medium for literacy development in nine areas.

— First, students develop affect through drama. Drama creates motivation for students to participate and facilitates students' responses in reading instruction.

— Second, dramatization is a source of scaffolding for emergent readers by providing rich background experiences for future reading.

— Third, dramatization leads students to develop symbolic representation, which is the same concept children require in order to understand the alphabetic principle.

— Fourth, dramatic activities provide students a meaningful environment where they can practice oral reading repeatedly to develop fluency.

— Fifth, new vocabularies presented in the drama context provide students opportunities to acquire the meanings visually, aurally, and kinesthetically.

— Sixth, drama helps students acquire the knowledge of word order, phrasing, and punctuation that contribute to the meaning of a written sentence.

— Seventh, drama activities help students read different forms of discourse, especially in familiarizing children with nonfiction.

— Eighth, students monitor their own comprehension in drama and develop effective reading strategies.

— Ninth, teachers can use drama as an assessment tool since it provides immediate feedback about students' understanding of new reading materials.

For adolescents, dramatic activities provide meaningful contexts and motivation to practice literacy use. Worthman explored the writing done by a teen theater ensemble and showed that the aesthetic activities provided adolescents opportunities to see writing as a means for communication other than solitary practice. Ferree documented how two British secondary language arts teachers engaged students with literature by producing soap operas. During the production, teachers engaged students in various language usages, spelling and writing instruction. Students were motivated to participate because they had ownership over the product. Students also had opportunities to study realistic materials, use technology, learn actively, and to collaborate with peers in the production process.

10

COMPUTER

COMPUTERS IN DISTANCE EDUCATION

In recent years, educators have witnessed the rapid development of computer networks, dramatic improvements in the processing power of personal computers, and striking advances in magnetic storage technology. These developments have made the computer a dynamic force in distance education, providing a new and interactive means of overcoming time and distance to reach learners. Computer applications for distance education fall into four broad categories:

— *Computer Assisted Instruction (CAI)* - uses the computer as a self-contained teaching machine to present discrete lessons to achieve specific but limited educational objectives. There are several CAI modes, including: drill and practice, tutorial, simulations and games, and problem-solving.

— *Computer Managed Instruction (CMI)* - uses the computer's branching, storage, and retrieval capabilities to organize instruction and track student records and progress. The instruction need not be delivered via computer, although often CAI (the instructional component) is combined with CMI.

— *Computer Mediated Communication (CMC)* - describes computer applications that facilitate communication. Examples include electronic mail, computer conferencing, and electronic bulletin boards.

— *Computer-Based Multimedia* - HyperCard, hypermedia, and a still-developing generation of powerful, sophisticated, and flexible computing tools have gained the attention of distance educators in recent years. The goal of computer-based multimedia is to integrate various voice, video, and computer technologies into a single, easily accessible delivery system.

Advantages of Computers

— *Computers can facilitate self-paced learning.* In the CAI mode, for example, computers individualize learning, while giving immediate reinforcement and feedback.

— *Computers are a multimedia tool.* With integrated graphic, print, audio, and video capabilities, computers can effectively link various technologies. Interactive video and CD-ROM technologies can be incorporated into computer-based instructional units, lessons, and learning environments.

— *Computers are interactive.* Microcomputer systems incorporating various software packages are extremely flexible and maximize learner control.

— *Computer technology is rapidly advancing.* Innovations are constantly emerging, while related costs drop. By understanding their present needs and future technical requirements, the cost-conscious educator can effectively navigate the volatile computer hardware and software market.

— *Computers increase access.* Local, regional, and national networks link resources and individuals, wherever they might be. In fact, many institutions now offer complete undergraduate and graduate programs relying almost exclusively on computer-based resources.

Limitations of Computers

- — Computer networks are costly to develop. Although individual computers are relatively inexpensive and the computer hardware and software market is very competitive, it is still costly to develop instructional networks and purchase the system software to run them.
- — The technology is changing rapidly. Computer technology evolves so quickly that the distant educator focused solely on innovation "not meeting tangible needs" will constantly change equipment in an effort to keep pace with the "latest" technical advancements.
- — Widespread computer illiteracy still exists. While computers have been widely used since the 1960's, there are many who do not have access to computers or computer networks.
- — Students must be highly motivated and proficient in computer operation before they can successfully function in a computer-based distance learning environment.

THE INTERNET AND DISTANCE EDUCATION

The Internet is the largest, most powerful computer network in the world. It encompasses 1.3 million computers with Internet addresses that are used by up to 30 million people in more than fifty countries. As more and more colleges, universities, schools, companies, and private citizens connect to the Internet either through affiliations with regional not-for-profit networks or by subscribing to information services provided by for-profit companies, more possibilities are opened for distance educators to overcome time and distance to reach students.

With access to the Internet, distance educators and their students can use:

- — *Electronic mail (e-mail)* - Like postal mail, e-mail is used to exchange messages or other information with people. Instead of being delivered by the postal service to a postal address, e-mail is delivered by Internet software through a computer network to a computer address.

— *Bulletin boards* - Many bulletin boards can be accessed through the Internet. Two common public bulletin boards on the Internet are USENET and LISTSERV. USENET is a collection of thousands of topically organized newsgroups, covering everything from supercomputer design to bungee cord jumping, and ranging in distribution from the whole world to single institutions. LISTSERV also provides discussion forums on a variety of topics broken out by topic or area of special interest.

— *World-Wide Web (WWW)* -The WWW is an exciting and innovative front-end to the Internet. Officially WWW is described as a "...wide-area hypermedia information retrieval initiative aiming to give universal access to a large universe of documents". The WWW provides Internet users with a uniform and convenient means of accessing the wide variety of resources (pictures, text, data, sound, video) available on the Internet. Popular software interfaces, such as Mosaic and Netscape, facilitate navigation and use of the WWW. The central organizing feature of the WWW is the "home page". Every organization and even every individual user of the WWW can create a home page that contains whatever information they want to present. The hypertext capabilities of the WWW facilitate linking of information within your own home page and with all other home pages on the WWW.

Instructional Possibilities of the Internet

Distance educators can use the Internet and WWW to help students gain a basic understanding of how to navigate and take full advantage of the networked world into which they will be graduating. Some instructional possibilities of the Internet include:

— Using e-mail for informal one-to-one correspondence. Feedback from the instructor can be received more quickly than messages sent by mail. Students can read messages at their convenience and easily store them for later reference.

— Establishing a classroom bulletin board. Distant students often work in isolation without the assistance and support of fellow students. Setting up a class bulletin board can encourage student-to-student interaction. With a class computer conference, individual students can post their comments or questions to the class, and every other individual is free to respond. The conference can also be used to post all modifications to the class schedule or curriculum, assignments/tests, and answers to assignments/tests.

— Engaging students in dialogue with other students, faculty, and researchers by encouraging them to join a bulletin board(s) on topic(s) related to the class.

— Developing a classroom home page. The home page can cover information about the class including the syllabus, exercises, literature references, and the instructor's biography. The instructor can also provide links to information on the WWW that would be useful to students in the class (e.g., real research data on agricultural markets, global climate change, or space missions). Other links could access library catalogs or each student's individual home page.

Teaching Considerations

When incorporating the Internet into a distance delivered course, remember that:

— All students in a course must have Internet and WWW access to ensure equal opportunities for computer interaction and feedback. Also, convenient access to a computer at home or work may influence student success.

— Students may face the concurrent challenges of learning basic computer skills, new software, and appropriate online communication skills. Trouble-shooting student computer problems will probably become a part of normal instructional responsibilities. Setting up a specific classroom conference for ongoing discussions of specific hardware and software problems may help students to work through these problems on their own.

— Some students might hesitate to contribute to computer conferences or to send e-mail because of a lack of familiarity with the proper protocols. Encourage students to use e-mail, classroom conferences, electronic bulletin boards, and the WWW early in the course so they overcome inhibitions. Specifying a minimum number of e-mail communications per week will encourage active participation.

— Using e-mail can help the instructor provide feedback more quickly than surface mail or telephone. Prompt response generally increases student motivation and performance.

— Prompt responses might not always be appropriate. Computer conferences can foster student-to-student interaction. To ensure that this interaction is sustained, work towards a facilitative role. It might be appropriate to delay response to a query in a classroom conference in order to allow students to respond to the issue and to each other.

— Becoming familiar with the resources available on the Internet and the most effective ways to use them will be part of the instructional challenge. A number of helpful guides to the Internet and WWW are available.

DISTANCE EDUCATION AND THE WWW

The Internet is the world's largest, most powerful computer network connecting personal computers, sophisticated mainframes, and high speed supercomputers around the globe. Current estimates suggest that over four million computers are part of the Internet. Because a myriad of computers and programs are part of the Internet, incompatibility problems can result because information is created using different computers and software. In 1989, a group of scientists at the European Laboratory for Particle Physics (CERN) in Geneva, Switzerland began developing an Internet tool that would link information produced by all of the CERN researchers. The tool provided a way to link textual information on different computers and created by different scientists.

The object was to overcome issues of incompatibility and utilize a new way of linking made possible by computers, called "hypertext". Rather than presenting information in a linear or hierarchical fashion, hypertext permits information to be linked in a web-like structure. Nodes of information can be linked to other nodes of information in multiple ways. As a result, users can dynamically criss-cross the information web using pieces in the order most convenient to them. The CERN project resulted in an innovative front-end to the Internet, now referred to as the World-Wide Web (WWW).

The WWW provides users with a uniform and convenient means of accessing the vast resources of the Internet. In 1993, the National Centre for Supercomputing Applications (NCSA) at the University of Illinois pushed the CERN scientists' idea further by creating a software tool called Mosaic. Mosaic is an easy to use graphical user interface that permits text, graphics, sound and video to be hyperlinked. Mosaic was the first of the Internet tools that are now referred to as " Web browsers". Other well-known browsers include Netscape (the first commercial browser developed by some of the programmers involved with the Mosaic project) and Microsoft's Internet Explorer.

Web browsers permit users to connect to the Internet and facilitate accessing information located on another remote computer. The Web browser links to the remote computer just long enough so that the information you need can be sent to your computer for you to view. Documents created to be viewed by a browser are formatted using Hypertext Markup Language (HTML). HTML solves incompatibility problems by using standardized tags which indicate such things as whether a piece of text should be plain, bold, italic, or linked to another piece of text. Pages of information on a computer formatted with HTML and accessible to someone with a Web browser, are referred to as "home pages" or "Web pages".

The WWW and Web browsers have made the Internet a more user-friendly environment. The ability to integrate graphics, text, and sound into a single tool means that novice users do not have to struggle with such a steep learning curve. In addition, organizations and individuals can create home pages independently and link to other home pages on their own computers or to pages created by others on different computer systems. For educators, the WWW provides an exciting new opportunity for distance teaching and learning.

The WWW can be used by the distance educator to build a classroom home page. The home page can cover information about the class including the syllabus, exercises, literature references, and instructor's biography. The instructor can also provide links to information on the WWW that would be useful to students in the class (e.g., research data on agricultural markets, global climate change, or space missions). Other links can access library catalogs or each student's individual home page. In addition, the home page can link students to a discussion list or listserv that set up for student communication. It is also a relatively simple matter to use the homepage to create forms that students can fill out and that will end up being sent to you as an e-mail message.

Developing a Home Page for Distant Students

Distance educators who are ready to develop a web presence, should avoid the following pitfalls:

— Rushing in without a master plan. Don't get so caught up in learning HTML and developing the home page that the purpose for developing your presence on the WWW is lost. Spend less time struggling with HTML, developing amusing graphics or playing with possible background and more time considering the purpose and content of the home page. Before you start your home page:

- Think about your reason for developing a Web presence. Will your home page be a stand alone course or will you be using it in conjunction with other technologies such as video or audio? Sound instructional design principles apply to home pages just as with any other materials prepared for a course.
- Become familiar with new software tools for developing home pages. Computer software tools such as HotMetal and HotDog mean that anyone familiar with using word processing software can develop a good looking and functional home page. Reviews of other such computer software tools are available on the WWW and many of them can be downloaded for a free trial.
- Utilize information that already has been developed for your course. If you already have your notes and syllabi in word processed form, make use of tools such as HotDog to format them for distribution on the WWW.
- Look at what is already available. Hundreds of home pages have already been developed for courses. Some of these home pages allow students to complete an entire course from the WWW and others are developed in conjunction with lectures delivered on-campus or by video or audio.

— Laying out home pages poorly and inconsistently. To avoid ugly and confusing home pages, consider the following:

- Consulting sites on the WWW which provide information on home page layout and style. A popular site is the Web Style Manual.
- Utilizing a consistent format for each of your pages. Based on suggestions made by the above mentioned style manuals, develop a consistent format for each

web page. While coloured or patterned backgrounds can be used on homepages, plain grey or white backgrounds make text easier to read.

— Keeping page lengths short. Your main index should jump to a lot of shorter pages. In cases where page information is long, index internally so that the student can jump to specific information as needed.

— Maximizing links to internal information and minimizing links to external information. The purpose of your home page is to provide information on a specific subject area. Only provide external links to home pages that provide useful related information for your students.

— Using unnecessarily large graphics or including sound/video clips. Consider that while graphics can add appeal to a home page, a large number of Internet users are still accessing the Internet using a 14.4K modem. Graphic images which are 20K to 40K are acceptable for people with 14.4K modems. Pages which take too long to download frustrate students and may force them to beat a hasty retreat. If your home page requires extensive use of graphics to demonstrate points, warn your students. If you plan to use sound or video clips, you will need to be sure that all of your distant students have access to computers that have sound and video cards installed in them.

— Letting the home page become out-of-date. The home page should be an ongoing part of course development. Make sure that you add or change information as necessary. Periodically verify whether other home pages to which you are linking still exist.

What Should I Put on the Home Page?

The home page should help your students to find necessary course information, learn the material, and get involved in thinking about the course material . Properly designed home pages will encourage thought, discussion and active participation by your distant students. The following elements can be included in your class home page:

— Course & Instructor Information — Include such items as course topics to be covered, your office hours, textbook information, course objectives, and grading policies.

— Class Communication — Provide access to your e-mail, link to discussion groups that you have set up for student-to-student communication, and create forms that your students can use to report problems or provide biographical information about themselves.

— Assignments and Tests — Distribute assignments and tests, provide for online completion or submission, and give solutions, hints, or samples of what you expect.

— Material covered in the classroom — Make lecture notes and handouts available either as web pages or as downloadable files.

— Demonstrations, Animation, Video, Audio — This is more complex than other suggestions and will require that your students have access to computers with sound and video cards.

— Reference Material — List materials in print and electronic form that supplement the textbook. To avoid copyright problems, electronic articles should either be written by you or in the public domain (e.g., government documents or are already available on the WWW with author's permission to distribute). In addition, provide links to other pages which cover information on the topic, similar courses that may also be available on WWW, your university library, and other on-campus resources that may help your student complete the course.

MULTIMEDIA TEACHING STRATEGIES FOR THE OPEN CLASSROOM

As the number of learning resources to enhance the K to 12

curriculum increases each year, practising teachers are challenged to access effectively what they need for their classrooms. Incorporating computer-based multimedia technology into the school setting is the focus of a two- year project currently underway in St. John's. The project brings together Memorial University's Department of Computer Science and Bishop's College, a local high school. The goal is to develop a single, user-friendly multimedia interface and support materials which will be accessible to all teachers regardless of their curriculum area or technical skill level.

Multimedia computer systems combine sound, image and text in an interactive style to provide more effective communication. To truly utilize multimedia, teachers need the flexibility to arrange, modify and incorporate selected components of multimedia materials and technology into their instruction. Current multimedia materials present problems of accessibility and design. Remote locations present access difficulties in the education system of Newfoundland and Labrador. Funding for upgrading is usually insufficient.

The result is a reliance on machines of older design, which often makes the use of latest software or equipment impractical. Without guidance in adopting multimedia materials in the classroom, many teachers are unlikely to have the time to learn technical skills and prepare the necessary materials. Typically, they have to develop successful strategies for incorporating multimedia into their classroom environment, at the same time that they are discovering the capability of the technology. The design of existing multimedia material also causes problems. While teachers want to use the multimedia package most effectively in instruction, this is not always possible. Most multimedia material is pre-packaged as a complete presentation and cannot be modified by instructors to meet the needs of their students.

In addition, software requires specific technical skills that must be learned before the multimedia package is used. The software may restrict how the multimedia material is used. This multimedia project has five components. It began with researching and identifying the most successful and beneficial strategies for integrating multimedia tools into the classroom. The proponents have developed a guidebook for teachers in the uses of multimedia."Multimedia in the Classroom", contains teaching strategies, teaching aids, multimedia examples, and technical information. As a practical guide, it offers alternatives to conventional classroom materials by using multimedia resources in several ways. For example,

— as a source text to enhance textbooks, providing tutorial sessions, self-testing, review and remediation

— as a source for independent and group activity, replacing some of the conventional written essays and assignments. Students, for example, can work on their own multimedia productions.

— for multimedia demonstrations to enhance lectures by using visual and sound images

— for multimedia experiments in science

The guidebook will also provide prescriptive suggestions to help teachers choose the appropriate use, based on the objectives of the lesson and the needs of their students. It offers a step by step guide to multimedia strategies and identifies the resource requirements for each strategy, including the hardware and software needed, technical information on how to use them, the time required to use the resource and the skills required of teachers and students. Examples of the use of multimedia provide a general model for the teacher. The third component of the project is the development of a single, unified multimedia platform which enables technical information and multimedia materials to be shared among all users on both IBM and Apple applications.

The integrated multimedia platform is a software program or set of programs which provides a common system for all multimedia users. This was a challenge given the variety of multimedia products used in schools throughout the province.

Current programs needed to be evaluated and new software designed. Once the new multimedia platform is developed, teacher in-servicing will begin. Teacher training materials and pilot projects have been developed to explore the possibilities of on-site, remote, and self-instructional training sessions. Training materials include instructor- conducted sessions, multimedia instructional unit and a training institute. Finally, by the fall of 1996, a bank of multimedia materials will be available on a wide area network.

A central depository of multimedia materials will be available to the school community and will be comprised of several types of material, including raw sound, image and data files, collection of finished productions, information on other sources of multimedia material, a database system to assist in selecting material, and a collection of suggestions on using multimedia materials. Information on the use of the depository is included in the guidebook as part of the multimedia teaching strategies. The practical outcomes of this project over a two-year period will be to develop multimedia teaching strategies, create and evaluate multimedia resources, and provide teacher training in multimedia use. The products will simplify access to the wealth of resources available in multimedia format, and will encourage both teachers and students to make more frequent and productive use of those resources in the classroom.

The computer skills which will be developed under the training component are essential in the modern electronic workplace. The final products will be adaptable by teachers to suit their teaching environment and methods and the technology available to them. It is hoped that the techniques pioneered by this project can be adapted to allow for the delivery of courses through distance education using multimedia tools. Courses, once developed, can then be shared with other schools within the province.

MICROCOMPUTERS IN THE SCIENCE CLASSROOM

In considering current and potential uses of microcomputers,

Tamir examines three modes of microcomputer applications: tutorial, tool, and tutee. In the tutorial mode, drill and practice is the most common use, although the tutorial function may also appear in the form of remedial programs. Tamir also includes testing as a part of the tutorial function because it is such an integral part of the science curriculum. Homework tasks similar to those described under remediation and testing represent another form of tutorial use if the homework is systematically evaluated and feedback provided. The microcomputer as a tool can serve many management, administrative, and instructional functions. In calculations and statistical analysis, an important function of microcomputers is in performing time-consuming or complex calculations, especially in those cases involving relationships of two or more variables over time.

Microcomputers can also be used to perform standard statistical analyses such as frequency distributions, t-tests, Chi squares, regressions, analyses of variance and the like. Word processing is another important tool function of the microcomputer that represents a major time savings to both students and teacher. Not only can science reports be produced in less time, but reports generated with a word processor have been found to be better written as rated by independent raters in five categories: spelling and punctuation, organization and design, sentence structure, clarity, and overall quality. Drawing and graphics display capabilities involving the microcomputer as a sophisticated visual aid incorporating colour, animation, and sound still need much exploration. The potential for combining such graphic cues with other forms of instruction would seem to be promising.

Data accumulation and processing represent still other tool functions. The microcomputer can be used to collect, analyze and display data in the form of graphs and charts, showing relationships that change as the values of the variables change. The interactive capability of the microcomputer makes possible problem solving and decision making applications. In some programs students identify variables, define hypotheses, determine methods of measurement, treatments, procedures, and proposed techniques of data analyses. Data drawn from research can be stored in the computer's memory so that students can process and examine the data, test predictions, and draw conclusions. Simulations and games can allow the students to examine models and relationships of the real world under controlled conditions, to study variables which might otherwise be inaccessible. This capability of the microcomputer to provide models of scientific phenomena or systems has significant potential for science teaching.

The microcomputer as tutee is different in both kind and emphasis from the tutorial and tool functions. In the latter cases, the student uses the microcomputer as an aid to learning, with communication in the student's language. In the tutee function, the student "teaches" the microcomputer, using the computer's language. Perhaps a more important difference is in the nature of the task. In the tutorial and tool modes, the student is attempting to learn by using existing programs. In the tutee mode, the student attempts to clarify a problem in order to communicate it effectively to the computer. To be successful, then, requires that the student come to understand the problem that is to be "taught" to the computer. Much more work is needed on the effect and potential of this mode.

Effectiveness of Microcomputers

Some examples of recent research on the effectiveness of the microcomputer in the science classroom will be briefly summarized. The effects of alternative ways of using microcomputer simulations on the achievement and attitudes of sixth- and seventh-grade science students were studied by Shaw and Okey. Nine classes were randomly assigned to one of four treatments: (1) microcomputer simulations, (2) laboratory activities, (3) a combination of simulations and laboratory activities (simulations presented first), and (4) conventional instruction. Topics covered during lessons included the process skills of observing, hypothesizing, testing, classifying, and recording data. Results showed that laboratory activities, simulations, and a combination of these two strategies yielded higher achievement than did conventional instruction; there were no significant differences in achievement among the non-conventional treatment groups; and there was no attitude differences among the four groups.

It was also found that students at middle and high levels of logical reasoning outachieved students at the low level of logical reasoning ability. Hands-on activities and computer simulation methods in chemistry were examined by Bourque and Carlson to compare the cognitive effectiveness of a traditional hands-on laboratory exercise with a computer-simulated program on the same topic, and to determine if coupling these formats into a specific sequence would provide optimum student comprehension. Three laboratory experiments (acid-base titration, determination of the equilibration constant of a weak acid, and determination of Avogadro's number) were designed to correspond to three computer simulations. The data indicated that the hands-on activities produced higher scores for the acid-base titration and for the ionization constant, and no significant difference for the determination of Avogadro's number. The results further showed, however, that the highest cumulative scores were achieved for the format of hands-on experience followed by the computer simulation for the first two experiments, but there was no apparent advantage in sequence of performance for the derivation of Avogadro's number.

Mokros and Tinker reported on the impact of microcomputer-based labs (MBL) on children's ability to interpret graphs. In a longitudinal study, seventh- and eight-grade students worked with MBL units on illusions, heat and temperature, sound, and motion for a minimum of 20 class sessions. The data indicated that there was a significant change in students' ability to interpret and use graphs (an effect size of 81 percent). Brasell studied the effect of a very brief MBL treatment with a kinematics unit on high school physics students' ability to translate between a physical event and the graphic representation of it, and the effect of real-time graphing as opposed to delayed graphing of data. Overall posttest scores form the treatment in which the graphs were displayed in real-time were significantly higher than scores from all other treatment groups.

The evidence showed that a single class period was sufficient for high school physics students to improve their comprehension of distance and velocity graphs when compared with a paper-and-pencil control treatment. Most of the improvement (90 percent) was attributable to real-time graphing. A delay of only 20-30 seconds in displaying the graphed data inhibited nearly all the learning. Computer simulations used by high school biology students in attempts to enhance their problem solving skills were studied by Rivers and Vockell. The simulations were administered under two conditions: guided discovery, and unguided discovery; a control group received no simulations.

The results indicated that: (a) students using the simulations met the unit objectives at least as well as the control students, and (b) the students using the guided simulations surpassed the other students on subsequent simulation pretests, on tests of scientific thinking, and on a test of critical thinking. The evidence suggested that students using the computerized simulations were developing generalizable problem solving strategies which transferred to novel settings.

USING THE WORLD WIDE WEB WITH ADULT ESL LEARNERS.

Developed for the military and adopted by universities as a medium for research, the Internet—a network that links computers all over the world—is now used widely by businesses, educators, government staff, and individuals for information gathering, entertainment, commerce, and communication. Much has been written about the use of Internet technologies such as e-mail, listservs, bulletin boards, and newsgroups in English as a second language (ESL) and foreign language classroom. However, another feature of the Internet, the World Wide Web, is also an excellent source for authentic language learning experiences.

Skills Developed Through the World Wide web

Websites cover a wide variety of topics and interests including health, entertainment, news, and sports. These sites provide information with which learners can interact in order to build basic language and employability skills.

Language Skills

A number of websites were created especially for English learners and contain exercises in grammar, vocabulary, writing, or reading (e.g., Lingua Centre Grammar Safari <http://deil.lang.uiuc.edu/web.pages/grammarsafari.html>; Frizzy University Network (FUN) <http://thecity.sfsu.edu/~funweb/>; Weekly Idiom <http://www.comenius.com/idiom/index.html>; and Grammar Self Study Quizzes for ESL Students <http://www.aitech.ac.jp/~iteslj/quizzes/index.html>). Other ESL sites provide practice in listening (e.g., Randall's ESL Cyber Listening Lab <http://www.esl-lab.com>; and Dave's ESL Cafe <http.//www.eslcafe.com/>).

To develop reading skills, learners employ skimming and scanning skills to find the information they need. Hyperlinked menus—where readers click on highlighted words, phrases, or images and move to another section of the page or site—facilitate the use of these skills. Web reading includes both prose literacy (narrative) and document literacy (charts and graphs). Instructors can introduce learners to sites that may be relevant to course content and personal interests. Since most English language websites are written for English speakers, the language may be more appropriate for intermediate and advanced learners.

However, if instructors choose websites that include graphics and pre-teach the vocabulary, even learners with limited English can take advantage of the Web resources. Writing is a natural response to Web reading as learners respond to articles, request further information on topics, register complaints, and provide information about themselves. Websites prompt learners to complete forms, send e-mail messages to political representatives, request information on travel destinations, and write comments for bulletin boards and guest books. Engaging in these authentic tasks make writing meaningful. The large amount of information available on the Web requires learners to synthesize what they have read as they write reports and opinion pieces and make oral presentations.

Individuals can also create their own websites as a way to publish texts and projects. Studies have shown that computers can also facilitate oral communication between learners. Learners want to talk about their research and what they are learning. One study reported that communication occurred among students when they were using computers both individually or in groups. The Web also makes it possible to listen to news broadcasts, historical speeches, and films. These sound files can easily be replayed as needed for comprehension.

Employability Skills

Employability skills are the skills needed to find, get, and keep a job. The SCANS Commission (Secretary of Labour's Commission on Achieving Necessary Skills) names the following skills required for effective workplace performance—three foundational skills which include basic skills (reading, writing, speaking, listening, mathematics), thinking skills (creative thinking, reasoning, decision making, problem solving, representing information, learning how to learn), and personal qualities (individual responsibility, self-esteem, sociability, self-management), and five workplace competencies (use of resources, interpersonal skills, information, systems, and technology) for solid workplace performance.

Many of these skills are addressed in well designed Web-based lessons. For example, effective use of the Web requires skills in problem solving, as learners need strategies to sort through the flood of information. The analyzing and evaluating of information that learners must do to separate the wheat from the chaff is similar to what employees do at today's workplace as they gather information from remote sources. Projects that require learners to use the Web to gather information about specific topics (e.g., health insurance) provide practice in many SCANS workplace competencies. If learners can work in teams on these projects, they will have experience working cooperatively, solving problems as a team, and coming to a consensus.

Further, using the Web in the adult ESL classroom gives learners opportunities to "develop technology skills and experiences in contexts that are similar to those in which technology is used outside the classroom". Learners become familiar with technology as they use the mouse to point and click and navigate from screen to screen. Icons that were once unfamiliar now have meaning that will transfer to a variety of computer applications. As learners type information into online forms, they improve their keyboarding skills.

Preparing Learners for Searching the World Wide Web

Preparation can turn an overwhelming experience into a manageable one. Learners should be introduced to the use of the mouse, the browser, and the modem or Internet connection. A lesson in how to use icons and a mouse will make learners feel more comfortable as they approach the World Wide Web. If they have used computers before for word processing, they may already be familiar with many computing conventions. One of the greatest challenges of searching the World Wide Web is finding appropriate information.

A lesson on Web searching will give learners more control over the process. This lesson should include brainstorming keywords and concepts, adjusting these terms as needed, using search engines such as Yahoo, HotBot, and Alta Vista. Learners can keep logs to see which keywords yield the best results for particular searches. Because Web-based materials are not necessarily accurate or truthful, Web searching can also help learners develop their critical literacy skills. Learners can be taught to consider the source and question the veracity of what they read, a critical lesson in an age when tabloids and even legitimate news outlets print stories that are not completely true.

Guidelines and criteria for evaluating the accuracy and quality of the information at a given website can be found at Kathy Shrock's Guide for Educators (http://discoveryschool.com/schrockguide/) and in Cowles. Finally, learners should be prepared for the possibility that, because the Web is an uncensored medium, searching it can yield unwanted results. Sites containing pornographic photographs and videos may appear. If found, these sites can stimulate class discussions about freedom of speech, whether or not children should have unlimited access to the Web, and whether public libraries and schools should allow censorship.

Procedure for a Web-Based ESL Lesson

Web-based activities can include electronic field trips to museums and historical sites; comparison shopping online; and finding information about health, home buying, and travel. However, as with any language teaching tool, there must be clear objectives, focused activities, and evaluation. There are three essential steps for Web- based activities:

— Prepare learners for the activity. Ask learners to define a problem and then identify possible sites or sources that may contain information that will help them to explore that problem. Be sure that learners have familiarized themselves with the use of search engines. Brainstorm keywords to be used in the search. Be sure that learners know how to use the browser and hardware (such as a CD-ROM drive) or software (such as Sound Card) that might be needed for audio or video. Establish how learners will record the information. Will they print pages, make notes, or complete a survey form? How much information will be enough?

— Perform the activity online. Locate the sources and gather the relevant information from each source.

— Process the information. Ask learners to organize the information collected from multiple sources. They may present this information in an agreed upon format. Have learners evaluate the information gathered as well as the information gathering process.

The following is an example of a Web-based lesson adapted from Bogarde. Although written for K-12 learners, the lesson is also useful for adults, especially if the analysis and evaluation of both the product and the process is stressed.

Sample Lesson: Monitoring the Weather

— To prepare learners, review weather expressions (e. g., hot, cloudy, rainy). Teach or review the formula for converting Fahrenheit and Centigrade temperatures. Choose the cities that the class will monitor and locate them on the map. Decide whether to monitor the weather daily, weekly, or monthly. Ask learners to suggest some Web sources for weather or brainstorm some keywords for finding weather sites through a search engine. Decide what information will be tracked (e.g., temperature, precipitation, or other conditions). Record the information on a chart in the classroom; groups may choose to keep individual charts for different cities.

— To perform the activity online, have individuals or groups search for weather sites that contain information on the selected cities and record this information.

— To process the information, learners can organize the information they have gathered and make bar charts and graphs that illustrate the temperature or rainfall for each city. Ask learners to evaluate the various weather sites they used. Were some better than others? Why? Ask learners what part of the activity they would have changed. Was the process appropriate for their product?

COMPUTER USES IN SECONDARY SCIENCE EDUCATION

Computer use by any teacher is a function of his or her computer experience and expertise, availability of hardware and software, and perceived need. An excellent science course may be taught without the use of a computer. However, the careful incorporation of computers into a science course can and does add an important level of enhancement. Although not as conclusive as one might hope, studies do indicate that computer use in science education can improve learning and positively influence students' attitudes and self-esteem.

The importance of using computers in a science class may not be limited to the ability of computer assisted instruction (CAI) to improve learning. Rather, computer use adds another dimension to the teacher's repertoire of strategies, which may improve overall learning. Another important reason to include student computer use in a science course is that most (if not all) students, especially those planning a career in science, will be required to be computer literate. As students interact with computers in a variety of ways within their science courses, their degree of computer awareness and literacy will increase. The following studies found positive effects associated with microcomputer use in science education applications:

— Higher achievement and more positive attitudes were observed in a high school biology course that was "computer-loaded".

— Scientific reasoning skills were found to be enhanced using a microcomputer-based curriculum.

— Specialized computer programs were found to help develop inquiry skills while also increasing scientific knowledge even when strong "misconceptions" were present at the start.

More than one study found that computer use by students enhanced their self-esteem. This may also account, in part or in whole, for the increased interest in science by lower achieving students who have computers incorporated into their curriculum. Whatever the reason, the effect is positive and adds another reason to use computers in the classroom. Some studies, however, find CAI to be of limited value in science applications, especially when the control group is given equivalent non-computer support. For example, a study by Wainwright showed that a control group using worksheets scored significantly higher than did an experimental group using CAI.

Wainwright suggests that paper and pencil worksheets allowed the students to more easily experiment with trial and error in balancing chemical equations. A major problem in evaluating the results of studies designed to measure the value of CAI is the elusive factor of the quality of the software used in the study. Not only should the software be well designed, but there also must be a match between the objectives of the software (or courseware), the understanding of the teacher as to how to apply it, and the needs or interests of the students.

How Science Teachers are Using Computer

Most teachers are willing to incorporate computers into their curricula when the obstacles are not overwhelming. The desired uses, however, include more than CAI. In fact, a relatively small number of science teachers use computers for CAI and lab applications because there isn't enough hardware and because lab applications require both specialized hardware and software. A study of secondary science teacher needs revealed that, of the nearly 800 respondents, 70% wished to know more about using computers to deliver science instruction, 64% to manage instruction, and 60% to use a test item data bank. The most widely used application appears to be wordprocessing. Test and worksheet production takes the lead in this area, and customized laboratory activities are produced as well.

Many science teachers employ spreadsheet or customized or commercial grade book programs to record, calculate, and post student grades. Using test item banks to sort and select questions is becoming more popular as software and banks become more available. Finally, a small number of teachers are using computers to produce items such as crossword puzzles, word searches, posters, signs, and diagrams to support instructional activities. A small but increasing number of science teachers are using computers as a component in selected laboratory activities. Microcomputer-based laboratories (MBLs) employ computers interfaced with commercial or "home-built" transducers.

Using the appropriate software allows the computers to measure, record, graph, and analyze a variety of physical quantities: temperature, light, pH, pressure, and electrical and magnetic parameters, to list the most common. Some teachers create their own programs, in a computer language such as BASIC, that allow both students and teachers to evaluate the accuracy of laboratory data and/or calculations. On the cutting edge of classroom computer applications, interactive videodisks are making their way into many science classrooms. To date, the most popular subject areas have been biology and earth science, and interactive video programs with related courseware have recently been produced for physics and chemistry. A physical science curriculum project in Texas purports to have had significant success with a videodisk-based program.

The report states that even though the effects of using this curriculum varied considerably by teacher and other factors, the overall results were positive, with the greatest achievement gains being for "low-ability" students . Finally, students are increasingly being introduced to computer database searching at school. Many high schools subscribe to databases on CD

ROM (compact disk, read-only memory). In addition, modems are used to access university and government databases at remote locations. Such databases range from libraries' online catalogs to scientific data being gathered from spacecraft and satellites.

Constraints to Classroom Computer Use

By far the major factor inhibiting computer use in the classroom is the insufficient amount of computer hardware and software available due to budgetary constraints. It often takes a science department three to six years to obtain even the minimum number of computers necessary for one teacher to effectively incorporate CAI and MBLs into the curriculum. Although just one or two computers can be incorporated into classroom activities, this number will support a very limited number of strategies. Moving computers in and out of a classroom is time consuming and significantly inhibits their use. Moving students to a "computer lab" also has several constraints, the two major ones being that the typical computer lab is too small and that teachers must compete for limited lab time.

The Ideal Computer Environment

An ideal computer learning environment, possible with current technology, might be an arrangement where each student has access to a "friendly" computer station consisting of high quality computer managed instruction (CMI), touch screen colour displays and interactive video. At such a station each student could proceed at his or her own rate. Motivated students of the very highest ability might learn at three to four times the average classroom rate, completing two or three high school science courses a year. Students who seem to learn more slowly could be given extra months to complete a course without failure. The "average" student might elect to proceed at a pace equivalent to the conventional course.

An important feature of the CMI would be the learner's ability to choose whether to proceed or to review when attempting to master course objectives. Research has shown that learning increases when the learner has some control over the CAI program. In addition, students would be encouraged to repeat for themselves demonstrations observed on the interactive videodisk. And, regardless of the degree of computer involvement, there must also be a substantial hands-on laboratory component integrated into each science course. MBLs would also play a major role in the labs of the future.

Students in the ideal computer environment would also be encouraged (or required) to participate in cooperative activities as part of the complete science course, perhaps in the form of problem solving activities that would not require that all students in a group be at the same level of instruction. Indeed, it might be very beneficial to create cooperative problem solving groups composed of students currently studying topics in different areas (i.e. earth science, biology, chemistry, and physics), or at differing levels of an integrated science curriculum. The role of the teacher in a room of 24 such individual stations would be to discuss questions and concerns brought to them by the students, as well as coordinate and oversee laboratory activities. The role of the science teacher would be dramatically different, yet just as valuable and rewarding as it is now. The teacher's job might become even more rewarding as ideal learning conditions replace the disadvantages of group instruction and more time becomes available for meaningful student contact

COMPUTER-ASSISTED WRITING INSTRUCTION

Anyone who has learned a word-processing program and uses it regularly on a computer at work or home might be disappointed with reports to date on the impact of the computer on student writing. Features of word processing which allow a writer to revise quickly produced hard-copy drafts should, it seems, effectively serve writing instruction; but until the time students have enough access to computer work-stations to practice and become comfortable with word processing while they are learning to process written language, it is probably too early to judge how effective the computer will become in improving student writing. Computers are becoming more common in schools.

In 1983, Withey predicted that the computer "may have a firmer hold on the future than do English teachers." That same year, a survey estimated that there were over 200,000 microcomputers in U.S. elementary and secondary schools; and it predicted a 60-percent annual growth rate for the following years. That would suggest that well over two million computers are now accessible to elementary and secondary students and teachers; and in the light of initiatives launched by Federal agencies and some states to develop computer-assisted instruction, that figure may be conservative.

How Much Time on Task?

The presence of computers in regular classrooms may not guarantee that students will have ample opportunity to use them. A Canadian study of 90 teachers and 180 elementary students in three grades placed computers in regular classrooms. Each teacher worked with one student learning to write on the computer and with one writing in longhand. Students who logged the most hours on a computer averaged about 60 hours over six months. Several of the reports in the database indicate that many students learning to write with computers are lucky to get 30 minutes experience a week. Whether the atypically larger amount of time and experience the students in the Canadian study had with the computers was sufficient to allow them to become very proficient word processors is not clear.

Why Don't Computers Encourage Revision?

Limited time-on-task may explain why so many of the reports in the database fail to mention the benefits of computer-assisted instruction in encouraging revisions and why several reports specify that the students did not get opportunities to print and see their efforts in hard copy. Such applications provide no opportunity to evaluate the feature of computer writing that recommends itself to many practiced writers: the almost immediate opportunity to see and react to what one has written and then to make changes which can be quickly reprinted. Yet the studies which have focused particularly on revision do not support the notion that writing on computers should encourage a student to revise.

Daiute found no difference either in quality or quantity of revision for junior high students writing with and without computers. In another study, Daiute found that students writing on computers revised less than those using pens and pencils. The computer writers, however, got higher scores on their finished products after getting lower scores on their first drafts, suggesting that computers may have led to more effective revision. Nor did the college students in Hawisher's study revise more than those not using computers; but, interestingly, this study found no positive relationship between revisions and quality of writing.

For younger children, there are several simplified word-processing programs available, but even with these, it appears that students who are being taught to write on computers do not get enough time-on-task to become comfortable with simple word-processing features like "insert" and "delete" or to use them freely in making revisions—let alone enough time to learn to "block" text, move it for reorganization, and then print and analyze the results for subsequent revision. A recent guide from Phi Delta Kappa outlines the teaching of writing with the microcomputer as a seven-year procedure. Although students in classes following this process are learning simple revision commands in the second grade, the program sensibly reflects the fact that it takes a reasonable amount of time for students to learn word processing.

Dickinson found that when collaborating on a writing project at a computer, first-grade children developed language skills while planning and evaluating their project. Heap reported on a program that teamed a writer with a peer as "writing helper"—a kind of in-process editor—and another classmate as a "technical helper" to advise and discuss solutions to word-processing problems. Piper, Smutek, and Heap each found the computer effective in assisting teamed writing instruction for students learning English as a second language.

Is Word Processing the Only Approach?

Also in the database are reports on the use of computer software which assumes a strong instructional and interactive tutorial role. Most of these programs guide the student writer through the identification of topic, the brainstorming and then organizing of jot notes on the topic, and the application of the resulting outline to produce a written document. Strickland conducted a case study using such a program and found it effective. Styne reported on how a computer program that guides students as they compose poetry generated enthusiasm among college freshmen. Some teachers of writing at higher levels involve students in the development of their own software programs to guide their writing.

Walton and Balestri discuss studies that link instruction in computer programming and college freshmen composition which they feel help students understand writing as a design discipline. Bruce cites such approaches as the precursors of the computer's potential in facilitating thinking, creativity, and language development. In addition to computer software which guides a writer through the formation of his or her own ideas, there are, of course, programs of preformatted exercises that many teachers consider important to writing instruction. Smith discussed "a plethora of skills and drills software" that often lacks quality because it is not theoretically based. Such programs present, in effect, a kind of electronic workbook, which may have the potential to hold student interest through programmed practice but which may not relate to the process of writing.

When Can We Know?

The computer's great promise to writers who know how to compose on one is its facilitation of revision. As Withey described it, the computer can be "a blank page on which the student can write, revise, and edit...." What the writer who uses a particular word-processing program needs to keep in mind, however, is how long it took him or her to become comfortable with the new tool. What kind of familiarity with both the keyboard and the written word did the writer have before sitting down to learn word processing? How many hours of writing in front of a computer monitor did it take before the writer learned how to use the features o the program comfortably? When did focus on the computer software stop competing with getting the best words in the most effective order? After how many hours did word processing first begin to serve effective composition?

The ratio of computer stations to students may have to provide more time-on-task before we can adequately evaluate the computer as a tool for writing instruction. That kind of access, it seems reasonable to point out, is going to involve considerable investment in expensive hardware that has an annoying way of becoming obsolete; it also means that teachers interested in using the technology need to be trained to use it productively. With those factors in place, writing instruction will—as has always been the case—rely on the enthusiasm, abilities, and effective methodologies of good teachers.

The teachers and other researchers who are now experimenting with computer-assisted instruction are building an important database that will be analyzed for guidance in developing effective methodologies. The computer is a technology that will almost certainly become more and more accessible in the lives of students, including the young writers involved in the studies reported to date. Many of these students will be writing regularly using computers. Whatever the limits of the experience they got using computers, it can become a valuable one.

GUIDELINES FOR COMPUTER-ASSISTED READING INSTRUCTION

Discussions concerning computer use in education have rapidly passed through a number of phases. The first phase centered on the need for "computer literacy," generally defined as computer awareness and computer programming. At the height of the computer literacy debate, emphasis shifted to the role of the computer as a tool, and as a method for teaching problem solving. Most recently, attention among educators has turned to yet a third phase. This third phase addresses issues related to computer applications in support of the curriculum.

Research studies indicate clearly that computer instruction is effective for a wide variety of reading skill and concept areas. The level of popularity of computer-based instruction in reading may vary, but few will dispute the fact that computers have won a permanent place in most classrooms. The most common concerns of educators now have to do with the effectiveness of computer-based education, and with the appropriateness of the many possible roles computers can play in language arts instruction. The emphasis should not be on using computers to increase reading and writing achievement, but rather on whether teachers use computers for meaningful reading and writing instruction, or are locked into computer-based drill and practice software.

The following guidelines may also be used as a checklist to help teachers of the language arts match their use of computers with what is known about the reading/writing process. We hope that the checklist will be used in a context where students are given opportunities to work in all the various computer modes: tool, tutor, and tutee.

Guidelines for Computers and Reading

1. Computer instruction in reading should focus on meaning and stress reading comprehension.

   — Learners should have opportunities to work with whole, meaningful texts. Programs that offer learners a chance to process large chunks of related text, rather than bits and pieces of unrelated language fragments, allow students to use and extend what they know about reading comprehension.

   — Learners should have opportunities to work with word-recognition programs that stress the use of word meanings in conjunction with phonics and structural analysis. Care must be taken to make sure that, when programs feature the study of individual words and phrases, they are offered within a contextual framework that help them make sense to the learner. Assessment programs for teachers should also be provided in meaningful context.

   — Learners should have the opportunities to apply the skills being taught in some meaningful way. Programs that deny the learner an opportunity to make use of what is being "taught" are merely assessment tools and do little to further the learner's growth.

   — Learners should have the opportunity to work with computer materials that use content and language that are within the range of their conceptual development. Tasks should be challenging but not frustrating. Student interests, previous experiences, and purpose play a role in determining whether or not a computer task is comprehensible and worthwhile.

2. Computer instruction in reading should foster active involvement and stimulate thinking.

— Learners should have opportunities to discuss the purpose of the computer task or program as well as its nature. They should be aware not only of what they are supposed to do but also of why doing it is important.

— Learners should have opportunities to make decisions that control or influence the computer task. Programs that build in opportunities for students to make choices and test predictions help them learn to think and act on their own rather than merely react to someone else's thinking.

— Learners should have opportunities to monitor their own learning. Tasks that offer students opportunities to self-check and correct their own errors support the development of independent learners.

3. Computer instruction in reading should support and extend students' knowledge of text structures.

— Learners should have opportunities to encounter a wide variety of text structures upon which to apply and refine their comprehension skill. A variety of narrative and expository structures should be provided. Commercially prepared, teacher-authored, and student-authored materials should also be included. Reading instruction can take place through all kinds of computer-based materials, not merely those designated specifically for that purpose.

— Learners should have opportunities to experiment with text in creative ways to suit their purposes. When students reorganize a story or an informational piece on the computer, they are employing and strengthening what they know about the structure of texts.

4. Computer instruction in reading should make use of content from a wide range of subject areas.

— Learners should have opportunities to use the computer as a means of applying reading strategies to all areas of the curriculum. Programs related to science, social studies, and math require the use of strategies for reading comprehension.

Unless students are being helped to use what they know about reading comprehension under these circumstances, they are not progressing as competent readers.

— Learners should have opportunities to use the computer in conjunction with other modes of instruction. The computer should not operate as a separate and isolated means of learning. Its use should be integrated with that of books and other learning materials. Students need to think of the computer as one additional means of sharing and retrieving information and practicing skills in interesting and meaningful ways.

5. Computer instruction in reading should link reading and writing.

— Learners should have opportunities to create text with the computer for sharing and use by others. When students enter information into the computer for someone else to retrieve and use, they must compose with the reader in mind. This frequently involves making explicit use of what they know about what makes a text comprehensible. Revision and proofreading strategies clearly involve the combined application or reading and writing skills.

11

Skills Related to Electronic and Non-electronic Media

MEDIA LITERACY

Children spend the majority of their days consuming mass media. On average, children spend four-and-a-half hours a day using television, video games and computers. Yet children are not provided with the tools needed to evaluate and analyze the media messages they see. Teachers have the ability to engage students in media literacy — the ability to access, evaluate, analyze and produce both electronic and print media — by dissecting pop culture and advertisements. Media literacy education can help students build critical thinking and analytic skills, become more discriminating in the use of mass media, distinguish between reality and fantasy, and consider whether media values are their values.

> Media literacy empowers people to be both critical thinkers and creative producers of an increasingly wide range of messages using image, language and sound. It is the skillful application of literacy skills to media and technology messages. As communication technologies transform society, they impact our understanding of ourselves, our communities and our diverse cultures, making media literacy an essential life skill for the 21st Century.

Media literacy goes beyond the idea of reading and writing. It requires media consumers to effectively analyze and evaluate the numerous media messages we encounter. Media education can facilitate students' reflections on their media experiences and help them develop critical thinking skills.

Tips for Using the Teacher's Guides

— Television is a compelling medium. When showing program or commercial clips to students, keep the segments very short — one or two minutes — so that students stay with the task at hand. Tell students that they will be seeing only short clips, and play with the media to keep attention from wandering.

— To concentrate on images, turn off the sound.

— To concentrate on sound, put a towel over the screen. Use the "pause" button on the remote and the "closed-captioning" function.

— Throughout many of the guides, there are suggested open-ended questions to encourage students to think cortically and problem solve. Provide students with information and allow them to build the skills to interpret these messages for themselves.

— Keep in mind that people understand and interpret media messages differently. Students may gather different messages than you or other students. There is not necessarily a "right" way to interpret a given message, as we all filter messages through our own lenses

BASIC COMPUTER SKILLS FOR TEACHERS

Turning Your Computer Off and On

Yes ... you turn the power on to start and off to stop. (You are now an expert. Pick up your certificate at the door.) Well, don't turn the page just yet because there's more!

On

Almost all computers are made with a power switch in the front. However, some older machines may have a switch on the back of the box. Normally, after you turn the computer on, it will "boot up" (or load the startup software and the operating system) and bring you to the computer's desktop (a place where you can access the computer's services).

Exceptions:

1) If the computer wasn't shut down properly, it will probably run a program to scan the hard drive for errors and try to fix them if found. (Windows users: If the computer prompts you to fix a problem, allow it to do so and choose "Skip Undo" if it becomes an option.) (MacIntosh users: You won't have to do anything except click "Done" or "Ok" to continue.)

2) If the computer prompts you to enter a password, do so if you know it and click "Ok". If there isn't supposed to be a password, click "Ok" to go on (hopefully). If that doesn't work, you will need to find out what the password is. NOTE: If you click "Cancel", you will go on but you'll lose most, if not all, of your network functions (possibly the internet).

Off

When you have quit your programs and are ready to shut down the computer, click on the proper sequence (below) for your machine.

Windows: Start > Shut Down > Shut down the computer? > Yes

Macintosh: Special > Shut Down

Your computer may display an extra screen, but will ultimately do one of two things:

1) Turn itself off (including the power) You'll need to turn off any devices that need to be turned off (printers, monitors, speakers, etc.) and you should be done.

2) Display a screen saying it's ok to turn the power off (or shut down). Go ahead and turn the power off. You'll need to turn any devices off that need it (printers, monitors, speakers, etc.) and you should be done.

Starting and Ending Programs

Starting the Program

If you can't find an icon on the desktop to double-click on, try these steps:

— Macintosh:

  — Double-click on the "Macintosh HD" (or whatever the hard drive is labeled)

  — Double-click on the folder that contains the program. Look for a folder with a name similar to what you want to start.

  — Double-click on the icon that starts the program (probably a similar name).

  — From here, just run the program as per its instructions

— Windows:

  — Click on the "Start" button

  — Click on "Programs"

  — Click on the folder that contains the program. Look for a folder with a name similar to what you just installed.

  — Click on the program name

  — From here, just run the program as per its instructions

Starting an MS-DOS Program: Click on "Start" and then "Run". In the window you'll have to type the proper command path to start the program. It will probably be something like C:\blaster\math.exe but you really should refer to the program's instructions or someone who is familiar with the program to help you.)

Ending the Program

Make sure you save your work (if necessary). Click on "File" then "Exit" (or "Quit"). That's the standard way. Now for a few exceptions:

— Mac/Win—There are the occasional programs that will exit if you hit the escape key (Esc).

— Windows users can click on the "X" box in the far upper right-hand corner of the program window to exit.

— Macintosh users often click on the upper left hand box to close a window but forget that the program is still running. Use "File" and Quit" to shut the program down.

Shortcuts

— Windows—Holding "Alt" while pressing "F4" is the same as "File" and "Exit".

— Macintosh—Holding "Open Apple" while pressing "Q" is the same as "File" and "Quit"

Memory Trap!!!

— If you minimize a program (Windows) or hide a program (Mac), the program is still running and is still using RAM (Random Access Memory). Make sure you exit/quit programs when you're done

Finding Programs and Files

Possibly the hardest thing to do on a computer is to keep the files you create, load, or save organized. You work hard something and then can't open it up to work on it, or print it, because it's not in the folder you expect it to be.

Navigating through folders works if you have an idea of where you are going. Sometimes you just need a little help finding files. Both Macintosh and Windows machines have a "find" type of program which work in the same manner: type the name of the file, (if the "find" program finds the file) double-click on it to activate it.

Windows: Click on "Start", then "Find", then "Files or Folders". Type the file name and click on "Find Now".

Macintosh: Click on "File", then "Find". Type the file name and click on "Find".

Macintosh 8.0 and above users have "Sherlock" which opens when you click on "File" and "Find". Sherlock will search for files and programs on your computer AND search for sites on the Internet using many of the popular search engines available.

Saving Files

When you start working on a file, save it on the hard drive right away and then continue to save your work every 10-15 minutes. To save a file, click on "File" and "Save". If it is the first time to save the file, you will see a window which will let you choose which folder to save in and what file name to choose. Then click on "Save" to complete the process. As you continue to work, click on "File" and "Save". This will update you work. If you want to save the file into another folder, click on "File" and "Save As". This will to open a window and allow you to save to a different folder or even another computer.

Opening Files

Opening up a file is similar to saving files. After you start the program, click on "File" and "Open". A dialogue box appears that will let you find the folder and then the file you need. Click "Open" to see your saved work. Another way to open a file is to double-click on the file from within your hard drive.

Windows: From the desktop, double-click on "My Computer", then double-click on your hard drive (probably drive C or D), then keep double-clicking on the appropriate folders until you find your file (i.e. "My Computer" > "Drive C" > "My Documents" > "Sampletest.doc"). By double-clicking on the file, you'll automatically start the program that created it.

Macintosh: From the desktop, double-click on "Macintosh HD" (or equivalent), then keep double-clicking on the appropriate folders until you find your file (i.e. "Macintosh HD" > "Applications" > "Microsoft Office" > "Sampletest.doc"). By double-clicking on the file, you'll automatically start the program that created it.

Deleting Files

You cannot do this from within a program. You must be at the desktop to delete files. Deleting files is almost identical to opening files except for the last step.

Windows: From the desktop, double-click on "My Computer", then double-click on your hard drive (probably drive C or D), then keep double-clicking on the appropriate folders until you find your file (i.e. "My Computer" > "Drive C" > "My Documents" > "Sampletest.doc"). Then click on "File" and "Delete" then "Yes" or click and drag the file to the recycle bin or right-click on the file and then click on "Delete" and "Yes" (shortcut).

Macintosh: From the desktop, double-click on "Macintosh HD" (or equivalent), then keep double-clicking on the appropriate folders until you find your file (i.e. "Macintosh HD" > "Applications" > "Microsoft Office" > "Sampletest.doc"). Then click on "File" and "Move to Trash" or click and drag the file to the "Trash" or click on the file and hold down the "Open Apple" key and press "Delete" (this is the shortcut).

Remember to empty the trash (or recycle bin). The files won't be permanently deleted until you do so.

Installing Software

There are 3 ways to install and use software:

1. You don't install—just run the program from the CD (rare)
2. You install the software and never need the disks or CD to run the program
3. You install a portion of the program and need the CD in the machine to use the program

You often don't know which type it is ... you just have to put the CD in the machine and find out what kind of program it is.

Method #1. You don't install ... just run the program from the CD

— Open CD tray

— Insert CD label side up and close tray

— For Macintosh:

  — Most CDs will open automatically. If it doesn't, double click on the CD icon that appears on the desktop—I'm using a CD called "Aesop's Fables".

  — If there isn't an installer icon in the window that appears then double-click on the icon that starts the program.

  — From here, just run the program as per its instructions

— For Windows 95/98:

  — Double-click on the "My Computer" icon on the desktop.

  — Double-click on the CD icon that appears in the My Computer window.

  — If there isn't an installer or setup icon in the window that appears then double-click on the icon that starts the program.

  — From here, just run the program as per its instructions

Method #2. You install the software and never need the disks or CD to run the program

— For both Macintosh and Windows, follow the same instructions for method #1 all the way up to starting the program. This time you're looking for and double-clicking on an icon that's labeled "Start Here", "Installer", "Setup", or something like that.

— Follow the installer's instructions. You usually just accept all of the defaults that the installer gives you. This means you may be clicking on "Next" or "Ok" or "Install" a lot of times.

— Once the installer is done, you may have to restart the machine ... go ahead and let the machine restart. Remove the disk or CD.

— To run the program,

— Macintosh:

  — Double-click on the "Macintosh HD" (or whatever the hard drive is labeled)

  — Double-click on the folder that was just installed. Look for a folder with a name similar to what you just installed.

  - Double-click on the icon that starts the program (probably a similar name).
  - From here, just run the program as per its instructions
- Windows:
  - Click on the "Start" button
  - Click on "Programs"
  - Click on the folder that created for your program. Look for a folder with a name similar to what you just installed.
  - Click on the program name
  - From here, just run the program as per its instructions

Method #3. You install a portion of the program and need the CD in the machine to use the program

This method is identical to Method #2. The only difference is that in order to run the program, you have to have the CD in the machine. If you don't, you'll receive an error message saying something like "Please insert CD into drive". What happens with method #3 is that you are installing just the program but you still need the CD in the machine to access all the data the program uses.

Creating an Alias (Mac) or Shortcut (Win) on Your Desktop

An alias (Mac) or shortcut (Win) is an icon that, if clicked on, will start a program or file that is located somewhere else on your hard drive or even on another computer on the network. This type of icon on your desktop (or folder on your desktop) is advantageous because if you or your students throw it into the trash (or recycle bin) then your program is still intact ... only the shortcut was eliminated. Here's how to create an alias (Mac) or shortcut (Win) on your desktop:

Windows: From the desktop, double-click on "My Computer", then double-click on your hard drive (probably drive C or D), then keep double-clicking on the appropriate folders until you find the file you want to create the shortcut of (i.e. "My Computer" > "Drive C" > "Windows" > "Pbrush"). Single-click on the file. Click on "File", then "Create Shortcut". (Or right-click on the file and click on "Create Shortcut".) Click and drag the icon onto your desktop.

Macintosh: From the desktop, double-click on "Macintosh HD" (or equivalent), then keep double-clicking on the appropriate folders until you find the file you want to create an alias of (i.e. "Macintosh HD" > "Applications" > "Microsoft Office" > "Word"). Single click on the file. Click on "File", then "Make Alias". (Or click on the file and then hold down the "Open Apple" key while you press the "M" key.) Click and drag the icon onto your desktop.

That's it. Close your windows and double-click on the alias (Mac) or shortcut (Win) to start the file.

Trouble-shooting

If you can perform some basic troubleshooting before you call your tech coordinator or the Help Desk @ 830-8080, then 1 of 2 things may happen: 1) you fix it yourself, or 2) you'll help the technicians be better prepared when they come to help you. Here are some general tips/concepts for trouble-shooting problems with your computer:

Restart the computer - This clears the memory and usually reloads the settings (preferences) you normally start with. Be sure to save your work (if you can) before you restart.

Plug it in - Almost all of us have called a tech person in only to find the keyboard (or whatever) came unplugged. Sometimes you can solve a problem by unplugging equipment and carefully plugging it back in.

Did you just install a piece of software (or a driver)? If you did, and the problem occurred right after, you should try uninstalling the software and restarting the machine to see if it is the new software that is the problem. There usually is an "Uninstall" program that came with your software. Use that program to uninstall. If there isn't that option, you'll need to delete the folder that was installed by the software. There may be other files installed into the system, but these steps will help either fix the problem or give a tech person extra information to solve the problem.

If it's software or the system, try to find out what happens immediately before the problem occurs. Does the problem happen over and over? If you can take note of what happens before the problem, then the tech person will have a better idea of the actual problem. If an error message appears, be sure to write it down. (Sometimes error messages aren't enough to trouble-shoot. You have to have a better idea of the whole picture to solve many problems.)

Exchange the bad parts with good parts (turn off the computer if needed) - A problem: A device attached to my computer (mouse, keyboard, printer) doesn't work.

— Is the it broken and needing to be replaced?

— Is the connection in the computer to the device shorting out?

— Is the driver (a software program) that controls the device corrupt and needing to be replaced?

There is no way you're going to know the answers to these questions until you do some basic steps: Restart the machine and check to make sure it's plugged in. If it still doesn't work, borrow an identical device from another computer (a neighbor perhaps), plug it in the same spot and restart the computer. If it works, your device is bad - get a new one or get it repaired. If exchanging didn't work, call a tech person because either the system software or the connection needs to be repaired.

If the Computer Freezes ...

Do NOT just walk away mumbling something about the computer's questionable parentage. Restart the machine somehow and let it run the disk scanning program. Here's how:

Windows: First try holding down the "Ctrl" and the "Alt" keys while pressing the "Del" key. If you don't get an option to end the task that's stalling the computer, then perform this sequence a couple of times to restart. If that doesn't work, turn the power off, wait 10-12 seconds and turn the power back on. There should also be a restart button somewhere on the machine that reboot the computer.

Macintosh: Holding the "Open Apple" and the "Option" keys while pressing the "Esc" key will force any program to quit if its stalling your computer (choose "Yes"). If the computer doesn't respond (frozen), hold the "Open Apple" and "Ctrl" keys while you press the power button on the top right-hand corner of the keyboard to restart. If that doesn't work, turn the power off, wait 10-12 seconds and turn the power back on.

Some Macintosh machines have a restart button somewhere on the machine. Press this button to reboot the computer.

iMac users: Either unfold a paper clip and insert the end into the restart button or press the restart button (on newer iMacs) on its side to restart the machine. You're looking for the hole or button by the triangle.

Laptop users: Try removing the battery to completely turn the computer off.

Installing and Maintaining a Printer

There are so many different printers on the market and ways to configure them that it's difficult to cover usage issues for all of them. But there are some general rules to keep in mind.

— Read and use the manual. Lately, printer setup manuals have become more graphic and easier to understand. By following its directions, you'll be able to have directions specific to your printer and not violate the printer's warranty.

— Be gentle when pulling the printer out of the box. Unlike a lot of "rough 'n tumble" educational equipment, your printer has a lot of delicate parts. The wrong jolt can knock parts loose that won't easily be replaced.

— Make sure that printer cable is securely installed in BOTH the computer and the printer.

— Turn the ink cartridges back and forth a half-dozen times before you install them to get the ink/toner flowing.

— When installing the printer software, it's usually ok to accept all of the "defaults" that the program gives you. That works when the printer is attached to your computer. If you are trying to use a network printer, see your technology coordinator for instructions/help in configuring for the network.

"Help! My printer won't work!" This is one of those statements that makes tech coordinators run away in frustration because they hear it so often. Here are some steps for you to take before you call for help:

1. Double check to make sure the cables are attached correctly. You might even want unplug and plug them in again to make sure.

2. Run a self-test to see if the printer will actually print if it receives a command. There is usually a button or a combination of buttons on the printer that, if held down for about 5 seconds, will force the printer to print a test page. (Check the manual that came with the printer to find the specific instructions for running a self-test.) If you can do this, check the test page to make sure the lines are coming out clear and the colors (if any) are correct.

If you run into problems at this step:

— Was the printer not able to send a piece of paper through? Make sure there aren't any foreign objects in the paper's pathway.

— Was the printout fuzzy or smudged? Take out the print cartridge and gently clean the print head with a damp, soft cloth. (The cloth will get ink on it— so make sure it's disposable.)

— Was the ink spotty or non-existent? Take out the print cartridge. Look at it and try to weigh it in your hand to see if it is light and needing to be replaced or refilled because it's out of ink. If it has ink, ask your tech coordinator how to get the ink flowing for that particular ink cartridge. (In many inkjet printer cartridges, you can place the print head on a wet cloth for about a half-hour and then run a few test prints to get the ink flowing again.)

3. Check to see if your printer is set as the default printer. (The computer needs to know what printer it is supposed to print to.)

   Windows: Open up "My Computer" on the desktop and then open up "Printers". Click 1 time on the icon that matches your printer and then click on "File". If there isn't a check by "Set as default", click on it to make it the default printer.

   Macintosh: Click on the apple in the upper-left corner, move the cursor down to "Chooser" and release. In the Chooser window, click 1 time on the icon that matches your printer then see if the highlight in the box to the right is on the printer option (there should be a picture of a printer). If not, click on the printer option and close the Chooser window.

4. Clear previous print jobs. Sometimes if a print job was sent and the printer stopped functioning for your machine, then the people printing may have sent more jobs thinking

that the previous attempt was simply "lost" by the computer. The problem with this is that now you have a bunch of jobs backing up the computer. Go into the print monitor for that printer and get rid of those jobs before you send any more.

Windows: Open up "My Computer" on the desktop and then open up "Printers". Open up the icon that matches your printer and see if there is a list of print jobs. Click on "File" and "Purge Print Jobs" and then click on "File" and see if "Pause Printing" has been checked. If it has, uncheck it.

Macintosh: If there is an icon for your printer on the desktop, open it up. Click on a print job and then "Cancel printing" or the trash can (or another equivalent). If the print queue has been stopped, click on "Printing" and select "Start Print Queue".

5. Sometimes restarting the computer (and maybe the printer) is necessary.

One final tip:

"My inkjet printer sounds like it's in the final stages of death when it tries to print!" When your printer was made at the factory, the assemblers didn't apply much lubricant to the bar that the print heads move back and forth on. Take and apply 3 or 4 drops of a lightweight household oil along the bar. As it prints it will distribute the oil and reduce or eliminate the noise.

Your Internet Connection

In order for you to see web sites on your computer, a long series of connections need to be made and working correctly: If any part of any link in this long chain fails, you won't see your web pages. Here is what you can do:

— Make sure the CAT V (Category 5) cable (or whatever type of cable you were given) is plugged into the wall. The cable looks like a thick phone line with wide plugs.

— Make sure the cable is plugged into the computer. In the back of your computer, you can only plug the cable into 1 place. (For many computers, you should see a GREEN light come on near the plug. This means you are getting a good connection and all of the hardware that you can control is probably working correctly. If you don't see a green light or the light is orange, stop and have your tech person look at the connections to figure out what action should be taken.) 1 other step to take is to try another plug in the wall.

— Restart and Log in (if needed)—if you have a good connection (a GREEN light (maybe)), restart the machine and log in correctly if prompted to do so. Many computers give you a log in screen. Make sure you provide whatever password is needed and click the "Ok" (or equivalent) button. Don't click on the "Cancel" button or you won't be recognized on the network.

— Check to make sure you can see other computers on the network

— Windows machines—double click on the "Neighborhood Network" icon on the desktop. When the window opens, you should see other computers or servers underneath the "Entire Network" icon.

— Macintosh machines—Click and hold on the apple icon in the upper left hand corner. Scroll down to and release on "Chooser". When the Chooser window comes up, single click on "Appleshare" and look to the right to see if other computers or servers are shown.

If you can't see other computers on the network, call a tech person to check settings and even cable connections. If you can't see other machines on the network, your computer won't be able to access the internet.

Connecting to a TV or Projector

Your computer is a powerful tool to demonstrate your thoughts, but often the screen is too small for a whole class to see. There are several options for projecting your screen and they all follow some basic hook up procedures. The main options are:

1. Scan Converter which shows your computer desktop on a TV screen
2. LCD panel to place on strong overhead projectors
3. Projector which shows your computer desktop on a screen projection
4. (Different setup procedures not listed) Software to broadcast to other computers (see your tech person for availability)

Any computer with a separate CPU (the computer box) and monitor can usually support a projector, LCD panel, or scan converter because they already have a port to plug the monitor in (this is where you'll plug the device(s) in). The "all-in-one" computers (monitor and CPU in one box) will not support a projector, LCD panel, or scan converter unless a separate external monitor port has been installed.

Here's what you do:

— Read the instructions that came with the projector, LCD panel, or scan converter.

— Plug the monitor-type cable from the input port on projector, LCD panel, or scan converter into the monitor port in the CPU.

— Plug the actual monitor cable into the monitor output port on projector, LCD panel, or scan converter.

— Turn on the projector, LCD panel, or scan converter.

— Turn on or restart the computer. This will allow the computer to sense the device if it needs to.

— If it's a scan converter, plug the smaller, video cable into both the scan converter (video out) and the TV (video in).

— Turn the TV on and turn to channel 3 (or 4 or Aux). For newer TVs, you can scroll through a menu where you can choose the input type—choose "Video" or "Ext" or an equivalent

— If it's a projector or LCD panel, there's probably a "sleep" or "power" button that will turn on the lamp. Once it's on, use the menu buttons on the projector to select the input settings so that you can see the desktop being projected.

Scanners

— Make sure that the scanner is plugged in and on when you turn the computer on.

— Start the software program that came with the scanner (i.e. "Ofoto").

— Place the photo or document to be scanned in the scanner (usually like you would for a Xerox copier).

— Click on "Scan" or equivalent to begin scanning.

— Make whatever adjustments you need to make once the scanning is complete.

Digital Cameras

— Digital Cameras come in 2 varieties: with or without a floppy disk drive.

— If yours has a floppy drive, take your pictures as per the cameras instructions, remove the floppy disk and insert it into your computer.

— In your word processor, click on "Insert" (or equivalent) and "Picture > From File" (or equivalent). Navigate to the floppy drive and your picture file. Insert your picture into your document.

— If yours is without a floppy drive, take your pictures as per the cameras instructions, connect the camera to your computer, and start up the software that came with the camera.

— Use the software to download the picture files as per its instructions.

— In your word processor, click on "Insert" (or equivalent) and "Picture > From File" (or equivalent). Navigate to the picture file and insert your picture.

Since most digital cameras take the pictures in a JPEG format, their pictures are internet ready. Be careful about its size! You may have to reduce it to make it more accessible

Word Processor Quick Start

Word Processors are typing programs that allow you to type text, insert pictures, format the way the document looks, and make changes without having to retype entire pages. There are basic word processing programs that come with every operating system: "MS Write" ("Word Pad") in Windows and "SimpleText" in MacIntosh. These simple processors will handle the basic features covered in this quick start guide. However, more advanced programs like "MS Word" and "AppleWorks" (the newer version of "ClarisWorks") have more sophisticated graphics and formating features.

The first thing to keep in mind is, "A word processor is a word processor is a word processor". They are all basically the same in any operating system and any program.

— You start the program.

— You type what you want.

— You click on "File" and "Print" to print a hardcopy.

— You click on "File" and "Exit" (or "Quit") when you're done.

USING INTERNET PROGRAMS - SURFING THE NET (A QUICK START USING NETSCAPE 4.5)

Start the Program—

Windows: Start > Programs > find the folder and then click on the program or just click on the program

Macintosh: Hard Drive > find the Netscape folder and then double click on the program

E-Mail Quick Start

E-mail (electronic mail) is much like it's real-world counterpart (affectionately known as "Snail Mail"). If you have an e-mail account, you type the recipient's address, type a message, send it, the recipient "gets" his mail, reads it and can reply to you. The differences are in the way the process looks, the fact that you usually include a subject, and the speed at which the mail is delivered. (That doesn't mean your recipient will read his mail any faster—but it's a possibility.)

First ... Get an E-mail account

APS provides free e-mail service to all its employees. Fill out a Staff Password Request Form (the Internet individual account—Create a new Username for me), have your principal sign it, and send it to the Help Desk @ the Resource Center. Once they process it and send your user name and password, configure your Netscape browser preferences to access your account. You now have an e-mail account with an address in this format: myusername@aps.edu .

Go to www.mailstart.com to access your e-mail account. Follow the directions they give you. You can read, reply to, and delete messages on the server from this internet site.

Or

Get an e-mail account from one of the many e-mail service providers on the internet. One such provider is Yahoo. Go to www.yahoo.com. Click on the mail icon and then "Sign Me Up". You'll be asked to provide a username (ID) and a password. The username (ID) must be unique or you'll be prompted to choose another one. Continue filling out the information and submit the form when done. If all the information is correct, you now have an e-mail account with an address in this format: myusername@yahoo.com .

Accessing or "Getting" Your Mail

As mentioned before you can go to www.mailstart.com to access your e-mail account. Follow the directions they give you. You can read, reply to, and delete messages on the server from this internet site. The problem with this option is that it tends to be slow.

If you have configured your Netscape browser to access your e-mail, find and click on the mailbox in the lower-right corner of the window. Type in your password, if prompted, and your program will go and "get" your mail from the server.

If you have an internet e-mail account, go to that site's home page or e-mail page (i.e. www.yahoo.com and click on the "Get Mail" button), sign-in with your username (ID) and password and the program will go and "get" your mail from the server. There's a massive amount of information out there for you to use and the browser is your window to view that information.

The Parts of the Program

Back Button If you need to go to the screen (or "Web Page") you were just on, click on this button and it will take you there. Reload or Refresh Sometimes the web page is taking too long to load or didn't get all of the button or pictures. Sometimes you just need to update the page's information. Click on this button to load the page again. Home Button Every browser has an Internet address that it uses as its "Home". You can program yours to take you to a specific page each time you click on it. Try Edit > Preferences in Netscape 4.5 to set your home page's address. Here are some common homepages:

Print Button Sometimes you'll need to print an internet site. Click on this button to do it. Be careful! There could be many pages to the printout! Try highlighting the text you need and pasting it in a word processor. Stop Button Too many pictures? Can't seem to load the movie clip? Taking too long? Click on this button to stop the loading process so you can move on to something else. Location (URL) Box When you see an add on TV or in the newspaper that says "Visit the Smithsonian Institute on the Internet at www.si.edu", click in the box and get rid of the old address that's in there, then type the new address in its place (don't worry about the http:/ / - the browser will insert for you) AND THEN PRESS ENTER.

Configuring Your Internet Browser To Access Your E-mail

1) Make sure you have an internet connection.
2) Start up your internet browser.
3) Click on "Edit" and "Preferences" and then find the section on "E-mail" or just "Mail".
4) Begin filling out the boxes providing the information it asks for. There might be more than one window to fill information with ("Identity" and "Mail Server"):

   Your Name—That's your actual name (i.e. John Doe) Incoming or Outgoing Server—That's the last part of your e-mail address (i.e. APS.EDU) Username—That's the first part of your e-mail address (i.e. DOE_J)
5) Click "OK" or "Done" when you're done.

Listservs and Address Lists

Listservs and Address Lists are two e-mail tools that allow you to send 1 message to many people with 1 basic step.

Listservs are groups of people with similar interests or jobs that can send and receive the same messages as everyone else. If you sign up to be on a listserv, you and anyone else that signed up on that listserv can send an e-mail message to 1 e-mail address and everyone signed up to that listserv will receive that e-mail message. The advantage to listservs is that 1 message is easily sent to a group of related people (i.e. job, hobby, education) and the responses to that message are viewed by everyone in the group so that a type of forum or open dialogue is created. The disadvantage to listservs is that people commonly use the listserv for personal one-on-one communication and everyone in the group receive those personal comments that aren't normally meant for mass distribution.

Address Lists are lists that you can generate on your computer. The list contains the e-mail information of all the people you include in a group. For instance, if you have a book club that you often send e-mail messages to, you can create a list and drag on the new list the e-mail information from your address book for all of the people in club (naming it "Book Club"). When you want to send an e-mail message to everyone on your list, start a new message and go into your address book. Select the list with the title you gave it before ("Book Club"). Type the message. When you send it, it will be sent to everyone on the list. The advantages: you control the list and any standard replies (not "Reply to all") will only be received by you ? and not the whole group! The disadvantage: you can't conduct an open forum type of dialogue with an address list as easily as with a listserv.

INDEX